≪   **FEASTING WITH CANNIBALS**   ≫

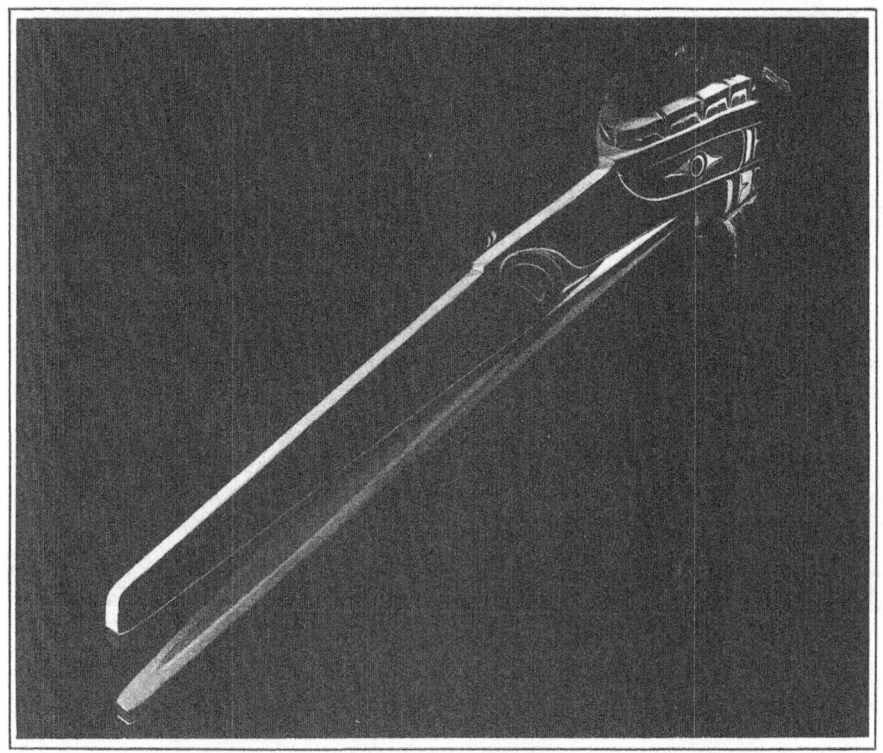

Feasting with Cannibals

An Essay on Kwakiutl Cosmology

≼ STANLEY WALENS ≽

Princeton University Press

Published by Princeton University Press, Princeton, New Jersey
In the United Kingdom: Princeton University Press, Guildford, Surrey

Library of Congress Cataloging in Publication Data will be
found on the last printed page of this book

Publication of this book has been aided by a grant from
The Andrew W. Mellon Foundation

This book has been composed in Linotron Times Roman

Printed in the United States of America by Princeton
University Press, Princeton, New Jersey

Designed by Laury A. Egan

**For Stefani
and the three chiefs**

*Io la vidi, al suo sorriso
scintillar mi parve il sole*

◄ CONTENTS ►

⟨ LIST OF ILLUSTRATIONS ⟩

PHOTOGRAPHS

(Following page 82)

1. Alert Bay (Courtesy of the Milwaukee Public Museum)
2. Northern Kwakiutl box (Courtesy of the British Columbia Provincial Museum)
3. View of a house in Alert Bay (Courtesy of the American Museum of Natural History)
4. Houseposts (Courtesy of the American Museum of Natural History)
5. Shaman's raven rattle (Courtesy of the Brooklyn Museum)
6. Nakoaktok man (Courtesy of the Provincial Archives of British Columbia)
7. *Tsonoqua* mask (Courtesy of the British Columbia Provincial Museum)
8. *Bukwis* mask (Courtesy of the British Columbia Provincial Museum)
9. Thunderbird/*sisiutl* transformation mask (Courtesy of the Brooklyn Museum)
10. *Hohok* mask (Courtesy of the British Columbia Provincial Museum)
11. *Hamatsa* multiheaded mask (Courtesy of the British Columbia Provincial Museum)
12. Dancing costume (Courtesy of the Field Museum of Natural History, Chicago)
13. Diorama showing a *hamatsa* dancer (Courtesy of the Field Museum of Natural History, Chicago)
14. Masked dancers (Courtesy of the Provincial Archives of British Columbia)

◄ ACKNOWLEDGMENTS ►

I WOULD LIKE TO EXPRESS my gratitude to all those people who have helped in the creation and completion of this work: Ethel Albert, who guided me through the difficult process of defining the direction my ideas were to take; James VanStone, who provided invaluable suggestions and assistance; Victor Turner, whose advice and enthusiasm have been as beneficial to me as they have been to the many others he has inspired; Roy Wagner, whose cogent and insightful contributions to every stage of this work place me forever in his debt; and my wife, Stefani, whose intellectual contributions and steadfast encouragement and support have played an active and significant role in the writing of this book.

The writing of this work was partially supported by grants from the Ford Foundation, the Woodrow Wilson Foundation, the National Institutes of Mental Health, and the University of Virginia.

≪ FEASTING WITH CANNIBALS ≫

> To no-one among us is it given to liber-
> ate himself from the course that life has set
> before him. We think, feel and act faith-
> fully to the traditions in which we live. The
> only means by which we might be freed is
> the immersion in a new life and under-
> standing for a thinking, a feeling and an
> acting that has not grown up on the soil of
> our own civilization, but that has its sources
> in another cultural stratum.
> —Franz Boas, *Kwakiutl Ethnography*

$\mathbf{A}$NTHROPOLOGISTS have long realized that a people's worldview is composed of two interrelated parts: first, a notion of how the world is structured, of how its parts have been fashioned into a cohesive whole; and second, a set of rules by which that structure is set into motion, and of how that motion can be controlled or directed. We may make a distinction between worldview and ethos, between ontology and morality, between a description of the world in which people act and the set of rules delineating how they ought to act (see Geertz, 1973:126-41 for a discussion of this idea).

Yet, with few exceptions, students of the Kwakiutl, and of other cultures as well, have used a model of the world that derives from Western concepts of the nature of the world and society—concepts that view the world as a universe of men whose operating patterns are the interactions between men—and not in terms that are appropriate to native ideas, in which the relations between men are not necessarily more important than those relations between men and the other inhabitants of the universe. Traditional anthropological ideas are so completely tied into ideas about man as the prime mover of the world and of behavior as the indicator of man's role in the shaping of his universe that we forget how limited is a perspective dealing only in human relations with other humans.

Furthermore, if we discuss Kwakiutl behavior in such terms as lineage, rank, kinship, marriage, and warfare, we are not depicting Kwakiutl culture as the Kwakiutl themselves lived and envisioned it, but are actually translating that culture into the particular limited set of concepts comprising our own anthropological worldview. From the very first, ethnographers have tried to fit the Kwakiutl into one of our schemes. Boas himself, who set as an intellectual goal the depiction of another culture in its own terms and not ours (Boas, 1966:xi-xx), wondered whether the Kwakiutl were really matrilineal or patrilineal or of some intermediate form. Later scholars argue about whether or not the Kwakiutl had rank or class, as if the naming of a category of our own somehow captures the essence of Kwakiutl thought. In such an analysis, we learn nothing about the Kwakiutl, for we are merely manipulating the elements of our own worldview, changing our conception of Kwakiutl culture until it fits our own categories rather than changing our categories to fit Kwakiutl culture.

This book is not an ethnography in the usual sense of the word. I shall not be presenting data and interpretation simultaneously in the balance that is typical in most ethnographic works. Instead, I am using Boas's works to constitute the ethnographic data, and this book should be seen as a guide and adjunct to those vast works. Furthermore, wherever possible I have avoided the defining of terms prior to a discussion of them. The meaning of a ritual or ceremony, a symbol, a character, can only be artificially stated in a definition. The true meaning comes upon us only when we see the ways in which a single act is related to the larger context of action and native interpretation of those actions. Most anthropologists will be familiar with such terms as potlatch, Cannibal Dancer, and Thunderbird, and will not need definitions of these.

For the reader unfamiliar with traditional anthropological studies of Northwest Coast peoples, I suggest an examination of the presentations in Drucker (1953, 1965), Codere (1950, 1961), Barnett (1938), Duff (1964), Goldman (1937), Hays (1975), or McFeat (1967). These works focus on social economy, however, and pay little attention to the intellectual content of Northwest Coast culture.

At the same time, I urge care in the use of traditional anthropological approaches to Kwakiutl materials, which all too often have reflected the intellectual concerns of anthropologists far more than those of the Kwakiutl. Even the most straightforward anthropological statements about Northwest Coast cultures subtly slant the ethnographic data in ways that, because they have become part of a long anthropological tradition, may not be easy to perceive. Concepts anthropologists have found useful or valid in the study of other cultures have sometimes been applied to Northwest Coast societies without regard for the ethnographic materials. For example, because anthropologists are concerned with social groups, with affiliation to a human social entity such as a lineage or a clan, they have both consistently emphasized these social units in ways that fail to note the particular character of Northwest Coast social principles and almost totally ignored the important corporate connections between humans, animals, and spirits. Because they are interested in the material aspects of economy, they have fundamentally ignored the intellectual and philosophical aspects of Northwest Coast economies. Because they are interested in the common functions of ceremonies, they have fundamentally ignored the critical differences and distinctions between dozens of Northwest Coast rituals, and have indiscriminately listed them all under the heading of "potlatch."

Of the many books about the Kwakiutl, only one, Irving Goldman's *The Mouth of Heaven* (1975), tries at all to deal with Kwakiutl institutions from within the context of Kwakiutl, rather than Western, ideas. Goldman's work with Boas's texts is a revelatory structuralist approach to Kwakiutl culture. He points out such previously unstated basics of Kwakiutl culture as the fact that all beings are considered to be united within a single, coherent behavioral system, that the potlatch has religious overtones far more important than its economic overtones, and that Kwakiutl behaviors seem to be imbued with a fundamental moral and religious sensibility.

Goldman demonstrates the important nature of metaphorical equivalence in Kwakiutl thought, and he delineates many of the same particular equivalences between various elements of Kwakiutl culture that I shall examine—for example, the equivalence between salmon and twins, between owls and souls, between the structure of the house and that of the universe, between skins and masks. Yet, the fundamental difference between my own approach to Kwakiutl metaphors and Goldman's lies in the centrality we give to the process of metaphorization itself.

It is my contention that for the Kwakiutl the process of metaphorization is the fundamental process of their cognitive mode, the process by which they delineate the world and their place in it. For Goldman, metaphor is a secondary aspect of the processes of culture, which include religion, ritual distribution and exchange, antagonism, shamanism, and the aristocratic principle. He relegates Kwakiutl metaphors to an appendix entitled "Analytical Index of Themes," where he lists references from Boas's texts to various items and beings in Kwakiutl myth and ceremony, much as Boas himself did in *Kwakiutl Culture as Reflected in Mythology* (1935). I do not consider these metaphors to be themes, to be incidental to our understanding of Kwakiutl cognition, or to be simply material for an appendix. To make them secondary is to propose that some other process is primary.

My aim is to examine the way in which fundamental ideas of Kwakiutl worldview and morality are structured, and the way in which they operate throughout the entire intellectual universe of the Kwakiutl. I wish to argue that for the Kwakiutl there is a limited set of metaphors by which they express their worldview and their ethos, and that all aspects of Kwakiutl culture can be best understood when we realize the nature of these metaphors and their utilization in Kwakiutl cognition and culture. For me, the dialectic of explanation is one in which the Kwakiutl focus on a conventionalized set of resemblances and analogies, drawn upon human and animal characteristics and predilections, and use these metaphors to model their conception of the world, of how it operates, and of how people must act within it. My goal is to point out those fundamental resemblances and to explore their ramifications throughout all areas of Kwakiutl thought.

Thus, I intend to show in the first chapter the basic metaphors by which the Kwakiutl describe the nature of causality as an inextricable link between man and the universe, and to indicate the moral responsibility which falls upon a person to act correctly because of the ineluctable effect his actions have. Further, I will show that the Kwakiutl use a single metaphor and its corollaries to describe the nature of geographical, personal, and social space, and that these metaphors all share the physical characteristics of indicating the assimilation of one item within the boundaries of another.

In Chapter Two I will show how the same assimilative metaphors the Kwakiutl use to describe their physical universe are used to delineate the particular mode of human relationships that is the foundation of Kwakiutl society. Further, I will show that at times when these assimilative metaphors are most visible facets of life—that is, in behavior surrounding the act of the assimilation of food—that the Kwakiutl pay especial attention to ensuring that correct behavior is maintained at all times, that the act of eating a meal is itself a metaphor for the way the universe is organized and the way it must be maintained.

In Chapter Three I will show that the Kwakiutl derive their own conception of the centrality of assimilative metaphors from the world around them, that they visualize the world as a place of eaters and the eaten, that they model human lives on the specific oral behaviors of animals, and that they model animal lives on the oral desires they feel as humans. Thus, the Kwakiutl moral universe becomes united, not by any vague religious sense but by the fact that the entire universe contains all beings within its bounds, and that all beings are subject to the principle of being both hungry and the food of other beings who are themselves hungry. The Kwakiutl universe is a universe of related beings, all of whom have the moral responsibility to control their eating. Eating is a universal property of the world, and thus it is the basis for morality.

Finally, in the fourth chapter I will examine a particular Kwakiutl myth and a single ritual performance as exemplifications of the ways in which oral, assimilative metaphors are used by the Kwakiutl to encapsulate their ideas of man's role in the universe. We shall see that they consider the very creation of the world itself to be the result of a single food-related act at the beginning of time, and that rituals today are meant to recreate that act. In this way, the myth acts as a metaphor for the ideas the Kwakiutl hold about themselves, and the ritual enactment of the myth acts as a metaphor for the myth. We shall also see that knowledge of the metaphors we have previously discussed is necessary if we are ever to understand the purpose and meaning of Kwakiutl myth and ritual performance, both of which provide the context in which the Kwakiutl metaphorical system can be realized and displayed in a single, coherent, intense gestalt. And finally, we shall see that it is oral metaphors upon which the Kwakiutl found their ideas of moral ideology and moral action, ideas that lie at the center of their worldview and ethos.

Our task is to gain understanding of how the fundamental postulates of Kwakiutl ontology and morality are created and how they operate. To do this we must consciously ignore traditional concerns of anthropologists in order to gain a picture of the model of the universe and man's role in it as it is developed through Kwakiutl metaphors. I have thus chosen to ignore, for the most part, the standard anthropological analyses of Kwakiutl culture such as those by Codere (1950), Drucker and Heizer (1967), and Rosman and Rubel (1971). As excellent as these may be as anthropological studies, they do not address the subject of how, in Kwakiutl thought, man is related to the universe. Nor have I extensively utilized most of the works on the Kwakiutl that were based on fieldwork after 1935, for by this time the more traditional values and ideas Boas recorded between 1888 and 1931 were drastically altered by the demographic and economic collapse of Kwakiutl society. Instead, I have concentrated on one set of sources, the extensive ethnographic and textual materials Boas and George Hunt collected over a period of more than forty years.

Certainly, Boas's collected works on Kwakiutl culture constitute one of the monuments of American cultural anthropology, the achievement of a half-century of diligent research and careful scholarship. Yet, for all their scope and detail, few scholars have returned to them when discussing some of the controversial questions in Northwest Coast ethnography. This must, in part, be attributed to the very vastness of the work itself. Boas's published materials on the Northwest Coast tribes are almost ten thousand pages in length (Codere's list [1959:62] is quite incomplete), and the unpublished manuscripts in the libraries of Columbia University and the American Philosophical Society add several thousand more pages to the total. More than two-thirds of this material is specifically on the Kwakiutl. The task of reading through such a gigantic corpus of materials, let alone trying to colligate it into a cohesive whole, is so difficult and time consuming that even Boas himself was never able to create a unified picture of Kwakiutl culture.

The task is made even more difficult by the length of time over which Boas's materials were published and the large number of publications and serials in which they appeared. Even a learned student of Boas's materials can be completely unaware of Boas's treatment of a given subject. For example, Codere states (in Boas, 1966:358) that Boas published very little on Kwakiutl ideas and practices concerning death, and lists only those materials in *Ethnology of the Kwakiutl* (Boas, 1921), yet in a half-dozen works there are sections dealing with funerals and ideas about reincarnation and mourning. Indeed, one of Boas's very first publications on the Indians of the Northwest Coast (1887) contains a summary of Kwakiutl funeral customs.

The task of locating materials on a particular ethnographic subject in the Boasian corpus is made even more difficult by both the poor indexing which characterizes most of his works, with one or two notable exceptions, such as *Ethnology of the Kwakiutl* (1921), and by the fact that materials listed under a particular heading actually may be more directly related to other topics. For example, the section on pregnancy and birth in *Kwakiutl Ethnography* (1966) is replete with information about the symbolic nature of causality, the number of taboos expectant parents must observe, naming ceremonies, proverbs, statements about causal relationships between humans and animals, and pharmacological information, as well as the expected data on midwifery and other directly related topics. In fact, Boas was so diligent in recording every possible aspect of a topic that in some ways every given section of his ethnographies is a microcosmic realization of the totality of Kwakiutl custom and belief. Boas believed that even the most seemingly insignificant aspect of a people's culture was a key to their cognitive patterns (see Codere, 1959:65). Therefore, any given topic provides only a partial realization of those patterns and is interrelated to the rest of Kwakiutl culture in myriad ways which are far too complex to be indexed.

Thus, a given topical section may contain information relevant to dozens of special subjects. For example, Boas records an interview George Hunt had with a number of men concerning the nature of fire (1921:1331-33) that is important as a text on myth, the symbolic aspects of maleness and femaleness, the spiritual nature of the universe, the identity/embodiment/impersonation schema by which a given being can be both itself and something else simultaneously, eating behavior, prayers and supplication, and shamans. Furthermore, materials on fire, the fundamental mechanism of transformation in Kwakiutl thought, occur in hundreds of other places in the Boasian corpus, in hundreds of other contexts, and only when we have looked at the totality of these references can we begin to see the sense of Kwakiutl ideas about transformation.

The nature of the Boasian texts compels us to witness the process whereby he gathered the materials. Boas actually spent very little fieldwork time among the Kwakiutl. Instead, he trained an Indian, George Hunt, in the basic requirements of scientific research and in the phonetic transcription of the Kwakiutl language. It was Hunt who gathered the majority of texts and materials that constitute the Boasian corpus. Hunt's diligence and scientific meticulousness are obvious in everything he writes. In the above-mentioned text on the spirits of the fire (1921:1331-33), for example, one can see how Hunt solves the task of uncovering Kwakiutl ideas about the nature of fire, by choosing the experts on fire, recording their opinions, their specific knowledge, and the conflicting opinions of others, and by raising the question of whether the ownership of fire is a personal or a universal prerogative. Time after time we are made aware that Boas and Hunt are involved in the difficult process of trying to make an orderly scientific record of a highly esoteric and complex worldview.[1]

The task of delineating the fundamental metaphors underlying Kwakiutl thought is made more difficult in that it is the nature of metaphors to connote a wide variety of ideas and meanings simultaneously. The non-specificity of meanings in a metaphor gives it its creative dimension, for each individual brings his own associations to the interpretation of the relationship between the parts of the metaphor. Thus, metaphors, varying as they do from one interpreter to the next, must always remain vague. It is that very vagueness that gives them their meaningfulness, their power.

Take the case of the metaphors of smoke and fire used by the Kwakiutl to characterize themselves collectively, as in "Smoke from their Fires" (Ford, 1941), "Smoke of the World" (Goldman, 1976:19), and "Having Fires Moving on the Waters" (Boas, 1966:37). What do these metaphors tell us about Kwakiutl self-imagery and the moral role of humans? As we shall see, smoke is the visible transfer of material from the world of humans to the world of the spirits of the heavens. To light a fire is to communicate with the spirits, to provide them with food and the material necessary for their survival, and the spirits reciprocate by providing the food on which human survival depends. For the Kwakiutl to call themselves "Smoke of the World" emphasizes both the moral commitment they make, in that they are the particular people who provide smoke for the benefit of the entire world, and their sense of greatness, in that they see themselves as the central actors in the continuance of the cosmic

[1] Though Hunt's name is listed as coauthor with Boas on only two works, Boas freely acknowledged Hunt's contributions both in print and in public Even so, an account of the degree to which Boas's knowledge of the Kwakiutl arose out of Hunt's understanding of them and of the degree to which the excellence of Boas's work is the result of the meticulousness and diligence of both men has never been amply discussed. There is quite a lot of material in Boas's notes and letters that could give us insight into the nature of the Boas-Hunt relationship and into the critical role Hunt played in creating an ethnography of the Kwakiutl. I can only hope that this material will be brought to light in the near future.

cycle. "Smoke from their Fires" not only recapitulates these ideas, but provides a geographical locus, a territorial space, which characterizes the geographical nature of the Kwakiutl village, numaym, and family organization. Within the flux of the universe, a fire is a point fixed in space by the intersection of the pieces of wood from which it is constructed. So too is the human being a fixed point in the continuum of time and space, defined by the intersection of skeletal parts, which, as we shall see, are metaphorically equivalent to wood. Yet, at the same time as fire is fixed and permanent, smoke is impermanent and malleable. So too is the life of the individual, who vanishes as surely as does the smoke of the fire, who is as insubstantial as the smoke, whose life history is the product of the consuming of his wealth in the fire, just as smoke is itself the product of the consuming of wood in the fire. Equally as insubstantial is the house in which the fire is lit, for when its planks fall away and its posts rot, and when all its wealth is removed from this world and transferred through decay to other worlds, it too vanishes forever. Finally, the metaphor of fire is one of sociality and cohesion, as in the name "Having Fires Moving on the Water," a lovely image for the sight of a village as seen from the sea, which is the only means of approaching it, an image that, as the lights seem to reach out, conveys the feeling of coming from the cold, wet, foggy, dangerous seas across which fishermen and warriors must travel, back to a spot near the warmth of one's own family, friends, and fire. Yet, at the same time, what is more insubstantial, more unreal, more impermanent than the image of something reflected in broken lines upon the moving surface of the waters?

Thus, in the vagueness of Kwakiutl metaphors for themselves, we find encapsulated their entire image of their identity, their moral responsibility, and their social nexus. And for all their ambiguity, these metaphors capture more specific ideas about the Kwakiutl in just a few words than a less metaphorical description could ever attain.

The understanding of a culture's fundamental metaphors is an essential part of interpreting both the cognitive and behavioral aspects of that culture. A scholar can approach these metaphors unconsciously, hoping that the true connections between symbols will occur to him (though in this method, he is at the mercy of his unconscious biases and predilections, repressions, and sublimations). Yet it is an essential concept of Western philosophy that we must be at least as much aware of the process by which we analyze a phenomenon as we are of the phenomenon itself. Thus, if we approach the task with the awareness that we must discover these analogies, then we might hope to exert some measure of control over the process of determining the way these metaphors are structured and expressed. If we are aware that our interpretation of the symbols involves their integration into the totality of their cultural context, then we are more conscious of the need to keep our interpretations in close conformity with the Kwakiutl materials.

My task in this paper is to try to supply the particular analogic connections that explicate Kwakiutl thinking. These connections are not necessarily self-evident in Boas's writings, whose particularistic epistemology seems to reproduce closely that of the Kwakiutl themselves. At times, even the most fundamental of these analogic connections may be so ambiguous that the Kwakiutl themselves are unable to agree on them, as is the case in the discussion of the spirit of the fire (Boas, 1921:1331-33), the question of whether or not owls are the souls of men (Boas, 1930:257-60), and the fundamental basis of shamanic curing (Boas, 1930:1-56). While some of this ambiguity may be attributed to the growing influence of foreign ideas on the Kwakiutl during the last half of the nineteenth century and to the simultaneous decline of indigenous Kwakiutl culture, and some to the fact that most ritual and symbolic knowledge among the Kwakiutl is privately owned and secret, Kwakiutl epistemology is so characterized by the delineation of the particular that we must consider it to be one of their fundamental cognitive behaviors. That is, that the supplying of the analogies linking the particulars is as necessary an exegetical process for the Kwakiutl as it is for ourselves.

The key to the understanding of Kwakiutl worldview lies in the analysis of Kwakiutl ideas about those forces we might call causative, of how one action affects and effects another. The Western idea of causality is a matter of continuity in time and contiguity in space. However, for the Kwakiutl, causality is a relationship of sympathy, of analogy in form and motion. This sympathetic causality, often mistakenly called magic, is especially noticeable in behavior we do not share with the Kwakiutl: for example, a pregnant Kwakiutl woman must lie along, not across, floorboards so that her fetus will also lie lengthwise in the womb; she must not split fish in half or she will have deformed twins; she must not look at a dying person or her child will die. The essential process is one in which a human action is magnified and intensified into a power that alters the state of the world.

Since every act has the potential to magnify itself, it behooves each Kwakiutl individual to see that every one of his acts is consonant with the proper operation of the universe rather than with its destruction. Thus, every action is essentially a moral choice because its consequences affect the world. Almost by definition, then, the Kwakiutl universe is, as a totally interrelated causal system, a moral universe.

The moral codices governing Kwakiutl life are set down in myths, rituals, ceremonies, magical rites, prayers, and social organization. These provide a model for how man can play an effective and productive role in the functioning of the universe. They tell of how the world operates on a particularistic phenomenological level: how to become pregnant, how to catch a salmon, how to scare away witches, how to gather abundant wealth. These moral codices have been part of Kwakiutl studies for the last half-century, for they are discernible as cultural traits and thus fall within the traditional boundaries of cultural anthropology.

However, the other part of Kwakiutl worldview—the nature of the universe itself, its fundamental operating principles, the ultimate basis of morality—are not topics that have been dealt with, for these are not presentable as units of culture. Yet, in reading the Kwakiutl texts, one can hardly fail to be impressed by the way Kwakiutl ideas about what is the right way to act, what is the correct format for living, and what is the proper nature of the world and of man's role in it are all made plain. The Kwakiutl seem well aware that they have a moral responsibility to act in a certain way because the world demands it of them, and they clearly denote the ways of defining the world in which they live.

The Kwakiutl universe is predicated on a single, fundamental assumption: that the universe is a place where some beings are eaten by other beings and where it is the role of some beings to die so that other beings may feed on them and live. Theirs is a world where the act of eating becomes the single metaphor by which the rest of their lives is interpreted. Food provides for them a model of the nature of life; the act of eating provides a model of assimilation that recurs throughout every aspect of their culture; and the food chain itself provides the link between one human and another and between humans and the rest of the world. Metaphors of eating and assimilation provide the model by which the Kwakiutl can encompass items within a particular single rubric by which they can differentiate between items. Metaphors of assimilation and eating provide the cognitive model by which the Kwakiutl predicate the structure and process of their universe.

The Kwakiutl world is visually filled with mouths. It is a world where people, animals, spirits, sneezes, twitches, owls, dreams, ghosts, and even flatulence speak and sometimes forebode. It is a world where animals of countless variety all kill and destroy to satisfy their hunger, a world filled with the gaping maws of killer whales, the fearsome teeth of wolves and bears, the tearing beaks of ravens and hawks. It is a world filled with omnipresent man-made images whose mouths betray their greed for food: of Thunderbirds who bring sudden death from the sky, of Cannibal Birds with beaks nine feet long that crack open human skulls and suck out their brains, of wild women with pendulous breasts and protruding lips, who watch for unwary travelers and misbehaving children and rip their bodies to pieces in the frenzy of devouring them. It is a world where babies calmly sucking at their mothers' breasts suddenly turn into monsters and eat them.

An oral metaphorization of the universe is a cogent one since the mouth can be both a passive and an aggressive part of the body, and the processes of digestion and regurgitation mimic the processes of creation and destruction; at the same time, the powerful urges of insatiable hunger can be opposed to the controlled, learned, socialized nature of speech.

Various forces in Kwakiutl society act at all times to create and reinforce a high level of anxiety relating to food and to oral behavior, thus reinforcing the importance of oral metaphors and their moral character. The process of collecting food is itself of critical social and emotional consequence to the Kwakiutl. Food is plentiful, but access to food resources is extremely limited and in the hands of a small percentage of the titled nobility. Much of Kwakiutl social machination centers around gaining access to food-producing resources, both natural and supernatural; a commoner's food and life are dependent on his becoming successfully allied with a nobleman who owns food-gathering rights while the nobleman's success is achieved only through careful deployment of his food resources to create reciprocal obligation from those people whom he feeds. The judicious balancing of food against obligations is difficult and complex; one's life is securely in the hands of others, a fact that is validated every time one eats (see Ruyle, 1973; Adams, 1973).

The control of food is not any less troublesome within the family. Because of several peculiar rules of ownership, no one person ever controls all aspects of the food-collecting and preparing process (see Chapter Two). Since the right to collect food is the prerogative of men, and the right to prepare it the prerogative of women, no one can ever eat a meal without first obtaining someone else's permission. Kwakiutl marriage ceremonies conscientiously reaffirm the mutual obligations of husband and wife and emphasize their dependency upon one another. The food-related rights fostering this and other relationships are zealously guarded; encroachment upon them is punished by physical death and supernatural torment. The Kwakiutl individual, morally required to maintain the correct social formula, does so through the correct reciprocal distribution of food.

Etiquette at meals is also of great importance. Few Kwakiutl eat alone; to do so is to display vulgarity. If so much of Kwakiutl social relation is built on social control through food, eating alone expresses a disregard of social interdependency and, thus, bestial voraciousness. Even at feasts one is supposed to eat slowly, taking small bites, chewing unnoticeably, and swallowing as infrequently as possible. Women conceal their mouths behind cedar bark napkins to hide their chewing and swallowing, and drink from spoons rather than cups. Types of table settings are carefully prescribed according to the food being eaten, the number of guests present and their social relationships. Talking about food while eating is rigorously forbidden, and types of songs and permissible conversation are carefully delineated. Even such questions as when and what one can drink are codified, including the number of sips one can take after eating various types of food. Loud talk and rambunctiousness are forbidden during meals and are restricted to periods between courses, before, or after the meal. In short, among the Kwakiutl eating is a highly formalized, highly ritualized social interaction. This formalization betrays both a high degree of anxiety in relation to food and a mechanism for the constant reinforcement of these anxieties.

As we shall see, in the rituals of Kwakiutl meals we can decipher one of the basic paradigms of Kwakiutl moral thought: the mouth and the things it does are the representations of the bestial, antisocial, destructive aspects of human nature, which must be constantly guarded against, constantly obviated. People must either turn these primal forces to their advantage, or they must suppress them through the proper performance of social interaction. Whenever these forces threaten to bring destruction, people must actively counteract them.

The use of orality to counteract the destructive powers of the universe is most evident in Kwakiutl curing ceremonies. Here the shaman graphically recreates oral acts—chewing, sucking, moaning, spitting blood, vomiting—using the power created by his oral-expulsive acts to overcome the powers that are bringing death. He surrounds himself with oral images: rattles, covered with mouths, on which the tongue of man and life-bringing frog or raven are interconnected in a bridge of vital force; soul catchers through whose mouths the sickness-devouring spirit helper of the shaman emerges to devour the disease; charms made from the heads of reptiles and birds; and songs of power and death, expressed in metaphors of feasting.

Orality is also the basis for the totemic organization of Kwakiutl society. The oral peculiarities of animals play important roles in myths, rituals, artistic iconography, and social identification. Among the Kwakiutl, animals commonly used for major crests—beaver, bear, eagle, wolf, raven, and killer whale—have three similar traits: they are social, they are voracious, and they make a large number of vocalizations. Mythical extensions of animals are always carnivorous, such as the Cannibal Bird, which cracks open men's skulls, and the Thunderbird. In myths the actual oral behaviors of animals form an important part of their characterization: a mink's gluttony, a heron's incessant searching for fish, a killer whale's incredible appetite. Oral imagery also accounts for the magical potency of snakes, frogs, and lizards, for while these animals are not dangerous to man, the constant motion of their tongues and their abilities to strike rapidly and to eat large prey are easily transmuted into the idea of their death-bringing powers.

Just as death is metaphorized in oral terms, so is creation visualized as an oral process. The power of life resides not in semen but in vomit; fertilization is believed to occur only if the mother eats certain foods. In order to bring life to their unborn children, parents must perform rituals that transfer the life-giving power from the tongues of frogs into the mouths of children. Many rituals mimic acts of eating and vomiting, and are considered to directly affect the behavior of the child both in the womb and during labor; especially feared is breech birth, which is counteracted by a large number of ritual oral gestures.

Anxieties surrounding birth reflect fear of the potential destructiveness of children. Not only do children demand constant feeding, an attribute indicative of an unsocialized and therefore a primal and amoral greed, but they do so without the reciprocal obligation that is such an important part of Kwakiutl social relations. Furthermore, since parents are required to relinquish their privileges and rank to their children at specified times in the child's life, the birth of a child begins the inexorable erosion of its parents' roles in Kwakiutl social structure.

Since the acquisition of status is metaphorized in terms of eating, the primal amoral hunger of the child for food is extrapolated to its primal hunger for status and power. Thus, it is incumbent upon the parents to counteract their child's destructive voracity. Kwakiutl children are therefore swaddled so that all movement is impossible, with only their mouths, noses, and eyes exposed, and remain swaddled until they are about three years old. Weaning is harsh and abrupt, and is immediately followed by the imposition of a long series of self-chastening rituals on the child.

The child's destructive powers are believed to originate in the womb, where the fetus gorges itself on its mother's menstrual blood. The fear of breech birth, then, is not just a fear of difficult labor, but an expression of the fear that the child's hunger will be so intense that even when its feet have emerged into the human world, it will continue to devour its mother's insides.

The ultimate projection of the power of primal hunger comes in the Cannibal (*hamatsa*)[2] Dance of the sacred winter ceremonials (Benedict, 1934). Here the Cannibal's desire to eat human flesh is a manifestation of all the forces that can destroy society, and the ritual of taming the Cannibal is a metaphorical extension of child socialization. The Cannibal Dance is a sacred dance, not just an expression of secular relations and secular powers. It is the keystone to the entire interaction between mankind and the supernatural, between the bestial and humane facets of hu-

---

[2] I use the words Cannibal and *hamatsa* interchangeably. There are reasons for distinguishing between the two, and for discarding the pejorative term "cannibal," but I have maintained the use of it here to convey the important sense of the dancer's being a vehicle by which human flesh is symbolically "eaten" and thus transformed

man nature, and between the cosmic forces of creation and those of destruction. It both represents and is the moment of the utter taming of those forces that would send the world into the chaos of uncontrollable rapaciousness.

The cosmic force of the Cannibal Dance is created through the use of masks. Masks play a critical visual and religious role in all Kwakiutl ceremonies, and the importance of their mouths is immediately obvious. Not only are the various beings characterized by their mouths, but mouth shape may be the only significant difference between the masks of two different characters. Form lines become thin and meet around mouths, emphasizing the tension of the area; relief carving is done so that firelight will illuminate the upper lip, eyeballs, and eyebrows of a mask, suggesting a being with fearsomely omniscient eyesight and a cavernous mouth. Teeth are especially important, are present in a large proportion of masks, and are often inlaid with reflective materials to make them more noticeable by dim firelight; at times when they are not present, other mouth features are carved to suggest the potent rapacity of the being.

The Cannibal Dancer does not wear a mask; his own face has been grotesquely distorted by his uncontrollable craving for human flesh. He is so irresistibly drawn to the presence of human flesh that he trembles and gnashes his teeth; in his excitement he is rendered inarticulate and can utter only cries and moans. At first, he attacks everyone around him; so great is his passion that he bites flesh from the bodies of living men, until the opposing power of the Bear Dancers chases him away. Later he reappears, the old hunger having returned. The guests at the ceremony sing powerful sacred songs, but to no avail. Suddenly, from a side room emerges a naked woman, often the Cannibal's actual or classificatory sister, who carries a corpse in her arms. She dances lasciviously before him, but even the power of incestuous desire cannot distract him. He grabs the corpse and begins to devour it; his hunger is appeased but not negated. In the final dance, the negation of his voracity occurs only when the other dancers press a smoldering blood-soaked menstrual napkin into the Cannibal's face. Once the sacred smoke enters his body, he is satiated, for his primal desire has been satisfied by the primal food of menstrual blood. At this point, the Cannibal is thought to lose all knowledge of human behavior; he must be taught all the basics of human life as if he were a new-born infant: speech, walking, sleeping, eating, and drinking. All are taught to him in a ritual process lasting months, before he can again enter the world of other human beings. However, upon reentering society, he is magically more elevated than any other person, because he has conquered the destructive force of primal voraciousness.

Just as humans survive only because the spirits have given them food, so are the spirits dependent on reciprocal gifts of food from humans. In both secular and sacred relations, the gift of food is the gift of life, and thus in return for the food given them, humans must give lives, in the form of animal and human souls, to the spirits. Since the amount of food and the number of souls in the world are finite, the system works only because humans give to spirits the remains of their food transformed magically into souls, and the spirits give to humans the remains of souls transformed magically into food. This relationship is formalized under the rubric of named privileges, whose ownership carries with it the sacred obligation to provide, through magic transformation, souls for the spirits to eat.

This transformation is accomplished through the mediating action of two forces—vomit and fire. For the Kwakiutl, vomiting comprises the basic paradigm of transformation and rebirth; fire, like vomit, does not destroy, it transubstantiates. What seems to us to be the destruction of wealth items—animal skins, blankets (which are homologues of animal skins), and coppers (which are repositories of souls)—is in actuality the return of those items and the souls they represent to the spirit realm. Kwakiutl potlatches are filled with speeches reaffirming the eternal reciprocal bond between humans and spirits; indeed, reenactments of the original gift of food by a particular spirit to the ancestor of the present rankholder are a major facet of most ceremonials.

One additional point must be considered. The Kwakiutl man (or woman) who has owed his life to the beneficence of a spirit, owes that spirit his own soul. Therefore, upon his death, his soul is carried to the spirit world, where it remains for one lifetime. When its spirit-world body dies, the released soul once again returns to the human world, where it is reincarnated as the person's own grandchild, who has already inherited his grandparent's wealth, eternal names, and privileges. Thus, through cyclic reincarnations, the original ancestors of the Kwakiutl remain alive throughout all time, and when a Kwakiutl maintains that he is an ancestor, he is not speaking metaphorically. When the spirits come to reside in the sacred winter villages of humans, these reincarnated ancestors recreate the original gift of food and rank of which the myths speak. Such recreations are not merely dramatizations, but actually repeat and thus revitalize the ancient gift itself.

We shall see that for the Kwakiutl, metaphors of assimilation provide a model for both action and ontology, and these metaphors pervade Kwakiutl ideas of sociality, of human nature, of animal behavior, and of religion. While each individual symbol provides only a fragment of the total picture of orality, the interrelationship of the totality of symbols creates a web of metaphor that encompasses the entire universe. For example, those metaphors that derive from the Kwakiutls' primary concern over food and sociality come together in a powerful and immediate way in their model of animal behavior, while metaphors of animal orality come together in an equally powerful way in Kwakiutl rituals, art, ceremony, and psychology.

We shall see also that for the Kwakiutl metaphors express not merely likenesses, not merely similes, but equivalences, and that the central importance of transformation in Kwakiutl ontology is a statement not of how one thing is like another (and therefore not the same as the other), but of how one thing is another, of how it becomes another thing by being eaten by it.

The metaphorization of orality as the basis of Kwakiutl symbolism does more than just provide a single core image on which the Kwakiutl can focus. It is a symbolic process expressing the intricate differentiation of the world at the same time as it inherently limits the Kwakiutls' awareness of their universe to a single cognitive schema. As a depiction of the central role of assimilation and of its fundamental importance as the mode of being and becoming, orality is the Kwakiutl metaphor of how metaphors themselves are constructed, of how one symbol is transformed into another. Orality is not merely a metaphor for life, it is a metaphor for the process of metaphorization—a meta-metaphor. Orality, as assimilation, provides the model of how a symbol is formed and developed, of how one symbol becomes another by assimilating the nature of the other symbol within itself. Metaphors, like humans, animals, and spirits, become each other by assimilating each other's identities, by incorporating an old substance within a new skin, by putting a mask on it, thus giving it a new body, a new shape, a new identity on the outside while it retains its old identity on the inside. For the Kwakiutl a metaphor is a transformation, just as much as transformation is a metaphor.

Finally, we shall see that the Kwakiutl metaphorization of oral processes provides the pattern for and the power behind their cognitive orientation and their cultural institutions. Only when we become aware of these oral metaphors, their elaboration throughout all Kwakiutl thought, and their critical role in defining the moral laws of human relations with each other, with the spirits, and with the universe as a whole can we truly hope to understand Kwakiutl culture as the Kwakiutl themselves live it.

Before proceeding, I must express several caveats. First, it is a perennial mistake of anthropologists to believe that Boas's eclectic idea of culture prevented him from making any summary statements about Kwakiutl culture and precluded the kind of unified account of cultural character currently in fashion. The holding of such an idea is possible only if one has not read the corpus of Boas's materials, but has instead read isolated passages indexed under whatever particular topic is being considered. There is an implicit unity to Kwakiutl culture that is impossible to miss.

Second, I emphasize that this unity is metaphorized within the single rubric of assimilation. However, it would be a mistake to interpret this work as if I were saying that all Kwakiutl culture is reducible to a single idea and this idea only. To say that there is a single rubric is not to say that every Kwakiutl behavior or idea is obviously interpretable in oral terms, or that they do not embellish, transform, or metathesize oral images into highly complex, seemingly unrecognizable forms. Indeed, it is the nature of metaphor to transubstantiate meaning and form. Still, oral images provide the deep structure for Kwakiutl thought, and it is on this structural level that they unify Kwakiutl culture. Assimilative imagery forms the foundation for Kwakiutl thought, but only the foundation. In these pages, I can do little more than point out how this imagery can be found throughout a wide variety of Kwakiutl customs and behaviors, and that the ways in which anthropologists—members of a culture overtly concerned with wealth and the use of wealth to denote social status— have miscolored our view of the Kwakiutl by focusing only on the materialistic aspects of Kwakiutl action. We are talking in these pages of the experience of being a Kwakiutl. Boas amply documents the nature of this experience, and we must wonder at the efficacy of a discipline that in the last half-century has failed to look at any of these critical materials in a holistic fashion.

Third, for the sake of compactness I have chosen only one or two prayers, myths, rituals, feasts and other examples to illustrate the points I make. Boas has included many dozens of each of these and it is from the totality of these that I have made my conclusions. I have chosen the particular examples primarily for the clarity with which they illustrate the points I make, because the imagery is clear-cut and obvious. In the interests of scholarship, I have listed the locations of other supportive materials in Appendix Two, so that those who might wish to find other examples can do so readily. In addition, I have for the most part not discussed in detail the complex analogies that occur between many of the particular supernatural beings in which the Kwakiutl believed, and indeed, I have in this work presented only the most fundamental of the analogic chains that unify the Kwakiutl idea of the cosmos. Such areas as color symbolism, an incredibly important part of all Kwakiutl rituals, body part imagery, many dozens of particular animals, hundreds of spirit beings, scores of dances, thousands of mythological images defining the character of Kwakiutl culture have had to be set aside here so that my central thesis can be presented as clearly as possible. The data in Boas's works is so overwhelming that there are many lifetimes of scholarly analysis of it waiting to be done. This book can only be seen as prologomenon to that analysis, as the first step toward making sense of a culture whose customs have been misconstrued for the last forty years. Because this work is a prologomenon, I have organized it so that the reader may see the order and simplicity of design that underlies the intellectual complexity of a vibrant and creative people.

Fourth, though I talk here about the psychodynamics of the human mind, I do not in any way mean to imply that Kwakiutl behavior is any more motivated by oral desires than is anyone else's. Instead, I argue that of the myriad ways in which people can choose to describe and evaluate their behavior and the purpose of their existence, the Kwakiutl have chosen one particular format as their organizational metaphor for human action. We are talking here not of the causes of Kwakiutl behavior, not of psychodynamic motivating forces, but of the grammar of ethics and of the way one chooses to bring drama and poetry to one's life. Yet, there must be some link between one's chosen and one's daily life, and the ways in which the Kwakiutl deal with food do bring power and depth to their use of oral imagery by creating anxiety and conflict on both individual and social levels. This does not imply, however, that the Kwakiutl were in any way hysterically, compulsively or neurotically concerned about food. Such an idea is contrary to my central thesis that food is the metaphor of social relationships, and that morality comes out of the renunciation of self-interested desire, no matter by what specific name we choose to denote human desire.

Finally, for the sake of narrative clarity I have adopted the convention of using the ethnographic present. Although I will be using the present tense, I wish to remind the reader that this work is an interpretation of materials relating to the Kwakiutl of the nineteenth century as depicted in the works of Boas and Hunt. As such it can be tested against the original historic materials only. Contemporary Kwakiutl culture is vigorous and strong, but its quotidian concerns, its internal structure, and its place within the larger Canadian society have so drastically altered in the last century that it would be incorrect to apply my conclusions to contemporary Kwakiutl society or to look for confirmation or refutation of those conclusions in a contemporary context.

ONE

Metaphors of Structure, Process, and Identity

All perception of truth is the detection of
an analogy.
—Henry David Thoreau, *Journal*,
5 September 1851

IT IS IMPOSSIBLE to understand Kwakiutl culture, and the structure and meaning of Kwakiutl behavior, without first understanding their basic ontological system and the principles of causality on which it is based. These causal principles delineate the organization and operation of the physical world and man's role in affecting events and their outcome.

Western ideas of causality are fundamentally different from those of the Kwakiutl. Indeed, the two ideas of causality are so different that scholars who have failed to see in their correct context Kwakiutl behaviors that do not fit into our scheme of cosmic structure have been forced to interpret them as acts of primitive mentality, infantile psychological fixation, prescientific thinking (magic), or even the dissociated acts of psychotics. Even the most recent structuralist approaches (Rosman and Rubel, 1971; Harris, 1974:111-30), which attempt to discover the underlying principles of other cultures, analyze these acts of the Kwakiutl as if they were metaphors for reality rather than a different form of reality in and of themselves (Lévi-Strauss, 1971). The general import of these interpretations is that the patterns of Kwakiutl ritual display prelogical or nonlogical thinking. However, for my purposes here the question is not whether Kwakiutl thinking is· more or less advanced, more or less practical or logical, than ours; it is simply how the two systems of thought differ in their fundamental postulates.

The basic principles underlying Western ideas of causality are two: continuity in time and contiguity in space. Causality is seen as the interaction of two objects or forces whose relationship involves their direct contact. If either temporal or spatial contact is removed, the two cannot exist in a causal relationship, that is, the action of one will be unable to affect the behavior of the other.

This conception of causality is totally alien to Kwakiutl thinking if only, as we will see later, because Kwakiutl ideas of time involve the endless cyclical repetition of a single eternal moment rather than a succession of discrete events. It is impossible to include the idea of linear time as a fundamental postulate of causality when it is not even one of the basic postulates of existence.

Instead, causality for the Kwakiutl is a relationship of sympathy in form and motion. Two items stand in a causal relationship if they can be shown to have inherent similarities in their structure; if some action is performed that utilizes that underlying structural similarity, then an event will be caused. Kwakiutl principles of causal relationship operate not through systemic, syntagmatic contiguities, but through metaphorical, paradigmatic correspondences (see Wagner, 1972: chap. 3 and Williams, 1938 and 1940:374-401 for discussions and exemplifications of these concepts).

What is traditionally called magical causality takes two forms, sympathetic and contagious. In the former, syntonic similarities in motions and structures intensify until a single human act is repeated by the spirits, and thus this type of causality can occur only when direct communication with the spirits is established. This is achieved through the creation of a state that I shall refer to as sacredness. In the latter, the motion and structure of the resultant act are inherent in an object and not in the human action involving that object. The performance of the proper ritual action automatically transfers the power of the action from the original possessor, the object, to the human using the object.

Structural similarities prerequisite to causal ritual acts are created by the use of prayers, that is, ritualized, formalized speech. Prayers function to articulate the important formal relationships between the component parts. This may be observed in the case of the following prayer to the sun (Boas, 1930:182): "Look at me, Chief, that nothing evil may happen to me this day, made by you as you please, Great-Walking-to-and-fro-all-over-the-World, Chief. Ha!" Here a structural relationship between man and sun is established on the basis of the analogous relationship of a man to a human chief ("Look at me, Chief"), by the statement that the sun as chief has the same responsibility to care for his subordinates as does a human chief ("that nothing evil may happen to me this day"), that the sun creates and directs the events of the day as the chief creates and directs the behavior of the animals the commoners must hunt ("made by you as you please"), and that the sun is a spirit-power just as the chief is a spirit-power (the metaphor "moving to and fro all over the world" being the standard way of implying the pervasive spiritual influence of a being). Thus, in this brief prayer the single relationship of human to sun as commoner to chief is emphasized in four different metaphors. In addition, we should add that the metaphorization of the idea of chief, here set up as structurally equivalent to the sun, is now expressible in terms of the characteristics of the sun.

Structural similarity is also created by the metaphorical extension of human behavior and social organization to encompass that of all animal and spirit beings. The Kwakiutl believe that animals and spirits lead lives that are exactly equivalent to those of humans. They live in winter villages, perform dances, wear masks, marry, pray, and perform all other acts that humans perform. This similarity is itself often sufficient to create a suitable formal structure for causal actions. Thus, a word, "chief," "friend," "brother," "grandfather," or any other term by which humans refer to one another at the beginning of a prayer, is the mechanism by which the prayer maker sets up the structural form necessary for the effectiveness of his words. In fact, since animals are considered to be human beings who have donned the masks and costumes that created their animal forms, people are united with the animals by virtue of the fact that they are all actually human beings.

The opposite is also true—that people and animals are related because humans are really animals, but animals who have removed their masks and costumes to return to their human state. Thus, the ultimate similarity between humans and animals is that they are in form, in constitution, in behavior, in motivation—in all ways—exactly the same. If humans are hungry, so then do animals hunger; if animals kill for food, so then must humans; if humans pray and fast, so then do animals; and if animals eat the flesh of the dead, so then must humans. Thus, human behavior and animal behavior, being equal, always reflect and reinforce one another, and humans see in animals the ideas, motivations, relations, and personalities they see in themselves. This, in turn, makes the metaphor of human/animal duality self-reinforcing.

The second aspect of all Kwakiutl causal acts involves the performance of a physical movement that will effect an event. Once two entities have been related by prayer, by verbal formula, or by the similarities in their metaphorization, the ritualist can utilize and mediate this structural conjoining so that the power inherent in both entities will create the desired effect. Thus, for example, once a shaman, through prayer and the use of such ritual paraphernalia as rattles, relates his sucking power to that of the spirits from whom he received his ability to cure and begins sucking on the body of the sick person, the spirit powers to whom he is related will also begin to suck. Magic, therefore, involves the magnification and intensification of a human action to a greater level of power. Although this power never belongs to a human but always to spirits, humans can obtain the use of the spirits' power if they set up reciprocal relationships with the spirits. Just as all members of a numaym, a ritually related community, help one another in their tasks in return for the sharing of food, so do the spirits help humans in return for humans' performance of the rituals that will ensure the spirits' reincarnation.

In short, animals, spirits, and humans form a ritual community, a co-operative mutual-assistance group (indeed a corporate group, for its membership exists eternally, owns economic prerogatives, and shares the work and the profit of those prerogatives). Goldman puts this idea succinctly when he defines Kwakiutl social organization in terms of ritual congregations:

> The Kwakiutl see each community as an incomplete segment of a wider universe. No part, no person, no tribe, no species, no body of supernatural beings is self-sufficient. Each possesses a portion of the sum of all the powers and properties of the cosmos; each must share with all or the entire system of nature would die. . . . Kwakiutl religion represents the concern of the people to occupy their own proper place within the total system of life, and to act responsibly within it, so as to acquire and control the powers that sustain life. (1975:177; see also 31-34, and passim)

The characteristics of the physical movement made by the ritualist are of the greatest importance, for the particular qualities of the movement he makes during the performance of the ritual will be repeated exactly in form, but with greatly increased power, by the spirits. Thus, if a man (i.e., a witch) wants to kill another by magic, his motions must clearly indicate the act of death and its direction toward the intended victim. Once they have created the power to kill, inexperienced witches who fail to perform correctly those actions that will point the death towards the intended victim run the risk of unleashing an uncontrollable death that may kill anyone, even themselves.

It is impossible to understand Kwakiutl ritual behaviors without first realizing that the prime agency of causality is not human action but spirit-power action, and that humans control the action of spirit-power only temporarily, and then only if they observe perfectly every aspect of a ritual. This is evident, for example, in the subject of Kwakiutl shamanism.

One of Boas's most famous manuscripts (1930) deals with shamanism, especially with the theatrical ruses and sleight-of-hand tricks shamans perform during curing ceremonies. The shamans themselves, and the rest of the Kwakiutl as well, seem well aware of the artificiality of the tricks—that is, that they are meant to mimic actions. Anthropologists have often wondered why it is that the natives do not complain that the shamans are performing tricks and not real cures. They have found it difficult to explain the seeming paradox that while Kwakiutl shamans are admired for their abilities at legerdemain, if a shaman bungles one of these tricks, he is immediately killed.

However, in the Kwakiutl causal system the paradox is nonexistent. The Kwakiutl pay no attention to the thoughts of the shaman while he is performing the act because the spirits effect the cure using the shaman as their instrument and the shaman's thoughts are irrelevant to the efficacy of his cure. The critical part of the cure is the fluidity, skill, and physical perfection with which the shaman performs his tricks, for it is the motions of the tricks (reinforced through their exact duplication by the spirits) that effect the cure. As long as the shaman performs his actions fluidly, the spirits are enjoined by cosmic forces to use their power to cure. The shaman who bungles his tricks, however, forces the spirits to perform actions that are as disjointed, undirected, and destructive as his. Such a shaman does not cure, but kills by unleashing uncontrollable chaotic power on the world, and thus he must be killed immediately before he can do greater damage. His death also provides a new soul in the spirit world that makes redress for whatever deaths he may have caused.

One relevant characteristic of the Kwakiutl conception of the universe not usually noted by anthropologists is that the Kwakiutl consider themselves to stand in a superior/inferior, superordinate/subordinate relation to the spirits. This particular dyad, a fundamental concept of Kwakiutl thought, lies at the foundation of all social and ritual behavior. In this relationship, the shaman is successful not because he has a special power as an individual, but because the spirits have chosen to use him as their medium for helping humans. The shaman has the ability to summon the spirits only because he observes the correct ritual taboos and performs the correct prayers. He can direct the power of the spirits by the perfection of his actions, but he himself, as a human individual, never possesses that power. That megalomaniacal hubris, which we have come to associate with shamans in general and with the Kwakiutl in particular, is simply not a function of Kwakiutl shamanic behavior. The shaman is dependent at all times on the spirits; he is at all times reminded of his inferiority to them and aware that his ability to control spirit-power comes only from his willingness to endure the torments, abstinences, fasts, ritual tortures, and complicated taboos that prevent the power he controls from backfiring upon himself. For him to become egotistical about his abilities is to risk the loss of the power itself.

This two-part structure to Kwakiutl causal actions imparts a particular tone to all Kwakiutl beliefs in that: first, because of the emphasis on creating formal relationships, there is an idea that a human cannot succeed when he acts alone but must always depend upon the aid of allies; and second, because of the emphasis on the perfection of physical movements, there is pressure for an individual to learn carefully the techniques of a given task. The satisfaction that results from a successfully caused end can occur only when the individual both creates correctly the framework for and directs the action of the causal power he is calling into play. All other actions result from forces out of the control of the individual.

We can see this two-part format at work in gambling during the well-known Hand Game. Here the Kwakiutl use various methods to deceive their opponents so that they lose sight of the hand the bone pieces are in. Some of these methods depend completely upon the skill of the man handling the bones, who can fool his opponents by mastering the correct technical motions, but others seem to us to be underhanded—the making of loud distracting noises, the singing of songs, and the use of sorcery to weaken the power of the opponents. These latter acts are the means by which the magical relationships of the opponents to their spirit-helpers might be broken, and by which the actions of one's own team might be elevated to magic so that no opponent could safely depend only on his observational skills. Indeed, because of the crucial role of spirits and spirit-power in gambling, we might say that the Kwakiutl play games as much with the spirits as with their human opponents.

In sum, prayers act to create relationships of form, networks along which power can flow from spirits and spirit-objects to humans who, through carefully directed ritual actions, can then utilize the power in specific ways that will lead to a single inescapable conclusion. Neither prayer nor ritual can exist alone. If the formal relationship is not first created, then the motion of the performer will have no higher consequence; if the relationship is created but not reinforced by action, then it dissipates and has no effect.

The state of existence that is in effect when formal relationships between humans and spirits are expressed in prayer and thus activated we can call sacredness. Certain Kwakiutl prayers create miniature temporary states of sacredness by emphasizing only one particular structural relationship (as in the prayer to the sun); these states are in effect for only a short time ranging from several minutes or even seconds to as long as a day, as in the case of the prayer to the sun. During the summer season, ceremonies lasting longer than one day repeat these prayers daily to re-energize the relationships. During the winter season, special prayers, which last for the entire length of the winter ceremonial, are said; these prayers are reinforced by the fact that each Kwakiutl assumes special names for the winter season, and these names in effect act as signs of the eternal relationship of humans to the spirits (see Boas, 1897:418-19).

We should also mention that the Kwakiutls' repetition of their origin myths on many special occasions signifies more than their social magnitude. Rather it is a long statement of relationship to the ancestral beings and the spirits of the world, calling into play the energies involved in those myths. Myths, then, are structural equivalents of prayers.

But we must emphasize one further point: that once a prayer has been made—either in a form that Boas calls prayer or in the other forms of songs, speeches invoking spirits and ancestors, and myths—the actions immediately following that prayer (and lasting for the time period stated by each prayer) are magical actions that call upon the spirit-power for their successful conclusion and that influence spirit behavior. That is to say, all actions following prayers are sacred actions. Thus, for example, the fact that meals begin with sacred songs (Boas, 1909:427-43; 1921: passim) indicates that the actions performed during the meal are themselves sacred, magical actions and cannot be analyzed simply as eating behavior.

For another example, the saying of a prayer upon the catching of a salmon or halibut (Boas, 1909:478) automatically makes the actions following that catch sacred actions with magical consequences. In this case, the prayer signifies to the fish that humans will perform those actions that will ensure the reincarnation of the fish. Thus, certain motions must be made—for example, the fish must be hit on the head with the correct fish club once, but never twice. The woman who butchers the fish her husband has caught must repeat her husband's prayer (not exactly, but in the same form) so that the sacred state is continued; and thus the woman's butchering acts become sacred acts, again in this case, related to the release of the fish's soul, for the husband's prayer is in effect only while the fish is in the canoe and before it is put down on the beach. Therefore, when we read the recipes and food preparation texts Hunt collected (Boas, 1921), the seeming ritualization of the butchering process is a consciously maintained kinetic process in which it is believed that the butcher's, the cook's, and even the eater's actions, because of the magical power involved, will have consequences far greater than that of the actual physical act. Thus, these actions must all be ritualized into particular forms, and mastered by everyone lest anyone inadvertently, through physical incompetence or ignorance, release these powers in destructive form.

To describe that state of sacredness, I use the term from theology, noumenon, which is a gloss for the particular feelings of fear and trembling that are associated with the presence of divine power and holiness.[1] The fear that is associated with noumenon is differentiable from that which is associated even with the most terrifying phenomenon, for the latter is considered to affect only the life history of the body while the

---

[1] I am referring here not to the concept of noumenon as it developed in phenomenological philosophy (see Edwards, 1967: III, 38ff., IV, 315, VI, 135, VI, 237), but as it was developed in theology by such writers as Kierkegaard (1941), Otto (1939), Buber (1958), Bultmann (1961, 1962) and Eliade (1964).

former is a fear experienced in the depths of the soul. In the case of noumenal fear, the basic motivation is proposed to be a sense of awe at the overwhelming potency of the spirit-power, a sense of personal insignificance, and, most importantly, a sense of having transcended mundane reality (see Wyss, 1973:384-412).

Kwakiutl ideas of the qualities of the sacred state are consonant with those of Western theology. The dominant component of this state, which enables humans to recognize it immediately, is the overwhelming fear they feel at the great power that is in their presence. So deep is this fear that even the strongest people begin to shake and tremble. The *hamatsa* dancer, for example, has as a basic part of his dance step a trembling gesture meant to indicate the potency of the power (of Man Eater) that is possessing his frail human body. In other rituals, shamans or dancers are considered to loose power into the air or discharge it directly into the bodies of the spectators, sending them into frenzied trembling.[2] The Kwakiutl consider experiencing noumenal fear to be a basic part of all humans' lives, occurring not once or twice in a lifetime, but many hundreds of times; in dances, feasts, meals, visions, dreams, fasts, in short, in all ceremonial activities. The potential involvement of the spirits in all types of activities leaves no single activity immune to the possible presence of noumenal force.

Kwakiutl conceptions of the characteristics of supernatural power are complex and varied. Every human activity and characteristic is in some way participant in the world of power; similarly, every animal, spirit, and plant being participates to some degree in the possession and exercise of supernatural power; and finally, all world events are the consequences of the exercise of supernatural power. In brief, the entire world is directly involved in the acquisition, the use, and the experience of supernatural power.

The idea that the entire universe is founded fundamentally on the workings of supernatural power has an important effect on Kwakiutl perceptions of the nature of events, especially in regard to those types of phenomena our culture calls miracles. For the Kwakiutl all events result from the conscious exercise of power by some human or spirit agency. Events whose every characteristic cannot be traced directly to a human action are explainable only as the result of spirit action. This means that there are no unexplainable acts, no events that are not the result of well-known mechanistic forces acting through ritual channels, no "miracles" that can be differentiated in principle from normal acts. Instead, all events partake of this feeling that supernatural agencies play an important role at every

[2] An example of this was filmed by Boas in 1931, and can be seen in his *The Kwakiutl of British Columbia* (1973).

stage in the course of events. Rituals do not act as mere palliations for human inability to perform chains of actions successfully. Rather, they are considered means of forcing the spirits to exercise their power for the benefit of humans—that is, they are as practical and mechanical as techniques of wood-carving or fishing. At the same time, the fact that all acts can be explained in terms of magical power has a reflective effect in that all acts, even the most mundane and straightforward, are conceived as succeeding only by virtue of the concerted use of both human and spirit power. No matter how skilled a woodcarver is, his carving will be excellent only insofar as he is helped by the spirits and their power to carve; the fisherman, no matter how carefully he has constructed his weir, is doomed to failure unless he can invoke spirit-power to make the salmon come to the place where he is fishing; and most importantly, no matter how young, healthy, or sexually active one might be, only when the proper rituals have been performed to ensure the spirits' placement of a soul in a human womb can pregnancy result.

Because all acts involve the participation of spirits to come degree, either through their direct intervention or through their gift to humans of their power, humans are never capable of completing an action on their own. Instead, they must always act in order to secure the cooperation of spirits in human endeavors. Thus, humans are the subordinates of spirits, for the spirits can control events on their own and are dependent on human aid only in a relatively few, but significant, areas of action, while humans are always dependent upon the spirits. Therefore, one of the major components of noumena—the feeling of insignificance in regard to the power of divine being—is part of Kwakiutl belief. Humans are the subordinates of the spirits, and their prayers emphasize this. In the previously discussed prayer to the sun, for example, the human states his subordination by structuring his relationship to the spirit in the metaphorical terms of a chief/commoner dyad. Other prayers state directly people's dependence on the benevolence of the spirits and their subordination to them (see Boas, 1921:618-19). In fact, the basic relation of human to spirit is always that of subordinate and superordinate, and people are never considered to have complete control over the actions they perform. Even shamans are not in and of themselves powerful as individuals. They are receptacles of power through which the spirits can control human destinies. The coveted powers of life- and death-bringers are not so much possessed by a person as lent to him through the largesse of the spirits for his use. Kwakiutl myths relating to these most magnificent of powers always emphasize the human's deservedness of them—the ritual acts that preserve the power and inform the spirits that he is honoring those commitments demanded of him if he is to receive the powers. The very paraphernalia of the shaman, especially the rattle and charms, are symbols of the shaman's subordination to the spirits for they show clearly the body of a dead (i.e., powerless) man on the back of a spirit-bird in whose beak is held the image of sacred power, a small ovoid piece of red wood.

The dialectic opposition of superordinate/subordinate is fundamental not only to Kwakiutl rituals but to all Kwakiutl thought and endeavor. The structural relationship of spirits to humans is replicated in the relationships of chiefs to commoners, husbands to wives, parents to children, animals to humans, Kwakiutl to non-Kwakiutl. Codified intrafamilially in kinship terminology and extrafamilially in the hierarchy of ranked ceremonial positions, this opposition provides a basic formula by which any relationship of two beings can be represented. Whereas we tend to see all members of a social class as equals more or less, for the Kwakiutl there are no equalities, only comparisons. People, animals, spirits, all living things, are always unequal, not only in their identities and their abilities, but also in their rights and responsibilities.

Indeed, it is this fractionating of social statuses, this particularization of the individual and his role, that provides the model by which the Kwakiutl define their lifegoals and the means by which to achieve them. Every social position has its particular rights and rewards, and social advancement can be measured in terms of the divestiture of subordinate positions in the hierarchy and the assumption of superordinate positions.

All social relationships in the Kwakiutl universe are founded on the superordinate/subordinate concept. One chief is subordinate to another, a commoner subordinate to a chief, a wife to a husband, a person to his numaym, and so forth. Yet while in the relationship of one human to another these relationships are constant, in relationships between humans and spirits or humans and animals, the particular being who is superordinate at any given moment will vary according to the nature of the interaction. For example, a hunter is subordinate to his prey, for he can catch that prey only when the prey animal allows him to; but the prey animal, once dead, is subordinate to the hunter, who, through the distribution of the animal's skin and body, now controls its destiny. A chief is subordinate to a spirit during the secular season, when food is obtained through the spirit's largesse, but during the sacred season, the spirit becomes subordinate to the chief, whose body the spirit needs if he is to appear in the human world. Superordination and subordination define not only relative social status but also the definition of who in a relationship functions as giver and who as receiver.

The superordinate/subordinate dyad thus presents both a model of social structure and a mechanism by which the social fabric can be maintained through gift-giving. The very workings of reciprocity and redistribution in the Kwakiutl world make equality impossible. The system can work only so long as inequality exists. Indeed, in cases where people of similar social status and wealth are involved in close association, rivalries and antagonisms seem to be normal in the course of events. In the famous case of "The Rival Chiefs" (Hunt, 1906), the two rivals are originally friends; and in the case of rivalries between shamans reported in *Kwakiutl Religion* (Boas, 1930), the shamans are Hunt's colleagues until his successes give cause for antagonism. The Kwakiutl pattern of inequality and differentiation is incompatible with the concept of equality between two people.

Thus, in all ritual and social acts one participant must assume a superordinate role with appropriate attitude and behavior, and reaffirm his superordination to the other participant. The speeches Benedict quotes in *Patterns of Culture* (1934) so emphasize this concept that she attributed their tone to the megalomania of the individual speaker, rather than to the requirements of rhetoric and the foundations of social organization. Parents instructing their children about marital relations emphasize subordination to the spouse as an essential part of the marriage (Boas, 1967:55-56). The Kwakiutl wedding practice of staging a mock battle may be seen as one instance of the application of this principle of dominance, for the husband's numaym proves its control of the situation by its ability to muster force to take the bride as hostage; the unwillingness of the bride's relatives to fight hard for her is, at least in part, a statement of their inferior status in regard to the husband's numaym.

We may see this affirmation of subordination that occurs in Kwakiutl rituals as a moral requirement of Kwakiutl religion, for it is by virtue of his subordinate status in regard to the spirits that a person is able to obtain their help, just as it is by virtue of their subordination to their chief that the members of a numaym are able to obtain his help. Since rituals are efficacious only when the proper structural relationship between the actors involved has been set up, and since marriage and war are situations involving the spirits (especially since they are situations in which the ownership of spirit-given privileges changes hands), marriages and wars are sacred acts whose structures must duplicate those of other sacred rituals. And since all sacred rituals are acts whose fundamental structure comes from subordination, then marriage and war achieve their character from the expression of subordination that underlies them. It would be blasphemous for a person to enter into either activity without the proper religious attitudes and preparations because he would be indicating his disregard for the power of the spirits by acting on his own; and it would also be foolish, for as with all other acts, the desired effect can be achieved only when the spirits have been enjoined to cooperate. Marriages and wars, like curing and hunting, will fail unless the spirits are enjoined to become involved in them through the proper performance of the sacred rites surrounding them.

There are several ways, the Kwakiutl believe, to create a state of sacredness. First, as mentioned earlier, it is created by the use of prayers. Other forms of verbal acts, however, may also create this state. Songs, which are considered to be the gifts of supernaturals to humans and the individual property of the person to whom they were given, are a prime mechanism for establishing a sacred mediation. Using names is itself a sacred act. Not only are some names considered to have been the gifts of the spirits to the first humans and to have, consequently, eternal existence, but all names are granted as signs of a relationship to the spirits. The fact that the assumption of a new name and the divestiture of an old name must be celebrated in a potlatch is clear indication of the sacred qualities of names. Sacredness is also created through the giving of speeches, which, in formal rhetorical meter, repeat and validate the bonds of humans to spirits.

Sacredness occurs in all situations in which the spirits and/or their spirit-power is present. It can occur suddenly when a man is out hunting and a spirit comes into his presence. Such a situation is considered to be fraught with intense danger, and many texts speak of the blinding pain and death that the visits of spirits bring to unprepared and unprotected humans (see Boas, 1935:148; 1932:#568). The prayers, speeches, and songs with which a person codifies and thereby mediates his relationship to spirits are thus, in part, a defense against the overwhelming potency that spirit-power possesses, providing a framework for the channelization of the power present. Prayers thus simultaneously elicit the power of the spirits and direct it toward human benefit rather than destruction.

Various ceremonial and ritual activities combine these methods in differing proportions. Everyday acts, such as fishing and food preparation, may require merely a single prayer expressing the relationship of fisherman to fish; at the same time, however, the fish are willing to be caught because the chief, who holds the name giving him the right to permit his kinsmen to fish at that place, has performed all those rituals for which he is responsible. The sacred quality of potlatches and the winter ceremonials is indicated primarily by the assumption of special ritual names. In addition, within these ceremonies specific ritual activities require their own special verbal mechanisms for the reaffirmation of their sacred character. Thus, the potlatch involves not only the use of sacred names but also the giving of speeches, the saying of prayers, the telling of myths, and the singing of songs. The sacralizing of the winter ceremonials involves the complete dissolution of the secular social fabric, the assumption of names used only for the duration of the winter season, and the use of ritual paraphernalia, all of which reinforce the state of power inherent in the ceremonies.

The singing of songs and the recital of ritual speeches is indicative of the transcendental quality of the actions that will follow them. Actions following these ritual verbal acts should not be viewed in any way as secular acts. If we find a giveaway of blankets at a potlatch preceded by a recitation of a numaym's myth, we must view that giveaway as part of an extension of the myth, as if the giveaway were itself the natural and necessary conclusion of the myth. Myth and giveaway form a unit that is equivalent to that of prayer and action. The myth, like the prayer, creates the relationship between human and spirit, and the giveaway, like the action, effects the result. Furthermore, if the giveaway is itself part of a sequence of sacred acts influenced by and influencing peoples' relationship to the supernaturals, we cannot view it as merely an economically based, profit-motivated, secular transaction between groups of human beings. To do so would be to ignore those participants of the giveaway who are as important, if not more so, than the humans who perform the action. It would ignore those supernatural spirits who have given humans the wealth, the desire, the reason, and the obligation to perform potlatches and who have given them the rationale and the motivation for the ceremonial.

Despite the apparent economic motives of the potlatch, which ethnographers are careful to mention, the giving of a potlatch should in no way be seen as a profit-making activity. Although controversy has surrounded the problem of the double-return of interest on potlatch gifts, most ethnographers tend to doubt that such a custom could have ever existed; few would accept a gift with the knowledge that it would have to be returned in a year with a gift of double the value. Economically such an action would be bankrupting. The ethnographers look mistakenly only at the gifts that Westerners consider valuable and not at those invisible items that the Kwakiutl believe are also exchanged at potlatches. For the Kwakiutl, the spiritual welfare of the tribe is a costly commodity that can be preserved not by the accumulation of profits, but by the acting out of those sacred responsibilities to provide wealth for others at one's own expense because it is one's moral responsibility. The purpose of the potlatch is to lose money and thus to gain spiritual purity. The Kwakiutl eschew profit making at a potlatch to avoid being placed in social debt.

In addition, faced with the dilemma of a ceremony in which people lose money in their transactions, we must not resort to the economists' hypothesizing of a quality called prestige, which makes up for one's financial loss (Suttles, 1960). Instead, we must examine carefully those qualities the Kwakiutl themselves consider to be the return given to a person who gives to others at a potlatch. As we will see, this return is not considered to be given by humans, but is given by the spirits to humans: that is, the man who gives the potlatch receives his reciprocal gift in spirit-power, which will directly enable him during the coming years to secure, by the grace of the spirits, a plentiful supply of food. Prestige has nothing to do with it. The results are considered to be tangible, meaningful, and essential, and they can be achieved only by the giving away of wealth.

The unity of humans and spirits is considered by the Kwakiutl to be far more basic, more incontrovertible, and less mechanical than the mechanisms of prayer, myth, and song by which it is reinforced. Prayers, myths, and songs tell of the covenants that people have made with the spirits, of the artificial relationships that have resulted from historic accident: the chance encounter of a spirit and an ancestor or the chance inspiration of a song. But human and spirit are both united in a far more inextricable manner, for both of them are motivated and dominated by the overwhelming cosmic force of hunger. Just as humans must always search for food to relieve the cravings in their bodies, so the spirits too need food to survive; just as humans covet each other's food, may fight for that food, and struggle to acquire food, so the spirits struggle to get food and satisfy their cravings. No spirit is free from the demands of hunger, and no spirit is so powerful that he can escape hunger. Myth after myth tells of humans who meet spirits whose sole desire is the acquisition of food and in whom the desire for food is so strong that they forget the basic prescriptions of social interaction (see Boas, 1935b:1-12). Beings of all types take food from their children in order to satisfy themselves, and they may even kill strangers, relatives, and their own children just to obtain flesh.

No creature in the Kwakiutl pantheon or in the Kwakiutl universe is free from the overwhelming desires of hunger. From the smallest slug to the great Thunderbird, all animals, all humans, and all spirits search for food. Thus, the ultimate, eternal structural relationship of human to the universe is established through hunger. As we shall see in the next chapter, the mechanisms that create and reinforce Kwakiutl social structure are all directly related to the acquisition of food. In a sense no matter what aspect of sociality a praying Kwakiutl draws on to metaphorize his relationship with the spirits, it is only an aspect of the greater relatedness that comes from the need for food. Consequently, in Kwakiutl ritual affairs the greatest chiefs, the most powerful men, are those who in some way can control the forces of hunger and satiation (the obviation of hunger) to their own purposes. Thus, for example, shamans' charms, rattles, costumes, and paraphernalia are heavily ornamented with images of mouths and teeth indicating the shaman's relation to the irresistible power of the spirits' hunger, part of which the shaman can invoke for a specific curing purpose. The *hamatsa* dance involves many symbols of spirit hunger as well: the cedar bark ornaments, representing the flesh of trees (conceived of by the Kwakiutl as living beings); the models and simulacrums of human corpses; the violently hungry, destructive actions of the *hamatsa* dancer himself; and the large corpus of myths validating the ritual purpose and nature of *hamatsa* initiations as the expression in human life of those vast forces that originate in and emanate from the home of Man Eater, the spirit who personifies insatiable hunger and its destructive force.

The efficacy of Kwakiutl actions is related to the strength of the bond by which they have related themselves to the world of spirit-power, and actions performed after this initial structuring stage will be efficacious proportionally to the strength of the movements involved and the kinetic power inherent in them. Since the most powerful human-spirit relationship and the most powerful kinetic motions are oral, we might conclude that the most powerful ritual acts should be predicated upon oral metaphors and oral behaviors that play out the dialectic possibilities of oral metaphors. And indeed such seems to be the case for the Kwakiutl. The rituals with the greatest cosmic effect involve oral imagery and behavior—vomiting, chewing and swallowing, spitting, speaking, singing, and biting. Acts invoking and involving the power of orality are far more efficacious than those that do not because they utilize the basic motivating force of the universe. Since all humans and all spirits are involved in the search for food, the rituals involving food are immediately effective in enjoining the interest of the spirits, who are directly involved in all acts of hunger and feeding.

If the major way in which humans relate themselves to the spirits is in terms of their mutual need for food, a force so great that no human or spirit can overpower it, it would seem to follow that all acts in any way involving food or eating or in any symbolic way mimicking oral behavior would be especially ritualized, surrounded with religious acts, prayers, taboos, and other anxiety-releasing defense mechanisms. And as we shall see in the next chapter, such is certainly the case. The Kwakiutl imbue all acts involving food and eating with a great deal of ritual activity and ambiance, so much so that it is nearly impossible to see hunting and fishing and meals as merely secular activities. Instead, these seem to be sacred acts in much the same way as the winter ceremonials or the potlatch. In addition, once we realize that meals are sacred occasions, then all large ceremonials that have as one of their parts the eating of a meal, the distribution of food, or the ritual enactment of any aspect of the gathering or eating of food are reinforced in their religiousness by virtue of their association with that food-act.

As we should expect, Kwakiutl social commentary does not take the form of criticizing an individual for his peculiarly idiosyncratic traits. Instead it takes the form of stating that the correct social formulae, which foster the well-being of the group, are being ignored and contravened by the antisocial behavior performed. Thus, for example, one chief may criticize another by stating that the latter's wealth comes not from the performance of the correct hereditary rituals, which ensure the giving of wealth to man by the spirits, but by the chief's hiring out his daughters as prostitutes and then using the money to give a potlatch (Boas, 1925:93ff.). Here it is not the prostitution that is considered to be bad; it is the fact that the chief uses wealth gained in an incorrect way for ritual exchanges themselves directed toward the garnering of wealth. By using wealth gained inappropriately the chief flouts the rules of society—and, even worse, merely to gain status for himself.

Even within the family, criticism of other family members is rare and heavily camouflaged when expressed. Parents may not even mention their child's transgression, no matter how serious it may be, hoping that somehow the child will realize the error of its ways. In the case of the "Story of Naensxa of the Koskimo" (Boas, 1921:1256-60), Waned's mother, though horrified by her supposed son's statement that he is hungry, not only refrains from making any critical comment or criticism of him but also brings him a bowl of food. Her means of socializing him so that he no longer makes such terrible statements is to call in the chiefs and shamans to examine Waned and to find out why he is ignoring the fundamental basis of human interaction, the denial of self-interest. The discovery that the hungry Waned is actually Waned's ferocious dog in Waned's body, and that the real Waned has been bewitched, indicates that only beasts and people whose normal control has been contravened by the action of witchcraft can be expected to express antisocial desires. With the congregation of chiefs responsible for the criticism of Waned, the mother is relieved of the onus of having to make a direct statement about the behavior of her own child. Socialization is thus removed from the realm in which it is merely a contest between the conflicting demands of the child and his parents. Waned's supposed act is not conceived of as a transgression against his parents, nor is his supposed failure to conform considered to be a sign of the quality of their socialization of him. His behavior is considered a transgression against the group, and his punishment is a matter for consideration by the group. The ultimate decision of the group is that Waned's behavior can neither be blamed on him as an individual nor on the group itself, but is the result of the actions of shamans and witches. Finally, since these shamans and witches transformed Waned into a beast solely to teach him not to be, nor to permit anyone else to be, violent and destructive, the responsibility for their action is obviated because of the social good that motivated it.

The principle that underlies the story of Waned is one of the fundamental behavioral postulates upon which Kwakiutl interpersonal relations are based: human desires create conflict and destruction that can quickly get out of hand, and that as a result it is people's responsibility to work together to prevent conflict and destruction from ever beginning. The Kwakiutl philosophy of childrearing, Kwakiutl social organization, and Kwakiutl ritual and religion are founded on this postulate. The central position of this principle in Kwakiutl thought is maintained through the interplay of socialization practices and social institutions, the first promoting the suppression of the desires of the individual, and the second providing a milieu in which those behavior suppressing desires are rewarded. The suppression of desire is thus reinforced, making it adaptive and satisfying for the individual. The congruence between the inner suppressions of the individual and the social demands put upon him by the particular cooperative form of Kwakiutl social institutions creates a situation in which the Kwakiutl individual feels comfortable and guiltless only when he knows that he is acting correctly, and that means only when he is denying his own desires, which he sacrifices to the social good.

The social aspect of self-denial may be approached from another direction. As in Christian theology, where it is as much a sin to pridefully believe oneself to be pure as it is to be greedy or lustful, so for the Kwakiutl self-denial is considered to be self-seeking if it does not have as its aim a greater social good. The religious mendicant must remove all of his actions, including self-denial, from the taint of indulgence or he cannot rid himself of the impurities that beleaguer his soul. Thus, it is not enough for a Kwakiutl merely to purify himself so that he will feel better; the act of purification must have as its ultimate purpose the benefit of the entire social group.

In a similar way, the possession of wealth for its own sake is an indulgence among the Kwakiutl. Though the desire to acquire wealth is itself a noble desire, and the distribution of wealth is a fundamental responsibility, the mere possession of wealth is indicative not of greatness but of greediness. Chiefs count their worth not by what they possess but by what they have given away. Miserliness is not only a character fault, it is an indication of such a terrible self-interest that it denotes hatred of others. For the Kwakiutl the miser is a witch (and, conversely, Kwakiutl witches are often considered to be misers). Thus, it is better for a chief to impoverish himself, his family, and his numaym than to stop giving away wealth at potlatches. And it is worse to be poor than to be rich, not because life is easier for the rich but because the rich can give wealth away. The poor, lacking what they need, must be all the more envious and desirous of it, and thus must be all the more self-interested.

Kwakiutl rules governing food sharing mitigate against miserliness and provide a basic mechanism by which individual possessions may be used to implement social cohesion. Food must be shared; it cannot be denied. When a person demands food, or requests it (which is merely another form of demanding it), he must be given food. To deny food is to express selfishness and a lack of regard for the person who requested it. Thus, when children request food, they must be fed. Waned's mother, though horrified by her son's request for food, cannot refuse it (Boas, 1921:1256-60). To have refused his request would have been to state that she considered her own selfish desire to have him behave correctly to be more important than his need for food. At the same time, the act of demanding food is antisocial and destructive, and must be expunged from Waned's behavior. This can be accomplished only by making Waned aware that his desire must be suppressed, a conditioning that must be performed socially. Kwakiutl socialization therefore consists of two opposing forces: the need to feed a child when it expresses its hunger and the need to teach the child not to express its hunger. While an individual's demand for food cannot be countenanced in a cooperative society, it cannot be openly punished or refused. Therefore, the practices of Kwakiutl child-rearing focus on training the child never to request food.

The suppression of self-interest and self-gratification is a major factor in maintaining the social harmony of Kwakiutl society. As is true among other Northwest Coast peoples, Kwakiutl society has few legal institutions, and when disputes arise outside the numaym there are few institutional means for settling them. Boas's texts include a number of cases of conflict situations, the most famous being disputes between mountain-goat hunters (1921:1345-48), fights over fishing spots (1921:223-24), and disputes between hunters and chiefs over the proportion of the kill belonging to the chiefs. In each situation, violence or the threat of violence is the primary means of obtaining recourse. Chiefs use slaves, numaym members, or hired thugs to defend their demands, while commoners must depend on their individual physical strength or the cooperation of others. Because the potential for violence is present in any conflict situation, and because there are no means by which violence, once started, can be stopped, it behooves every Kwakiutl to see that disputes do not occur. The person who allows himself the indulgence of demanding his own way opens the door to the chaos of feud and warfare. Self-denial functions to preclude conflict.

Within the numaym, however, there is a means for resolving disputes, although there is no way to judge its effectiveness. The head of the numaym may make suggestions as to the resolution of the conflict, but his decisions are not binding on the disputants. Though in some ways a numaym head is also a political leader, the major component of his authority is his ritual ties to the supernatural spirits. The person who contravenes the chief's decision jeopardizes the spiritual well-being of his entire numaym, and we can assume that the informal pressures of his fellow numaym members are as important as the threat of violence in convincing a person to resolve his dispute in accordance with the chief's wishes.

Even so, there are numerous cases where an individual leaves his natal group and becomes an adjunct member of a different numaym in another village rather than submit to the chief's decision.

While a chief can arbitrate disputes between the members of his own numaym, and while all the chiefs of a village may get together to plan cooperative actions, although this is usually only in regard to the winter ceremonials (Drucker and Heizer, 1967:81-97), or to make decisions about behavior before the fact of a transgression, there are only two mechanisms by which disputes between numayms can be decided: warfare and rivalry potlatches. According to Codere (1950), warfare was far more prevalent aboriginally than it had been during the last century, and aboriginal rivalry potlatches were infrequent. The decrease in warfare as a result of white influence brought about a concomitant increase in rivalry potlatches that substituted for acts of war and provided an avenue for aggression previously released through fighting. However, it would be more consistent with the necessities of conflict resolution in Kwakiutl society to conclude that both warfare and rivalry potlatches existed in aboriginal culture. The potlatch fulfilled the purpose of settling disputes where recourse to violence would be unreasonable or where spirit intervention precluded the use of violence. Warfare was used in cases where the hostility involved was so great that the restrained formalities of potlatching were incongruent with the emotions underlying the dispute. To conclude that there were few rivalry potlatches in aboriginal times is to predicate a situation in which the Kwakiutl would have no means of dispute settlement other than feud. However, even if, as Codere suggests, with the end of warfare the potlatch did serve in part as a mechanism for conflict resolution, it may have subsumed this function because its original nature already possessed the imagery and machinery for directing and resolving conflict. We can imagine an aboriginal system in which the potlatch provided one format for the expression of conflict and warfare another. It is not necessary to conclude that the structure of the potlatch changed from peaceful ceremony to rivalry battle, but only that with the suppression of warfare the Kwakiutl came to rely on a particular preexisting form of conflict resolution. Although previously less effective than warfare, the potlatch gained in importance until by the end of the nineteenth century it had become the primary mechanism for expressing and resolving disputes. (Strathern [1971] comes to a similar conclusion about Mount Hagen moka exchanges.)

Confronted with a causational theory and a social system in which every human action has the potential to invoke the vast forces of power capable of destroying the universe, the Kwakiutl must also develop means of limiting the consequences of human action. We have already seen that by creating a demarcation between secular times (when the consequences of human action are minimal) and sacred times (when the consequences are overwhelming), the Kwakiutl can remove some of their behavior from the possibility of cosmic consequence while at the same time imbuing a specific, bounded set of ritual behavior with greater social, psychological, and causative significance. By virtue of the highly organized way in which these rituals are performed, with limitations on the forms of motion permitted during the rituals, human action is directed into positive, constructive channels that cannot unleash destruction.

The debilitating anxiety that could arise in a thought system in which no human activity is considered to be under direct control but is considered instead to be controlled by some higher force is mitigated in Kwakiutl thought through mechanisms by which humans are related structurally to the forces that govern their fate. By influencing the behavior of these forces, humans can indirectly control their own welfare.

The act of creating a state of sacredness is itself a method for the structuring of a human's relationship with the spirits who rule his life, and the state of sacredness has its own incontrovertible rules by which both humans and the spirits are constrained. At the same time, the antithetical state of nonsacredness is logically outside the binding force of the rules governing behavior in a sacred state. Thus, a person can control his behavior by setting up a period when the actions of the spirits are not in effect, and he can control the actions of the spirits by dealing with them only under conditions when the spirits are themselves constrained. Consequently, the state of sacredness cannot be seen as a chaotic period when the rules of life are suspended, but instead must be seen as a period when the lackadaisical attitudes than can be a part of normal life are no longer permissible. The state of sacredness is the ultimate form of behavioral organization, the most regulated, the most codified, and the most unchangeable. The state of sacredness is the state of order and perfection.

The evangelical tradition in Western civilization has fostered an idea that the state of sacredness is associated with ecstasy, with the abandonment of social forms, and with the transcending of normal action. For the Kwakiutl, however, there is a clear distinction between feelings of sacredness and feelings of ecstasy in which normal social behavior is overridden. Feelings of ecstasy are associated with neither sacred nor nonsacred actions specifically; various acts in either realm may involve ecstasy, which overpowers normal reason and control. In the sacred realm, for example, certain rites involving spirit-power induce ecstasy, as is the case with the Toogwid Dance shown in *The Kwakiutl of British Columbia* (Boas, 1973; see also, Boas, 1897:487-94). However, here the sacredness of the dance is independent of its ability to induce ecstasy (though we might consider the ability to induce ecstasy a sign of the dance's power). Indeed, the achievement and display of ecstasy is a rare occurrence even in the most violent-seeming sacred ceremonies. At such times, the potential destructiveness of the uncontrolled behaviors that occur during ecstasy is so great that vast controlling forces must be invoked.

The organization of behavior during states of sacredness is actually a well-known facet of Kwakiutl ethnography, though few ethnographers have developed the idea beyond a merely descriptive depiction of the ceremonies. Kwakiutl rituals are highly codified, and are carefully practiced and performed. For example, mistakes, even simple mistakes, made during ritual performances at the winter ceremonials may be punished by death; at the very least the giving of a potlatch, which re-establishes the structural rules broken by the commission of the error, is required. The belief that control is necessary during states of sacredness may be seen to originate in the idea that during such states every action of a human being is magnified to cosmic proportions, as we saw in the case of shamanism, and that mistakes create disorder. Indeed, with the possible consequence of actions being drastically magnified, caution and care far beyond that required in everyday secular life must be strictly exercised. As in daily life, carelessness in sacred states breeds chaos; that ecstasy is pleasurable in no way makes it less chaotic. Indeed, its very pleasurableness is one important reason why ecstasy must be suppressed at all costs lest someone create destruction through a narcissistic urge for pleasure.

Thus, we must make a distinction between the states of ecstasy and the states of sacredness in Kwakiutl religious ideology, a distinction Benedict failed to make. In their religious actions—the vision quest, sacred dances, potlatches, and ceremonials—the Kwakiutl seek not the transcendental feelings of ecstasy but the transcendental feelings of superhuman self-control and purity that characterize feelings of sacredness. The transcendental feelings the Kwakiutl seek are not in the least Dionysian, but are Apollonian. The Kwakiutl seek not excess but order.

The differences in secular and sacred behavior do not stand in opposition to one another so that if secular is controlled, sacred must be uncontrolled, and so forth. Secular and sacred behavior are conceived as two totally different states of existence. In a secular state, the relationships called to the fore are human/human relationships, involving individuals only as individuals. In a state of sacredness, however, analogies are created that abrogate or deemphasize ties between humans and replace them with ties that unite individual humans with individual spirits. We might diagram the differences between these two states in the manner seen in figure 1:

In the secular state, humans are related because they are kinsmen or affines or coworkers, or because they like one another, or because of any of a number of social principles. Similarly, spirits are related to one another for the same social reasons. The processes at work in the human

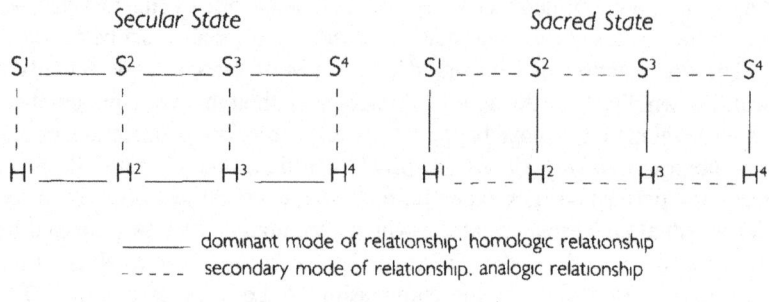

Figure I Human/Spirit Relationships

and spirit realms are parallel to one another (for example, spirits may be related as coworkers or kinsmen), but the two systems act independently of one another. In the sacred system, however, bonds such as kinship and friendship are dissolved, and instead, the analogies between humans and their spirit counterparts become the mode of structuring relationships. We might say that in a secular event groups are formed on the basis of social metaphors, whereas in a sacred event they are formed on the basis of spiritual metaphors.

This dual system has some important corollaries. First, the drawing of ties between humans in terms of a certain limited set of social metaphors creates a situation in which the relations of spirits with other spirits are metaphorized in those same terms. Thus we discover that the Kwakiutl consider the animals and the spirits to live in worlds structured exactly like those of humans, with villages, houses, tribes, marriages, and so forth. The particular ethnography of the spirit world is outlined in myths (the tales of *Oëmal* and *Q!aneqelaku* [Boas, 1935b:1-16], for example, and others that deal specifically and exclusively with spirits). However, the relationships between the spirits recorded in myths also define the relationships to each other of the humans who are telling the myths, for if the spirits live according to kinship, reciprocity, and social principles, should not people live by these principles as well? Myths thus provide a system through which humans' ideas are projected and then reinforced by their association with spirits in a self-contained feedback system.

A second corollary of the dual system of action is that the analogies uniting individual humans with individual spirits are also outlined in myths. The tribal, numaym, and household myths, which are a ubiquitous feature of Kwakiutl culture and one of its best-known aspects, are mechanisms by which the analogies between humans and spirits are made explicit by being made simultaneously history and gospel. Kwakiutl origin myths thus give definition and reality to the relationships between humans and spirits.

For example, since all people are united because they are all subject to the force of hunger and thus must learn to cooperate in the collection and distribution of foodstuffs, it naturally follows in the Kwakiutl system that spirits, in that they are generally like humans, also must be subject to the force of hunger and thus to the necessity of cooperating to procure and distribute food. This point is more than amply made in the myth of *Q!aneqelaku* (Boas, 1935b:1-12) in which *Q!aneqelaku*'s parents, Heron and Woodpecker, wish to hoard food and not to share it, but are discovered and punished, and in the myth of the stealing of the sun (Boas, 1887:423) in which a spirit-chief keeps the sun to himself in a box. Thus, we can say that if a behavior can be found in humans, it can also be found among the spirits; and similarly, if a behavior is described for spirits, it can also be discerned in humans.

The motivation of humans and spirits is equivalent. Thus, if Human H^1 is related to Spirit S^1, either secularly or sacredly, the behavior of S^1 in the myths becomes a perfectly natural part of the repertoire of acceptable behavior for H^1; and similarly, H^1 can project his desires into a form in which they become the desires of S^1, so that H^1's feelings of aggressiveness, for example, become projected as part of the character of S^1, and then are reintegrated as part of the justifiable behavior of H^1 because now those feelings can be attributed only to the character of S^1 and not that of H^1.

Humans in a secular state are related to one another by their humanness, whereas in a sacred state two humans are related only if they stand in analogous relationship to the same spirit. The individuality of human/ spirit relationships is codified in Kwakiutl thought by the use of names. Since only one person can embody a particular name, and since it is the name itself that links human to spirit (see Goldman, 1975), only one human can be related to a single spirit in a particular way. Only one aspect of sacred rites permits group identification with a single spirit— dance society membership (see Drucker, 1940). Here, several humans are related to one another not by social rules, but because they each stand in similar relationship to a given spirit or group of related spirits. Membership in these societies can be achieved only by performance of sacred rituals and the experiencing of a vision (an occasion during which the relationship between human and spirit is verified in a transcendental and numinous fashion). Members of the *hamatsa* Society, for example, are all related to one another only by virtue of the fact that they have each become related to the Cannibal spirits, especially to Man Eater. Rules of kinship have no influence on the relationships of these men. Indeed, even though membership in the *hamatsa* (or any other Kwakiutl dancing society) may be inherited, the heir cannot dance in the sacred ceremonies of that society until he has had a vision that incontrovertibly indicates his relationship to the spirit. The metaphor of the human/spirit relationship must be validated by the vision, which is itself a metaphor for the human/ spirit relationship.

The changing sets of metaphors upon which Kwakiutl activity is based are clearly denoted in Kwakiutl life. The year is divided into two seasons, and the activities that occur during each of those seasons are carefully prescribed. Ceremonies of the winter season, or *tseyka*, meaning "secret" (Boas, 1892:72), cannot be performed during the summer season, or *baxus*, and those of the summer season cannot be performed during the winter.[3]

The summer season is given over to secular organization. Group membership, daily life, food-gathering, and other activities are organized along idioms of locality, lineality, coresidence, friendship, and common interest. The patterns of group membership, of the individual's identification with a larger social whole, the bonds of kinship and friendship that operate in the summer are in effect only then; at the start of the ceremonies that mark the onset of the sacred season, they become secondary to those between individual humans and individual spirits. Yet, while the principal modes of affiliation switch during these two periods, at no time does either pattern of affiliation totally disappear; at no time is the operation of one pattern totally excluded. Both are always in effect, though one is always less important than the other. During the secular season men are united by their chief's ties to the spirits who provide food; during the sacred season they continue, despite their spirit connections, to reside and eat in groups organized along secular principles. For example, chiefs who stand at the head of their numaym by virtue of primogeniture, also are at the head of their numaym because of their connections to the spirits.

Obviously, since causality is a matter of relationship, it is necessary for the Kwakiutl to denote which pattern of organization is at work at a given moment so they can know what procedures will be causally effective. Thus, events are structured by those initial activities that serve to define the events as being sacred or secular. For example, as we shall see in the next chapter, meals, food-gathering, and cooking, indeed all aspects of the food-collection and preparation process, which we think of as secular activities, are defined by the Kwakiutl as sacred activities. This definition is achieved by beginning each part of the food-related processes with some religious act—a prayer, a sacred song, a penitential gesture that indicates the subordination of a human to a spirit on whose benefi-

---

[3] Indeed, the term *Baxus* (ba'qus) is translated as a "season when no Tsetsaeka [meaning winter ceremonials (1892:79)] must be held" (Boas, 1892.38)

cence he is dependent—denoting the analogy between human and spirit. The secularness of activities is marked by the absence of these preliminary sacred words or deeds. The weaving of a mat, the paddling of a canoe, and most of the other basic tasks in Kwakiutl life are performed without the introduction of sacred aspects, thus implying that action alone can achieve the desired end resuʀ.

Once we remember that all causal acts in Kwakiutl society are combinations of the setting up of an analogy and the subsequent performance of an action, we can see the distinction between sacred and secular as equivalent to the distinction between word and action. Rituals involving sacredness focus on the analogic aspects of causality, while rituals involving secularity emphasize the dynamic facet of causality. Of course, the most powerful, the most efficacious, causal rituals would be those combining strong analogic relations with vigorous but carefully structured physical motions. Indeed, this synthesis of powerful words and powerful actions is the fundamental characteristic of the major Kwakiutl rituals. Furthermore, since the greatest causal act people can perform is that of life-giving and life-destroying, Kwakiutl acts involving the creation or destruction of life always involve the synthesis of powerful metaphorical analogies (especially analogies between men, animals, and spirits) with the actions that derive from those analogies. These analogies center around the metaphors and the actions of eating: chewing, swallowing, vomiting, spitting, and biting. At all times, the analogy and the behavior must coincide if the rituals are to be efficacious. And of all the possible analogic links between people and the rest of the universe, none works so strongly as does the fact that human, animal, and spirit all experience hunger. As we shall see in the next chapter, the Kwakiutl view of human nature is one in which the bestial inner desires of the individual, especially the desire for food, are so powerful that only through strict control, both self-control and social control, can they be prevented from surfacing and destroying. As a result, much of Kwakiutl ritual activity and daily behavior is directed toward the structuring of activity in such a way that its dominant characteristic is orderliness and structural rigidity. Even when individual variation is permitted (as, for example, in the prayers to the sun discussed earlier in this chapter, the prayers to the salmon discussed in the next chapter, or in dances), the end results vary so little, one from another, that it is hard to believe variation was a factor in the first place. The structuring of action into modes of limited variation is a fundamental feature of Kwakiutl social organization and behavior.[4]

---

[4] It is difficult to tell whether the Kwakiutl theory of human motivation is one in which there is a basic desire that must be repressed, or one in which the energy of the basic desire needs to be rechanneled into a system where its destructiveness can be changed to constructiveness. Boas's materials are not detailed enough on matters directly related to personality

For the Kwakiutl, both the idea of sociality and the principles and units of social organization are metaphorized by a group of related symbols expressing the idea of containment: boxes, houses, numayms, villages, bottles, mats, canoes, baskets, weirs, bodies, mouths, and the like. All of these containers act as symbolic representations of the boundedness and the integrity of space, time, kinship, mutual interest, cooperation, and other social acts and ideas. While anthropologists have long recognized the importance of containers, especially boxes, as artifacts of Northwest Coast technology and have long appreciated the difficulty of making such boxes, they have paid scant attention to the social role these boxes play. Boxes are seen as storage areas for food, masks, or clothing, or as beautiful works of act and manufacture but their symbolic and ritual role in Indian life is virtually ignored. Yet, in actuality, boxes (and other containers) provide such an important metaphor for Kwakiutl social organization that we can see the ramifications of boxness, or the character and nature of boxes, throughout all Kwakiutl social and cosmological thought. Boxness forms the metaphorical basis in Kwakiutl philosophy for ideas of kinship and separateness, space and time, cooperation and competition, secularity and sacredness, self and other, life and death, and innumerable other dialectic oppositions. Humans are born from boxes, swaddled in boxes, catch, store, and serve their food in boxes, live in boxes, travel in boxes, and when they die are buried in boxes. Even the body itself is a type of box; humans not only live and die in boxes, but are themselves boxes. The universe is envisioned as a set of conjoined boxes. Time is envisioned as self-contained units that are as bounded and integral as boxes. Names act as containers for invisible spiritual matter in the way that wooden boxes contain material items. Social units act as boxes to contain people. Indeed, the metaphor of the box is so important that we must discuss it at length.

The structural characteristics of boxes as containers—with walls, an internal space, decoration on the walls, and lids—repeat again and again throughout all Kwakiutl life. Houses, bodies, costumes and masks, world levels, lineages, numayms and villages, animal species, names and souls, months and days, cradleboards and sites, dishes, storage containers, canoes, fishing weirs, and many other items of Kwakiutl culture are visualized and interpreted as though they were boxes or parts of boxes. Different items can be so similarly boxlike as to seem merely variations on a single visual template (see Boas, 1909:420-22, 444-45, 448 [illustrations]).

---

for one to reach a conclusion about which motivational theory the Kwakiutl espouse. However, as in Freudian psychoanalytic theory, where repression and sublimation are two aspects of the same psychic processes of ego defense, it is not really necessary to choose one of these two theories as the only one the Kwakiutl espouse. It seems more reasonable to accept both theories as reflections of one another rather than as mutually exclusive.

Three inherent characteristics of boxes are most noticeably manifested throughout Kwakiutl culture: the fact that boxes define space; the fact that boxes have an outer surface that separates inside the box from outside the box; and the fact that egress between the inner and outer space can be achieved only through some orifice that violates the integrity of the box's surface. A fourth important characteristic is determined by usage: boxes are used to hold valuable wealth items such as food, names, costumes, masks, coppers, animal skins, and the like—the supernatural treasures around which Kwakiutl activity centers. Thus, boxes are important both because they are containers and because of what they contain.

It cannot be maintained, however, that boxes provide a one-sided metaphor of Kwakiutl life—for example, that Kwakiutl ideas of the self are merely extensions of their idea of boxes—for metaphorization works in dialectic ways, defining entities as aspects of one another. Thus, at the same time as the characteristics of particular items are metaphorized as boxes, those items lend their characteristics to boxes as well. For example, an individual person is similar to a box in that he has a skin (wall) that differentiates space inside from space outside, a mouth providing an orifice through which matter may migrate between these inner and outer spaces, facial features (decoration), a stomach that contains food, and names. Boxes possess some of the qualities of individual humans and are considered to be alive; to be active forces in determining the flow of events; to have limited lifespans yet to exist forever, as humans do, through reincarnation; to have names, characters, souls, and idiosyncratic personalities; to be inextricably related to the spirits who bestow them and to the lineages and numayms upon which they were bestowed; to need nurturing and care; to demand respect and deference; and to need power if they are to influence the flow of events. As individuals are boxes, so are boxes individuals. Furthermore, as individuals are animate, so are boxes animate, and thus they mutually define each other's essential nature—the individual is a box that must be filled with some vital substance to bring it to life, and the box a container with substance within that must be given an individuality to bring it to life.

We could progress through a list of both Kwakiutl concepts and items of material culture to show how their essential characteristics are defined through the metaphor of the box, and in so doing provide fresh insights into many controversial concepts in Kwakiutl ethnography. For example, the numaym, a social group whose structure and functioning has been a perennial problem for students of kinship (see Goldman, 1975: chap. 2), is best visualized not as a lineage, nor as a local group, nor as the residents of a single house, nor as the relatives of a name holder alone, but as a box, invisible, but nonetheless real, whose boundaries are created by a set of walls (both the walls of a single house and the walls of lineality). This box has an inner and outer space defined through social oppositions (most noticeably manifested in the potlatch), and which possesses an orifice through which members of the numaym may enter or leave the numaym (that is, life and death violate the surface integrity of the box). Similarly, the members of the numaym are the treasure contained in that box, and their eternal supernatural possessions—their wealth—is the paraphernalia that is stored within that box for all time. Like the box, the numaym is named; has an individual identity; an eternal life and link with the spirit world; and a spiritual purpose in the universe. The members of the numaym create wealth through their power as the ritual items within the box create wealth through their power; the numaym protects its members as the box protects the items enclosed within its walls.

Kwakiutl social groups are denoted not only because they live in the same residential boxes (houses, numayms, villages, and tribes) but because they share the same food storage boxes. The members of a numaym give part of their food to their chief, who puts it into communal boxes, where it remains until its distribution during ceremonies. Individual families have their own food boxes, distinct from those that contain food intended for collective ceremonies, but no individual has an individual food box into which he alone puts and removes food for his exclusive use. Stored food removed from boxes is cooked in other boxes, and served in still other boxes (dishes, bowls, and trays) from which several people share. Travel is accomplished in canoes owned by a social group and containing that group as a bounded, static unit during movement through the water (which is the flux of the outside world). Fishing weirs, which are boxes for catching live fish, define cooperative groups because of the social rules that dictate who can use them. Of course, as relationships can be metaphorized through the sharing of food taken from a single box, separateness is indicated by the fact that the members of one group store their food in boxes from which the members of another group obtain no food.

This opposition between self and other is the means by which boxes become metaphors for corporate identity in Kwakiutl thought. Identity is composed of all those items that differentiate oneself from others (hence the use of hierarchical differentiation as the basis for social identity). In the case of an individual, identity comprises the aggregate of his body, his body as a spirit being, all his souls, and the ritual paraphernalia associated with these. All of these are the treasures stored in his name, or the box of his identity. In Kwakiutl terms, what we think of as individual identity is actually a corporate identity and exhibits the characteristics anthropologists usually associate with corporate descent groups. Obviously, this idea of corporation can be extended to include those groups anthropologists more traditionally consider as corporate—lineages, clans, numayms, secret societies—and boxes stand for their corporateness as well. This could hardly be more graphically displayed than it is in Kwakiutl wedding ceremonies, where treasures from one family are physically transferred from the mats and boxes of one family to those of the other, or in potlatches, where the transfer of goods from one box to another is a significant part of the proceedings.

The denotation of the numaym as an enclosed social group is reinforced by the fact that the numaym is analogous to the body (or box) of a man. It has an eternal name, a village bounded on all sides by sea, forest, and sky, a house with both an eternal name and an eternal skeleton that forms the body of the numaym and that will exist as long as a single member of that group survives to inhabit it. The members of the numaym are the soul of that house, for as long as they fulfill their ritual obligations to the spirits who helped fashion their group in mythic times, the spirits will continue to provide them with food and new souls to be incarnated as numaym children. As a human has a heart to rule his behavior, so a numaym has a chief; as a human has hands to work, so a numaym has commoners; as a human who needs food to survive must devote himself to the practical and ritual tasks that guarantee food, so the members of a numaym must work to ensure their mutual survival through unified, co-operative action in regard to the spirits and the food they bestow. As a human has a mouth that is the boundary between his inner self and the greater cosmos, so a numaym's house has a mouthlike snapping door that is the boundary between their own world and the greater realm of people; and so a numaym's village (in aboriginal times) has a beach that is its boundary between the numaym's place in the world of humans and the worlds of the sea, sky, and forest. Thus, the body as a metaphor for the numaym creates a structure in which the internal nature of the body/numaym is opposed to the external world of ''other'' and in which the organic unity essential to the survival of the body of an individual is extended to the idea of the organic unity that is necessary to the survival of the numaym.

Another social relationship that is clearly denoted through the metaphor of boxes is the chief/commoner relationship. For example, in the process of collecting dogwood berries (Boas, 1921:220-21), a chief, who owns the privilege of collecting, hires women to go and pick the berries. They take with them baskets of three sizes: small, medium, and large. Berries are picked into the small basket; when it becomes full the berries are poured into the medium-sized basket. This process continues until the medium-sized basket is filled, at which point it is emptied into the largest basket. The filling of the baskets continues in this manner until all the baskets have been filled. Then the women return to the house of the chief, where one of his retainers or relatives empties the contents of the medium and largest baskets into one of his house's oil-boxes. The berries in the smallest baskets become the property of the women. Here the process is one in which the size of the baskets metaphorizes the relationship of chief to food. The chief provides the food, which is stored in bigger and bigger baskets until all are filled; the chief's distribution of the food reverses the process—the berries are served in large feast dishes at first, then some are removed and placed in medium-sized dishes, and from these dishes are served individual portions of berries. The chief's association with large amounts of food is symbolized by his close association with large baskets and dishes, the role of commoners symbolized by their association with the small baskets. At all times, abundance and generosity are associated with the chief, and hard work and dependency on the largesse of others are associated with the commoners. The collection and distribution of food is a complete cycle, mimicking the cycle of reincarnation and its ritual enactment through the garnering and storing by chiefs of souls that they later distribute at potlatches.

Just as spatial and social relationships are metaphorized in terms of boxes, so are they metaphorized in terms of mats, which are a variant form of box. Mats serve to denote temporary sociospatial arenas within larger, more permanent arenas—they may be placed anywhere within that larger arena, thereby creating localized interactional areas.

Mats are used to define spaces for many different events (see Boas, 1909: photographs; also Boas, 1973). They define workspace for a wide variety of tasks and eating areas as well as food-collection and preparation areas. They are used to create sleeping areas for individuals and groups, to wall off rooms within a house, or to form the walls of a temporary summer dwelling. Placed on the floor during potlatches, they create a central collective locus on which wealth can be piled after it has been removed from its storage boxes. Worn as clothing, mats wall off the body from the world around it; used as menstrual napkins, they separate the world of the womb from the world outside. During the winter ceremonials, a variant form of mat, the painted screen, made either of wood or cloth, separates secret areas from public areas, forming a secret room (or box) that is the backstage arena of the ceremonial activities. The analogy between this sacred room and a box (or body) is intensified in the *hamatsa* dance by the painting of a mouth on the curtain, which is the only point at which egress from one room to another is possible (Boas, 1935:83).

Just as physical space is organized through the placement of mats, so is social space. At meals and feasts the number of people sharing a mat varies according to their statuses—the highest chiefs have a mat to themselves; lower chiefs and commoners must share mats. Kwakiutl recipes always note clearly how many mats must be placed on the ground according to the specific food served and the number and statuses of the people at the meal (Boas, 1909:427-43). At tribal feasts, special feast mats, which may be twenty or thirty feet long (Drucker, 1955:99), divide the room into areas that define the social oppositions between tribes. The sharing of mats indicates some similarity between the people who share them, while the placement of people on separate mats indicates dissimilarity.

The type of space mats delimit differs from the type of space boxes delimit. Mats are open on all sides but one, while boxes are closed on all sides but one. Thus, boxes act to define hidden, private, closed, secret space (as in the case of the sacred room), while mats define visible, open, public space. This may explain why the screen separating the sacred room from the rest of the house is often made of a curtain—because it is the social face of the room that is presented to the uninitiated public; why private family rooms within the larger communal house are made in the shape of boxes but with walls made from mats rather than wood—because they are private spaces but in a public area; and why clothing is made from mats—because the body, most of which is hidden and private, must also be presented in public.

Finally, mats, like boxes, are associated with wealth, for while wealth is stored and hidden in boxes, it is displayed and distributed on mats. This difference may be attributed to the fact that both are products of cedar trees, but with an important symbolic difference. Boxes are made from wood, or the inner flesh of the tree, which is the treasured wealth it gives to mankind; mats are made from the bark, the outer skin, which is the visible, social surface of the tree.

The geographical basis for Kwakiutl social organization lies in the sharing of both food-collecting space and residential space. Residential space is denoted by houses and villages (groups of houses), and perhaps no entity in Kwakiutl culture is more obviously equivalent to a box than is the house. Made of the same materials, both are measured with the same methods and the same proportions (Boas, 1909:412); both have a roof that is removable; both are described as having parts that coincide with parts of the body (Boas, 1909:415); both are decorated with their individual crest designs on the front or "forehead"; and both are named and alive. The boxness of houses is enhanced by the fact that within the house individual rooms are walled off with mats, and entrance to the rooms restricted in one of two ways: first, by the construction of very low doorways (essentially making them miniature houses within a larger house); and second, by the erection of rooms on a staging accessible only by a ladder, which is pulled up when the room's occupants are within it (see Boas, 1909:416). Houses, then, can be considered as boxes that act as receptacles for people; similarly, boxes can be considered as houses that act as receptacles for people's wealth. And people and wealth, both contained in boxes, are analogues of each other.

The central role of the chief in the household and its affairs is metaphorized by the placement of his rooms at the rear (forehead) of the house (Boas, 1909:416). This symbol is reinforced by his wearing during ceremonies of forehead frontlets carved in crest designs. The role of the chief as food provider for his numaym is stated by the fact that he sits on a settee (Boas, 1909:425), which is essentially a box (i.e., a receptacle for a chief). It is, however, an open, public box, whose openness perhaps symbolizes the generosity of the chief, who must provide his numaym comembers with some of the wealth stored in his boxes. These settees are placed on piles that not only raise the chief above everyone else, but also link the settee with the house, itself placed on piles (see Boas, 1909:415). Furthermore, the fact that settees are covered with mats reaffirms both the role of chief as property distributor, as mats are the place where wealth is displayed and distributed, and his value as a treasured item himself, since it is through his power that the numaym acquires its food. The metaphorical equivalence of houses and villages is expressed through the use of the same terms (such as upriver and downriver) for the description of both the interior geography of the house and the geography of the village (Boas, 1909:415; 1934).

Though formed on the principles of a box, a house can also be seen as a representation of the structure of the universe. The Kwakiutl believe the universe has four distinct levels. Egress between levels is possible only at points where some orifice (for example, the Mouth of Heaven) broaches the integrity of the level's surfaces. Travel between levels is accomplished by climbing up and down "ladders." The house too has four levels: the area beneath the floor; the area in which cooking and most communal social activity occur; a platform that runs around the inside walls of the house and provides the floor for individual family compartments within the house; and the roof. Ethnographers have long realized, but have seldom recognized the importance of, the fact that the roof of the house is clearly associated with the sky, and the great transverse housebeam with the Milky Way. The roof is reachable from the lower levels by ladder or by the cannibal pole, a ladder for the use of the spirits. The floor of the house can be associated with the level of the universe we call the ground. The Kwakiutl consider the ground to be the upper surface of the world of small mammals and underground beings. This level would have been far more extensive, of course, in the times when Kwakiutl houses were raised off the ground on stilts. Here access to the house from the ground was clearly gained by means of a ladder. The level of the cooking fire, which is the level of eating and dealing with food, forms the arena of social interaction. Kwakiutl individuals, in eating by the fire, are eating not in the world of humans but in a brief manifestation of the world of the sea, the domain of fishes and sea mammals. The space defined for social interaction, then, inherently relates humans to their food-animals at every meal. The social space that is defined as truly belonging to humans, including both the sacrosanct private rooms that are found along the upper platforms of a house and other private spaces in which individual activities take place, is symbolically equivalent to the part of the entire universe that is the world of humans. Ladders connect this platform to the cooking and eating area of the house. Thus, the house itself recreates the fundamental structure of the universe, and the structuring of activities within its space reaffirms the metaphorical relationships that people's actions have to the greater universe around them.

Of course, the universe is a house just as the house is a universe. Kwakiutl cosmology clearly depicts the universe as an enclosed space (a stasis) bounded on one side by a river (a flux). Such a description also applies to a house, itself a box with one side abutting a moving body of water. The outermost levels of the universe, sky and sea, constitute the natural realm of the spirits, just as the outermost levels of the house, roof and underfloor, constitute the ritual domain of the spirits. Humans can travel to these levels only when they have protected themselves with spirit power. The two central levels of the universe correspond to the two central planes of the house, the upper of which is the natural domain of man, the lower of which is the natural domain of the animals man uses for food. Again, humans, if they are going to travel to the world of food animals, must protect themselves with spirit power. Because house and universe are congruent, the house provides a point in space and time where all these domains, human, animal, and spirit, cosmic and social, intersect.

Social space is also metaphorized as a box on the village level since villages act like boxes that contain houses. A village is an entity separated by sharp boundaries (the walls of forest, sea, air, and ground) from other equal entities. We can even envision the village as a bubble of living space, with everyone in it linked by the skin of the bubble. Villages, which have skins just as individuals and houses do, also have skeletons. While the skeleton of a human consists of his bones, or the lasting internal parts of his body, and the skeleton of the house consists of its posts, or the eternal, named internal parts of its body, the skeleton of the village comprises the total number of houses existing in it—houses that exist eternally because their posts exist eternally.

Boxes play one more important role in Kwakiutl ritual—in the form of drums. Drums, made from boxes or from tree trunks that have been hollowed out, accompany Kwakiutl songs. During ceremonies, such as the arrival of the groom and his relatives during marriage rites, the canoes of the group are beaten upon with paddles so that the entire canoe becomes a drum (see Curtis, 1914). Containers of supernatural treasure, both boxes and canoes are made from wood (each necessitating the death of a tree and the capture of the tree's soul in the wooden item made from it); both have names, souls, identities; both are treasure items themselves, distributable at potlatches; and both are directly related to the accrual of food. Thus, they become interchangeable with one another. In rituals where communication with the spirits, an act achievable through singing, is necessary, the beating of drums is an affirmation of the food-based relationship of human and spirit, for the boxes contain food and food-based wealth.[5]

The entire Kwakiutl cosmos may be seen as a set of similar container/contained relations between objects, like a set of Chinese boxes, each smaller than the last and containing another box smaller than itself. We may conceptualize the Kwakiutl cosmos in the following structural manner:

(1) The cosmos as physical space
    Universe:Village::Village:House::House:Box
(2) The cosmos as social space
    Universe:Tribe::Tribe:Numaym::Numaym:Individual

These analogic relationships may be stated as follows:

(1) As physical space, the universe is a village that contains villages; the village is a house that contains houses; the house is a box that contains boxes.
(2) As social space, the universe is a box that contains tribes; the tribe is a box that contains numayms; the numaym is a box that contains individuals.

Or alternatively

the universe is a tribe that contains tribes; the tribe is a numaym that contains numayms; the numaym is an individual group that contains individuals.

Furthermore, the terms in one set of analogies correspond vertically to respective terms in the other set:

Physical Universe: Social Universe

as

Village: Tribe

as

---

[5] Drums made from a wooden hoop and a stretched animal skin are related to wooden drums in that the death of an animal is required to provide a skin and therefore a soul for the drum. However, I have not been able to discern whether these drums, though decorated with crest designs, are considered to be individuals with names and souls in the same way as wooden drums and canoes are

House: Numaym

as

Box: Individual

These equivalences may be stated as follows:

Physical Universe = Social Universe
Village = Tribe
House = Numaym
Box = Individual

where the relationship designated by the equals sign may be understood as congruence and/or identity. Thus we might say that the physical universe represents the physical form of the social universe, the village represents the physical form of the tribe, the house represents the physical form of the numaym, and the box represents the physical form of the individual. Or obversely, since people provide the souls that animate the physical space they inhabit, the physical universe is a living universe, the tribe a living village, the numaym a living house, and the individual a living box.

We have seen that houses and villages, which function as spaces where food is stored and distributed, are organized symbolically in terms of boxes. Similarly, food-collection areas are predicated as self-contained, bounded units, and as they are owned and worked by the same social group that own and work in particular houses, they also metaphorize social structure in terms of bounded space. Kwakiutl resource ownership patterns (like those of most other Northwest Coast cultures) are based on individual ownership of limited spaces from which only particular resources may be removed (see Piddocke, 1965; Ruyle, 1973). A chief and the members of his numaym might own the right to fish for salmon from a particular promontory, yet not own the right to collect berries that grow on that same promontory; or he might possess the right to fish for salmon, but not herring, at the mouth of a stream. Such areas, therefore, function as boxes from which food is removed, and just as the correct person only may remove food from the group's storage box, so the correct person only may remove food from the group's collection "box." Indeed, so much of food collection involves boxes that we might envision the process of collecting food as a long train of removing the fish from one box and placing it in another. The fish are removed from the "box" of the ocean world, placed in the "box" of the canoe or the weir, and carried in baskets to the village, where they will be stored in boxes in houses. In fact, since so much of Kwakiutl food collection is imbued with awareness of the changing status of the animal being caught, the Kwakiutl surround fishing and hunting with rituals that mark the changing environments through which the animal progresses. From the fish's point of view, being caught, prepared, and served involves a series of magical transformations, and the Kwakiutl clearly note these transformations in their food-collecting and preparation rites.

Just as food is collected and stored in boxes that demarcate social groups, so is it served in boxes that denote social groups. During feasts, potlatches, and ceremonials, food is served in special feast dishes, called "House Dishes" by Boas (1935:51). These dishes are among the most valuable of wealth items transferred in marriage and through inheritance. Every house has a number of them, usually four. Like the house posts, the house itself, and the chiefs who live in that house, feast dishes are all named. These names have the same eternal existence as those of the house, its posts, and its guardians. As a particular feast dish rots away, it is burned and another is carved in the same figure to take its place. Thus, a house with four feast-dish names will always have four large feast dishes in it, and always of the same four types. These four main dishes may be of gigantic proportions, capable of holding immense quantities of food (see Feder, 1969:#166). Every household also owns other smaller dishes in the same pattern as the large named dishes, but these smaller dishes are not named and thus stand in relation to the named dishes as individual members of an animal species stand in relation to their named spirit-chief. In addition, the fact that food is eaten directly from only the smaller unnamed dishes reaffirms people's dependence on the individual members of a species. At feasts where the large dishes are in use, food is ladled from them into the smaller dishes, which are set down in front of groups of people who share their food content; at small feasts, food is ladled from the small feast dishes into food trays. In both cases food is removed from a repository of a great quantity of it and dispensed into smaller dishes; so is food taken from the food-collecting sites and distributed among the tribes, and so is magical power taken from its source and distributed among the chiefs. The pattern of serving food at feasts, then, is structurally equivalent to the patterns of collecting food and obtaining power.

The carving of feast dishes in which food is served reinforces the fact that food is considered to be a gift of the spirits, and that the food-collecting and food-distributing privileges are all derived from the spirits. At every meal this connection is reemphasized by the presence of carved dishes. However, the serving of food in carved dishes also reaffirms the right of the human who is serving the food to be serving it, and reaffirms his links to the spirit represented in the dish. Thus, if a food-collecting privilege has supposedly been granted to one's ancestor by a wolf, and food is therefore served from dishes carved in the shape of a wolf, the act of serving the food reaffirms the chief's claim to the hereditary privilege. Furthermore, since feast dishes are considered to be animate beings in the way that the house and its posts and masks are animate, the act of taking food from a bowl is equivalent to taking food from the body of the animal the bowl represents.

Bowls also provide a direct link to the world of the spirits. Originally these bowls were the ones used by the spirits themselves in their spirit-world houses. However, though the ancestors of the Kwakiutl are given the bowls as gifts from the spirits to verify the ties between humans and spirits, when the bowls are brought through the hole-in-the-sky (Mouth of Heaven) they lose their divine essence, becoming only the lifeless hulks of the living beings they were in the spirit world. (Having changed the nature of their existence, they become dead.) As long as spirit-power is not nearby, the dishes remain lifeless carvings equivalent to the corpses of the original dishes. However, during those times when spirit power is present, especially during potlatches and the winter ceremonials, the spirit of the dish returns to the human villages, which, at that time, have become extensions of the spirit world. The dishes come back to life, forming a direct link between the household of the chief who owns them and that of the spirit who gave them.

Since the name of the dish is eternal, while the particular example of dish possessing that name can change, new dishes are carved to replace old ones. As animate beings, dishes are subject to the same characteristics as such other animate beings as humans. Just as a particular human soul that inhabits a particular body will leave that body upon its death and enter another human body, so the soul of a named dish can leave a particular incarnation and enter another. The original dish then becomes a lifeless corpse just as the first human body became a corpse; the soulless wooden residue of the first dish is then equivalent to the lifeless skin of the corpse. Significantly, just as a human soul cannot be released until its original body has decomposed, so the soul of a dish cannot be reborn until its original body has been destroyed. This act is accomplished by the burning of the first dish during the potlatch in which the new dish is officially unveiled. In this manner, the soul of a dish always has a body to inhabit. The dish acts, then, in the same manner as does a house post by providing a place for the powerful spirit incarnated in the dish (or house post) to come to rest during sacred rites. In providing such a body for the incarnating spirit, a human informs that spirit that he is faithfully maintaining his ritual responsibility to ensure its rebirth.

We should point out an important social ramification of the relationship between resource ownership and feast dishes. We have seen that feast dishes symbolize the connection between the abundance of a resource and a human's ability to obtain some of that abundance because of his relation to the spirits. If resource ownership were a corporate privilege of the numaym, these feast dishes would have to remain in the numaym for all time. However, feast dishes are prime objects of hereditary (individual) wealth, and are one of the most important items exchanged, along with other types of food-related privilege, in marriages. Boas found that the dishes had been exchanged in marriages so often that it was often impossible to determine to which numaym or even to which tribe their original owner had belonged (1935:52). Since it is the chiefs who have the right to exchange these privileges at the marriages of their heirs, would it be possible for a numaym to own a privilege and yet have the chief alienate that privilege at his own child's marriage? Obviously not, since that would entail the constant upheaval of economic relationships. Resource ownership, therefore, must be seen as an individual privilege, not a collective one.

The box, which in the form of the feast dish symbolizes social space, in Kwakiutl cosmology is the fundamental metaphor for all forms of physical space. As noted earlier, the Kwakiutl universe consists of four discrete levels of existence, each completely separated from the others except for specific points at which egress from one to the other may be made. In each case the "sky" of one level is the "ground" of the level above it. Thus, the sky of the human level (which is shared with the large land animals) is the ground of the level above it, the world of the spirits; and there is a hole-in-the-sky through which humans can travel to the world of the spirits, and through which spirits can descend into the world of humans. The ground of the human level is the sky of the world of small animals, especially insects, worms, reptiles, and amphibians.[6] Animals can travel from their level to the humans' by means of holes in their sky, which look like burrows to humans; and humans can descend to the world of animals by means of caves and pits. Finally, the lowest level of the world is that of the ocean, whose surface ("sky") is coterminous with the ground level of the animal world, and whose floor is the ground level where the fish-people live. The holes in the sky of the fish world, through which humans can travel to the world of fish, are whirlpools; the fish travel to the world of humans by jumping out of the water, which, in the case of salmon, takes place where there is turbulence.

Travel from one world to another is difficult and requires a great deal of power. While spirits can use their power to travel quite freely (which helps explain why Thunderbirds so frequently drop from the sky), humans and their animal compatriots in the human world have a great deal of

---

[6] Strangely enough, the growth rate of plant matter on the Northwest Coast is so rapid that new plants grow upon the remains of fallen trees far faster than those trees can rot away. The result is an accumulation of vegetal matter that is in some places more than twelve feet deep and so tangled and dense that its upper surface supports the weight of people. It is in this level that the small animals live (see Sanderson, 1961:71)

trouble traveling to the spirit world. (When the birds decide to travel to the sky, only Wren, which is small, fast, and active, succeeds [Boas, 1935:165].) Nor is it easy to travel to the worlds of small animals or fish. Without spirit-power to protect him, a human trying to enter these worlds will either drown or suffocate.

The key point here is that travel from one world to another involves a complete change of individual state of being. As the traveler passes through the various doors between the worlds, his nature changes. The Kwakiutl metaphorize this alteration in terms of the donning and removing of masks that conceal the inner character of the individual and give him an outer form adapted to the world to which he is traveling. By putting on a mask, a spirit changes from his true self into a special form adapted to the human world. Thunderbird, for example, who is a human in his own world, becomes a spirit-being when he puts on his Thunderbird mask and travels in that shape to the land of humans; the salmon-people, who look like, act like, and are humans in their own world, put on their salmon masks and travel to the world of humans, where they appear as fish. Similarly, humans, who of course look like humans in their own world, put on masks by which they can travel to the other worlds. If they put on salmon masks, they will look like all the other fish when they travel to the land of salmon; if they put on Thunderbird masks, they will look like the other Thunderbirds when they travel to the spirit world.

Masks are the metaphors of altered self, and as such they are inherently objects of immense power, around which great care and many precautions must be taken. They must be shown, as are all numinous objects, great fear and respect. It is all too easy for Western materialists to think of these masks simply as objects of artistic merit and beauty or even of social significance, but they are far more than that. To the Kwakiutl masks are living beings whose powers are literally those of life and death, for masks take people from one world and move them to another and, in so doing, bring about death and rebirth. The salmon dons a mask because he wants to die; the Thunderbird, the great death-bringer, dons a mask because he wants to find food in the world of humans; the human dons the mask of a spirit because he wants to seek the powers of eternal life that the spirits possess and that can be obtained only in exchange for another being's death.

Thus, in a sense the being who travels from one world to another dies. The human who goes to the world of the salmon is considered to have abandoned his body, to have died, to have visited with the salmon, and, if he should happen to return, to have been reborn. The salmon that is pulled from the water is becoming dead; and the fisherman's prayer to him to hold on tight (see Chapter Two) is in part a statement by the fisherman that he will aid the salmon in his quest to die.

The altered state of existence that accompanies travel across world boundaries explains why the Kwakiutl did not originally practice underground burial. (Later they did adopt the practice due to missionary and governmental pressure.) A person who dies and is buried in a tree still resides in the world of humans; as his body decomposes or is devoured by scavengers, his material existence disappears, but his soul travels to other places in this world. The soul of a hunter, for example, goes to live with the wolves, the soul of the average person inhabits a salmon, and so forth. Then, when that animal whose body is being inhabited by the human's soul dies, that soul can easily be reborn into the body of another human in this world. If the body is buried underground, however, the soul is released by decomposition into the world of small animals, and when the animal it inhabits dies, the soul will be reborn into the body of another animal in that world and not into a human body in this world. Death by drowning at sea, which the Kwakiutl fear greatly, has the same effect. As the body decomposes underwater, its soul is released into the world of fish, from which it cannot return to the land of humans. Similarly, the carcasses of salmon that are not eaten are thrown into the sea because the salmon otherwise could never be reincarnated in their own world; instead, they could be reborn only as some creature in the world of humans.

While animate beings can travel between worlds only by putting on masks, inanimate objects can be sent by the inhabitants of one world to those of another by a number of means. Objects may be physically transferred from one level to another. The most famous, and most frequently misinterpreted, example is that of the destruction of a copper.[7] Most scholars do not distinguish between the three methods of destroying a copper: burning it in a fire, throwing it into the sea, or breaking it into small pieces and distributing them to other people. Yet, when we realize that transcending the boundaries of the levels of the world alters the state of existence of the object, then the act of throwing a copper into the sea is not merely one of removing it from the human world, but of consciously sending it into the world of the fish-people. Similarly, the act of burning (melting down) a copper in a fire sends that copper to the sky-world of the spirits, as the smoke from the fire travels upward through the hole in the house's roof into the sky. The act of breaking a copper and distributing the pieces to other humans, however, does not release the souls in the copper, nor does it return them to the world from which they came. Instead, it merely redistributes them among the human coin-

---

[7] As we will see later, a copper is the repository of the skins of dead animals; its destruction releases those souls from human control and returns them to the inhabitants of the other world.

habitants of this world.[8] The former cases, then, represent sacrifice, a situation in which exchange and reciprocity between humans is considered to be at an end; the latter case represents a particular stage in the middle of a series of exchanges.

Just as the world has surfaces that hide a vastly different realm beneath them, so do all surfaces hide deep and alien worlds. The skin of a human acts as his surface in the same way that water is the surface of the ocean. Beneath that skin is the human himself, his soul, his heart, his emotions and intellect, and all those parts of him that define him as an individual and as a human being. Skin is, thus, structurally equivalent to a mask: when it is put on, the character of the individual underneath changes; when it is removed, the character underneath once again is altered back to its original form. One important corollary of this belief is the idea that the unborn soul, in choosing a body to inhabit, chooses an entire state of existence: if it chooses to inhabit a human's skin, it enters the human world; if it chooses to don the skin of a fish, it will become a fish; if it chooses to don the skin of a *tsonoqua*, it will become a *tsonoqua*. Much of Kwakiutl belief about the dead, ghosts, the soul, corpses, spirit/human relations, and world renewal cannot be understood without realizing two things: first, that people try to influence the choice of bodily incarnation souls will make in the future so that the demographic balance of the world's species can be maintained in equilibrium; and, second, that this influence can be exerted only in particular forms of coercion that figure as parts of the winter ceremonials, a ritual heavily oriented toward the redistribution of souls and skins throughout the cosmos.

Skin is a medium that defines the individual by giving surface character to the individual and by limiting his behavior; but it is also a medium that conceals the true self beneath it, and that acts as a barrier to that self. The true self may be manifest in the condition of the skin: fierce hostility makes the eyes widen and the mouth grimace, unhappiness makes the eyes tear, and so on, but the vast realm of the self is hidden and unknown to others.

There is one primary means of access to that self, only one way of traveling between the surface world of the skin and the inner world of the self. Just as the boundaries between the levels of the world are impassable except at specific orifices, so too there is an orifice in the skin that is the hole-in-the-sky between the world of the self and the world outside the skin, and that orifice is the mouth. Oral processes mimic exactly those of the magic orifices between worlds (though, from a psychodynamic standpoint, perhaps we should say that the actions of the cosmic orifices mimic

---

[8] There is a significant difference in the import, purpose, and motivation of these deeds. Only one is directly a human/human social interaction; the other two involve human/spirit interrelations.

those of the mouth). Just as material passing from one world to another is transformed in its fundamental character, so is food changed in its fundamental character as it passes into the mouth. As it is chewed, it is destroyed by saliva and teeth, then swallowed (the esophagus being analogous to the funnel of the whirlpool or the tunnel of a burrow). Inside the body it is even further transformed and can leave the body only by entering the world in two forms, neither of which is congruent with its original nature. Of these two forms, the most important magical form is that of vomit. The act of vomiting is graphic proof that the character of an object is unalterably changed as it travels between worlds. Vomit is food that has traveled down into the body and up again, a closed cycle involving two worlds and one orifice. The act of vomiting, to the Kwakiutl, is thus structurally equivalent to the act of bridging the gaps between the parts of the universe. It is an example of visiting the world of the spirits and returning again to the world of humans. The act of vomiting is a homology of death, a magical act, a religious, transcendental, creative act, not merely a physical act.

The second type of transformation is the changing of food into feces. In this case, the transformed substance leaves the body through a secondary orifice, the anus. Here the transformed food travels downward out of the body; it is buried beneath the ground or dumped into the sea. The treatment of the feces indicates that the Kwakiutl consider fecal matter a form of soil, or mud, and rightfully it should be incorporated into the mud, which is accomplished through its burial beneath the surface of the ground or the sea. Feces, then, is food that is transformed and sent to the world of the small animals. Interestingly, the Kwakiutl, like many other Northwest Coast people, have a fear of small animals (especially salamanders and snakes) being able to enter the bodies of humans through their anuses. This fear is explainable if we understand that the anus, like all orifices between worlds, can be passed through in either direction, so that just as humans can send their feces to the world of small animals, so too can the animals enter the world of humans through the same opening. It follows that there is no belief that small animals can enter humans' bodies through their open mouths. The mouth is not a door between these two worlds.

The transformation of food into vomit and feces is a magical, transcendental act. But the act of eating is itself also a religious act in that it involves the use by humans of the dead bodies of other beings. The body parts of a fish, for example, represent the inner self of the fish, which is its true being and its soul. These are the parts of the fish that are being eaten, and as they are being digested, they are transformed. The fish parts that are eaten are no longer present in the world as fish parts. They are instead transformed into vomit or feces. The eater has therefore removed one being from the face of the earth.[9]

In sum, we have seen that boxes are a cogent metaphor in Kwakiutl life, metaphorizing, defining, and structuring social relationships. We have seen that boxes simultaneously define the life span and the social and geographical environment of the individual. Born upon his removal from a box-womb, swaddled in a box-cradleboard as an infant, a person spends his life inside a box-house, in a box-village, traveling between villages in a box-canoe, and is in some ways a box himself, living in a world that is itself a box, and will leave that world at his death when he is buried in a box. Boxes create and define bounded space, and their inner/outer nature is translated into ideas of the dichotomy of self and other, skin and skeleton, conscious and unconscious, and a dichotomy between this life and outside this life that lies at the foundation of Kwakiutl ideas of resurrection.

As material items, boxes tend to define material space. However, another metaphor, which itself acts like a box in its functioning, deals specifically with invisible, spiritual items. That nonmaterial box is the name.

No characteristic of Kwakiutl names is more important than the simple fact that names are eternal and that although the holders of a name may live and die, the name goes on forever. In this sense, Kwakiutl names are more like our own titles of office, such as President of the United States, or Sterling Professor of History, than like personal names. The quality of permanence names possess is in part derived from the fact that the permanent topographic features of the environment are named. Indeed, one entire book of Boas's texts (1934) is simply a listing of Kwakiutl place names. Myths, which define the features of the social environment, may consist of nothing other than a list of people's names. But at the same time as names gain eternalness by their association with noticeably eternal items, these items gain identity because of their names. Items that are named are bounded because of those names, and because they are bounded they become individual entities. The obverse is true as well. If an item is bounded, if it is an individual entity, then it must be named; but even more so, if an item is a named entity, then it is eternal, because names are eternal.

[9] If people continue the process of eating fish after fish indefinitely, all the fish in the world will be transformed eventually into feces, and no fish will be left in the world of humans. It is therefore incumbent upon humans to ensure that the fish are reborn, either into the world of humans or into the world of fish. This can be accomplished in either of two ways: first, the parts of the fish that are not eaten, along with those that have been eaten and changed into feces, are thrown into the ocean, thus returning them to the world of fish; second, people must, in some way, save the soul of the fish until they can perform a ritual, for example at a world-renewal ceremony, that will redistribute fish in this world.

We find that houses, boxes, feast dishes, canoes, numayms, villages, times of the year, winter ceremonial positions, spirits, human beings, masks, and features of the environment are all named. All of these become individual and eternal through being named. As individual embodiments of a name die or rot away, they are ceremonially destroyed, and a new embodiment assumes the same name.

For example, the end of the summer season is marked by the blowing of sacred whistles, and simultaneously the winter season begins; the end of the winter season and the beginning of the summer season are marked by the catching of the first salmon of the first salmon run of the season. As each embodiment of time dies, a new embodiment takes its place. This cyclic replacement is of great importance for the cycle of reincarnation, which is predicated on the alternation of embodiments. Since a name is a box, and a box defines self/other distinctions, when the self dies, the other must replace it, and when the other dies, it must be replaced by the self. Thus, as the winter season cannot replace itself, so a person cannot replace himself. Instead, he must find someone else to keep his names for him so that when he is reborn at the death of the other (achieved ceremonially by divestiture at a potlatch), he can once again take up his names. A house may fall, and its walls may be taken away and distributed, but as long as the house's name exists, any new structure built on its site using its house posts or being lived in by the original residents of the first house or their descendents becomes the incarnation of the first house. Feast dishes may rot or be destroyed, but as long as their names exist new dishes are merely reincarnations of the old ones.

The idea of the perpetual reincarnation of houses, feast dishes, boxes, coppers, and canoes is further reinforced by the fact that these items, like all named items, are considered to be alive (see Goldman, 1975:55-62). Since people have names and are reborn, so items that have names are like people and are reborn. Further, since these items are alive, they are by definition active forces in the determination of events. They can, by their actions, create wealth or destruction, as can humans. They must be treated as humans are treated, and, like humans, they live and die, they grow and decline. And, although the lifespan of their individual incarnations is short, they exist eternally because they are named.

Another aspect of names is their permanent relationship vis-à-vis all other names. Like the positions of geographical places, which do not change, items that are named stand in a permanent and immutable structural position in regard to all other named items. This idea is heavily reinforced by patterns of ceremonial distribution in the potlatch, where the order of calling names is strictly adhered to at all times. To call someone's name out of order is both a grave insult to him, implying his unworthiness, and a blasphemy, for it implies the noneternalness of the name. The static nature of names is further reinforced by the fact that each name carries with it the privilege of collecting food at a particular geographical site. Since the topographical relationships of the sites are permanent, so are the relationships of the names. Of course, the metaphor of the name as a box is also reinforced by its association with food collection, since the name is a bounded site (box) from which food is collected; the box (which is named) is a bounded site in which food is stored.

Finally, individual human beings are named. However, they are not given names that define them as individuals only, but instead acquire names that define them as parts of the collective. A child's first name is always the name of the place where he is born. At his first naming ceremony, when he is ten months old, he is always given one of the names that has been in the family since the beginning of time. Most often the child is given the first name of his grandparent (who is the person whose ceremonial statuses the child will eventually inherit). Throughout his life, the child acquires new names and divests himself of old names, but these names are all eternal, ceremonial names; and since only one person can embody those names, a child can acquire a name only when the previous name holder has divested himself of that name. At first, names might seem to give individual identity to the child, but in actuality each new name only reinforces the social identity of the child. As holder of a specific name, the child has the same rights and responsibilities every holder of that name has had since the beginning of time, when the name was first created by the spirits.

A name provides a box, and people must provide the supernatural, spiritual treasure to fill that box. A name provides a body, and people must provide the soul to animate that body. Just as the act of filling and emptying boxes, of changing substance that is outside to substance that is inside, requires an act of transformation, so the assumption and divestiture of a name is an act of transformation. The potlatch provides a ceremonial mechanism that is the context for transformations in identity.

However, perhaps the most important idea behind the assumption of names, owing to the transformational quality of the act, is that the individual who assumes a new name is considered to be a different individual than he was before he assumed that name. If we look at the name as eternal and the person as the serial inhabitant of various names, it is not that the person is changing names so much as that the names are changing people. The assumption of a new name is the assumption of a new identity, a new self. It is a transformation of status, not an accrual of status. The name ingests a person and transforms him into the animating soul of that name. When the time comes for the person to divest himself of that identity, the name must vomit him forth and ingest a new person.

Names, thus, identify the self and deny the self simultaneously, for while the individual embodies the name, he is also only a manifestation of the name. Names act to deny the idea of an idiosyncratic self and foster the importance of an eternal social self. It is my belief that the Kwakiutl carry this idea to the point where they do not impersonate beings (in the sense that an actor impersonates Hamlet), but they become, by transformation, the being they are named. People bring vitality and energy to the world; but it is the eternal containers—the names, boxes, houses, and so on—that provide the identities, the constant verities, and the immutable structure of the universe. The names are superior, the people subordinate. The demands of the names are paramount, those of the people subsidiary. This suppression and de-emphasis of the self creates an expression and emphasis of the social. And, as we shall see in the next chapter, for the Kwakiutl, to be social and self-denying is to be moral.

TWO

Meals and
the Moral Basis of
Social Action

Es giebt gar keine moralischen Phänomene,
sondern nur eine moralische Ausdeutung
von Phänomenon. . . .
—Nietzsche; *Jenseits von Gut und Böse*

IN KWAKIUTL CULTURE, the process of analogizing, of symbolically assimilating one entity within the boundaries of another, comprises the basic metaphor of process. It is not surprising, then, that the procedures by which food is created from living matter and assimilated into both the individual and the society as a whole should be a critical facet of Kwakiutl life. Food collection, preparation, distribution, and destruction—the ways in which the body politic prepares and digests substance—are the visible manifestations of the nature of all process in the universe. The attention the Kwakiutl pay to every detail of the food-getting process is an essential part of a system in which one action represents microcosmically the sacral nature of the universe as a whole.

There are some important implications for Kwakiutl thought in the inherent dialectical nature of the analogic process. Just as in any dialectic the opposition between thesis and antithesis is collapsed by the resolution of the synthesis, so do analogies collapse connections of one kind precisely so that others can be constructed. In the Kwakiutl case, the homologic, syntagmatic connections between humans are collapsed so that the analogic connections between humans and spirits can be erected (see figure 1). Yet, since there are situations in which these syntagmatic connections between humans need to be reestablished, the structure of analogies must also inherently permit the deconstruction of the analogy itself. An analogy joins a thing and its symbol, but it can do so only because the distinction between a thing and its symbol is always implicit and emergent. The structure of an analogy must permit both the power of the analogy to encompass and the realization that an analogy is only an artificial construct.

The cycle of deconstruction and reconstruction of the analogies defining the universe as a whole and the homologies defining human society is an essential part of all Kwakiutl rituals. Yet, in studying Kwakiutl culture, anthropologists have focused only on the homological, "social" relationships between humans. Regarding Kwakiutl meals only as secular rites overlooks the essential dynamic, processual character of those meals. Not only is such a view inconsonant with the descriptions of meals in Boas's texts, but the relationships between humans can be understood only in the context of their dialectic opposition to the analogic relationships between humans and spirits. In their rituals, the Kwakiutl actively manipulate that contrast, continually deconstructing and reconstructing these relationships. Kwakiutl meals are not merely sociopolitical occasions; they are rituals about the relationship between the sacred and the secular, about the balancing of human desires with moral requirement. Meals are the arena in which humans confront and resolve the conflicts of their relationships with each other in the context of their mutual dependence on the spirits. Through the manipulation in ritual of the two alternating modes of relationship, the Kwakiutl bring power, drama, direction, and meaning to their ideas about the essential nature of human existence, its problems, and their resolution.

This continuous cycle of the simultaneous construction and deconstruction of homologic and analogic relations is a feature not only of individual Kwakiutl rituals, but of the entire culture as well. Analogies collapse human society by relating people to spirits; homologies destroy religion by relating people to each other. The social rituals of the summer deconstruct the ceremonial rituals of the winter, and vice versa; the changing of the actors who impersonate a name deconstructs the social process so that it can be remade later in its original form; the hierarchical distinctions that epitomize Kwakiutl society are possible only because all humans can distinguish between themselves and spirits; the identification of dancer with spirit is made over and against his obvious humanity. Each of these examples is a perfect realization of an analogy, containing within itself the framework of its antithesis.

In Kwakiutl thought the process of analogizing has to be controlled, for just as any process needs to be kept from swallowing everything, analogies need to be kept from assimilating everything. A metaphor, like a *hamatsa*, ingests, digests, and then regurgitates its "food," and there must be some way in which humans can prevent both the *hamatsa* and metaphors from swallowing everything. The power of the metaphor to create has to be weighed against its power to destroy. The drawing of distinctions offsets the process of collapsing distinctions. Humans maintain distinctions between themselves because otherwise the assimilative forces of the universe, reified in Man Eater, will bring about the final dissolution of the world, collapsing everything upon itself. The emphasizing of the rituals of hierarchical status at feasts, the giving of the first and best to the chiefs, ensures that man's drawing of distinctions can succeed in obviating his own assimilative propensities. Man, like Man Eater, is capable of devouring everything, of reducing the world to the primal substance from which it was first created. Hierarchy is the structure that mediates all cosmic analogic processes, yet (since all chiefs are analogous to spirits) it contains within itself the nature of the analogy as well.

The food-collecting process is therefore not just a social or ecological one, but is the primary mode of action by which humans exert control over themselves, their fellow humans, the animals, the spirits, the very processes of the universe. That the Kwakiutl should see the food-collecting process as a microcosmic realization of the nature of process as a whole fits with the analogic nature of their world; that they should ritualize and sacralize it are expected ramifications of the dangerous, potentially destructive character they see it as possessing. Man's moral responsibilities must balance the destruction of food with the construction of human relationships, the destruction of substance with the creation of ideational distinctions, and ultimately, the destruction of human relationships and substance for the creation of the nonhuman universe. It is precisely because eating is pleasurable and satisfying that it is able to function as a matrix for the obviation of satisfaction. It is only because eating is an individual assimilation that it can be the basis for the subjugation of the individual's desires to the welfare of others. It is only because eating is not in and of itself governed by an ineluctable morality that it can become the foundation for a system of ideas about how humans should act. It is only because humans played no role in the creation of the universe that they are able to play a central role in reconstructing it through their rituals.

For the Kwakiutl, food is not merely the inanimate edible remains of food-animals and plants, but is instead the substantial manifestation of the numinous nature of the universe. The relationship of humans with food as substance is not measurably different in structure from their relationship with the spirits and the animals by whose beneficence humans can survive. The eating of food, even when one is hungry and the food one is eating is delicious, is not a selfish act of personal gratification, but rather a stage in the complexly structured interrelationships of humans with each other and with the world around them. Every aspect of the food-collecting and eating processes, therefore, is imbued with an innate magicality and a special emotional intensity, because every aspect of these processes is simultaneously a social, a moral, and a religious act.

Once the analogic relationship between humans and food-animals has been set up, the actions of humans constrain the animals to act accordingly. So long as humans properly process the bodies of animals, animals will have to properly process the bodies of humans. Humans take care ensuring that the bodies and souls of animals are treated correctly because they thus ensure that their own bodies and souls will be treated correctly by the animals. Since analogy and action cause the desired results, the human/animal analogy coupled with man's actions automatically cause the result humans desire—their own deaths and rebirths.

Humans and animals work in balance and harmony. In many other American Indian cultures, the world is considered to be innately harmonious and man merely becomes syntonic with its orderliness. However, Kwakiutl cosmology is clearly based on the idea that the world is innately discordant, conflictive, and self-destructive, and only when its inhabitants agree to cooperate to maintain order at the expense of their own personal desires, agree to suppress their hunger, and to modify it into its proper proportion can the world operate.

Thus, humans' constraints on their own potentially destructive feelings and actions force the animals to be equally constrained in their behavior. The animals perform rituals and ceremonials in their own villages specifically because the humans are doing so in their villages. Through mechanisms of analogic causality humans maintain the order of the universe. Indeed, the orderliness of man's actions at the winter ceremonials constrains even Man Eater, the being who personifies the endpoint of world process, the alpha and omega of being and time, to find his proper place in the working of the world. In restraining themselves from eating as much as they might want, humans prevent the spirits from eating as much as they want. By denying themselves the indulgence of unrestrained killing and eating of animal flesh, humans ensure that the spirits cannot indulge in the unrestrained killing and eating of human flesh.

Ultimately, it is humans upon whom the entire burden of moral choice rests. The spirits have their natures, their fundamental feelings and desires, and without constraints they will naturally act out these desires. Only a human can choose to deny his wants, and in so doing constrain the spirits to act out their desires only in the pattern he sets for them. Maintaining harmony and order within the human group is thus a necessary part of the mechanism by which one maintains harmony within the cosmos. Only when the human order, the web of hierarchical, analogic relationships, is in good condition can the spirit world work properly. The Kwakiutls' awareness of the role their behavior plays in the working of the world is largely the reason for their carefulness, for they are thus ensuring that the spirits exercise the same care.

The Kwakiutl consider all humans to be united in their mutual dependence upon one another, and nowhere is that dependence more critical and more recognized than in the universal quest for food. Chiefs and commoners, men and women, and each numaym with every other are tied together because individually they cannot survive. Independent survival is impossible for two reasons: first, the food-collecting process is long, complicated, and exactingly detailed both technically and ritually, so that no one person could ever hope to master all the behavior necessary for solitary exploitation of resources; and second, Kwakiutl rules of resource ownership operate in such a manner as to prohibit each person from performing at least one critical part of the food-collecting process—refusing him, for example, the right to fish in a certain area, to prepare or eat a certain food, or to kill certain animals—so that even if he could master the requisite tasks, they would still be ritually forbidden acts.

No commoner, for example, can own the prerogative to fish in a certain river; this right is held by the chief by virtue of his elevated ritual status and his ability to interact with the spirit chiefs. Although he holds them in trust for the members of his numaym (see Goldman, 1975: chaps. 2 and 3), it is always the chief who owns the resource areas.[1] The chief is also responsible, to the spirits who granted the privilege, for ensuring that all those animals who come to die at that collecting area are captured. Because he could never perform this task alone, he is dependent on the labor of his numaym comembers for the proper utilization of those resources. No woman may hunt or fish, since menstrual blood purportedly repels animals, and so they are dependent on their husbands for food; yet no man may butcher a fish, which is an important ritual act with vast repercussions, so all men are dependent on women for the preparation and cooking of food.

Daily, every time a Kwakiutl goes to collect food, to eat it, or to interact with someone with whom he shares food or the work of collecting food, he is reminded that the entire social fabric is woven of the mesh of food-related privileges and responsibilities. Consequently, he believes that if a single step of the process is omitted or performed incorrectly, the entire fabric will disintegrate. Food, therefore, becomes the fundamental medium of social interaction, the fundamental symbol of human sociality, the fundamental template against which to evaluate human motivations and behavior, and, since human society is the metaphor for cosmic society, the fundamental metaphor of the cosmos.

There is a great deal of formalized, ritualized behavior involved in Kwakiutl food-related activities. We might see this formal emphasis on carefulness and correctness as similar to that involved in all Kwakiutl

[1] This rule, true in aboriginal culture, disappears by the late nineteenth century as a result of the drastic population decline and the subsequent restructuring of Kwakiutl society. Nevertheless, it is still considered the ideal.

manufacture. Careful attention to detail, to the ordering of tasks, and to the perfection of performance are all essential in any Kwakiutl task.

The ritual process regarding food operates not only during the procurement and/or eating of the food, but is in evidence during the entire range of food-oriented activities. It begins with the construction of a canoe, the building of a weir, or the carving of a fishhook, all of which are surrounded by ritual charms and prayers designed to ensure through analogy the efficacy of the objects' action in later food-getting activities. It continues in the ritual preparations, the fasting, self-denial, and ritual copulation, and in the prayers that must be performed before the food gatherer can leave his house to go to the food-collecting area. It remains in effect during prayers and rituals performed at the collecting site, during the time when a fish is on the hook but not yet in the canoe, after a fish has been landed, when the fish is brought to the beach, during the butchering and preparation, during the serving and eating, until the moment the guests finish the meal with a ritual hand washing. Even then the process of ritual does not end, but continues in all those rites organized toward the future attainment of food, the most important of which are the potlatch and the winter ceremonials.

The length and detail of the ritual process has not been apparent in the Boas texts because Boas sectioned Hunt's manuscripts, including portions of a single narrative account in different topical chapters, and sometimes even in different books published years apart. But we can reconstruct the order of these texts to see the process in its entirety if we combine the sequential portions from the different books (see Appendix One). When we do this, the picture is one of a coherent, unified attitude toward food, human control over food, and the control of humans through the distribution of food.

The entire economic system of the Kwakiutl is predicated on the idea that animals (and, to some extent, plants) are captured only because they are willing to be captured, and that they are willing to be captured only when they are sure that they will be treated in the proper manner. Humans must prove to animals that they will honor the animals' ritual needs. If they fail to do so, the animals will refuse to die, and the hunter will be unable to capture them.[2]

Animals are willing to die for one reason: without death there can be no rebirth in the eternal cycle of life. Without death, animals and humans grow old, feeble, senile, and powerless. They must die so that they can be reborn. Thus, an animal is willing to die; but it will let itself be killed

---

[2] The origin of human awareness that animals are willing to die is thought to have occurred in mythic times, when one of man's ancestors was first visited by an animal spirit chief. Such incidents are memorialized in myths, and are a constant feature of prayers, speeches, daily conversations, and all ceremonial presentations.

only by those hunters or fishermen who, by promising to perform the correct rituals, ensure that the animal's process of reincarnation will not be disrupted.

Since matter from one world level can enter an adjacent level at only a limited number of places, there are specific geographical points at which humans are able to remove animals, when they come to die, from their world and bring them to the human world. Thus, a Kwakiutl right to resource exploitation involves the right of a specific person to gather a specific food at a specific place at a specific time.

The rules governing the specificity of rights of resource exploitation fall into several categories. First, one might have the right to collect and/ or eat a particular foodstuff at a particular location (for example, all dog salmon at a particular fishing point, perhaps even only those caught there using one particular fishing method). Second, one might have the right to all of one kind of food (for example, certain types of berries, specific parts of porpoises and other sea mammals, or mountain goats) within the entire Kwakiutl domain, or any portion of it that can be specified by a name. And finally, in rare instances, one might have rights to all types of food in a particular locality, but only when the entire locality is one of those considered to have been created when one of the spirits was changed into a landform.[3]

We might imagine that in aboriginal times a chief's rights to food resources at a specific location would have been very important, since population pressure would limit the ability of people to travel to other locations to utilize food resources. As the population declined, however, many of these local resources were no longer near active villages and became open for use to anyone willing to travel to them (Drucker and Heizer, 1967:3-34; 81-117). Chiefs' speeches dating from the end of the nineteenth century frequently mention that the chiefs can no longer enforce their jurisdiction over all their rightful ancestral food resources, and that commoners and transgressors are taking food without properly asking, reciprocating, or sharing (Benedict, 1934:192).

Chiefs may have been less strict in guarding their ownership of and exclusive access to most types of food, other than foods strictly reserved by sumptuary right, when food was plentiful, allowing others to gather the surplus. It is also probable that they expected to receive partial reciprocation through later assistance in war, housebuilding, potlatch preparation, or other expressions of gratitude. It is incontrovertible, however, that prerogatives were zealously guarded when a chief felt strong enough

[3] It should be noted that the right to collect food at a given place and the right to serve it to humans other than the particular person who is the living incarnation of the ancestor to whom the right was first given are not the same. The right to collect food and the right to distribute it are carefully distinguished in Kwakiutl practice

to defend them and when food was scarce, and infringement upon them was punished by death. The family histories that Boas collected contain a number of such cases. Three separate sections of these texts (Boas, 1921:223-24; 1333-34; 345-46) speak of scarce resources, all owned hereditarily, in which poaching was a capital offense—seal hunting, mountain goat hunting, and salmon fishing upstream (where salmon would be both relatively scarce and relatively low in nutritive value).

No matter what the nature of the particular food right, it is the responsibility of every person involved with the process of turning living matter into food to prove to the animals that he will honor their ritual needs. Otherwise the animals will no longer make themselves available for food. It falls upon the carpenter, the canoemaker, and the weirmaker, who set up the apparatus that permits the animal to enter the human world; it falls upon the hunter, who is the instrument of the animal's corporeal death; it falls upon the woman who releases the animal's eternal soul from its body during the butchering process; it falls upon the chief, who, as the human liaison with the spirits, is the guardian of the sacred areas—the salmon rivers, the halibut grounds, the high, rocky mountains that house the mountain goats, and the forest where deer and bear wander—where animals congregate so that humans might catch them; and it falls upon all those people to whom the food is given.

Humans prove to animals that they will honor the animals' ritual needs in three ways. The first is the performance of rituals that maintain the analogy between human and animal at all stages of the food-collection process, whether these be prayers of thanksgiving that take only a few seconds, winter ceremonials that take two months, or marriage exchanges, which may take decades. These responsibilities fall primarily upon the chief, but are to some degree also those of individual hunters and fishermen. The second is the proper performance of collecting behavior, or what we would call work, but which is actually a specific magico-causal act utilizing the power of analogy coupled with directed movement to cause the food-animal to behave in the way man wants it to. The last is the correct performance of ritual butchering, preservation, cooking, and eating rites, the responsibility for which falls primarily upon women, who innately have the power to transform dead substance into living matter. Only when chiefs and commoners, men and women, all fulfill their responsibilities and perform correctly all three of these ritual activities will there be food. Ritual labor is as serious, important, and dedicated a part of food collecting as is physical labor.

Anthropologists unaware of the intertwining of the ritual responsibilities that are such a critical part of Kwakiutl economy have misinterpreted Kwakiutl economic relations, either overemphasizing the control of the chiefs over food resources or completely ignoring it. Yet the Kwakiutl are very particular in defining the changing ownership of food as it progresses from one stage to another of the process by which a living animal is transformed into edible matter. The entire process is a cyclic series of gifts of food, a cycle that begins when animals give themselves to humans, continues through gifts from one person to another, and ends only when humans give themselves to the animals for their food.

We might redefine the word "ownership" in a Kwakiutl sense. Specifically, it means only the right to accept some substance as a gift from someone else, and then only so that it may be given as a gift. In Kwakiutl culture, the entire point of the ownership of goods is to give the owner the chance to show that he is a moral being by giving away those goods. To own something is to have the right to give it away.

The delineation of the rules of the ownership of food produces a system of dependencies and differentiations that is one of the hallmarks of the Northwest Coast cultures. The hierarchical organization of Northwest Coast society is maintained through the principle that each food resource is owned by a particular individual. The people who have the privilege of ownership also have the responsibility of performing the rituals that ensure the abundance of food. Theoretically the hierarchical society is founded on the analogy of a particular person with a particular spirit. Yet, since analogy is only the first step in the causative process, there is also a principle by which the actions of humans give them some role in the production of food. Thus, people other than chiefs finish the process of creating food by performing labor that is the action complementing the spirit/chief analogue.

The division of access to food resources into these distinct but integral parts effectively makes the Kwakiutl aware that they are dependent on other people as well as on the spirits for their food, and this idea runs throughout Kwakiutl food-related rituals. However, it also serves to maintain the hierarchism of human organization by differentiating between people according to whether or not they have ties to the spirits. Thus every food-related act inherently reinforces the hierarchical distinctions between people, yet at the same time, because every human (whether chief or commoner) is dependent on other humans for some part of the performance of the food-collecting process, every food-related act also obviates the hierarchy of society by reversing the dependencies of one person on another in the shifting debts and obligations of the gift-giving exchange. Hierarchical division and dependence schismogenetically create each other.

The numaym is the nourisher of its members, for it is the corporate body responsible for the ownership, utilization, and ritual maintenance of a set of food-collecting sites and of the rights to certain types of food. The numaym is the box containing both the numaym head (who represents the analogic part of the ritual process) and the commoners (who provide the active part of the ritual process), without either of whom the ritual would be inefficacious. Although most scholars (e.g., Goldman, 1937:182) consider these rights to be the collective property of the numaym so that all members of the numaym have equal access to the resources, this assumption is not quite correct. The situation here is analogous to the control of power in a democracy, which, though said to reside in the people as a whole, actually resides in the hands of a limited number of individuals. While the numaym is the repository of these food rights, the rights to that food were given originally to an individual—an ancestor of the chief—by his guardian spirit, and they remain in the hands of an individual. The current head of the numaym is considered to be the reincarnation of the original ancestor, and his numaym comembers stand in relation to him as did the relatives and coresidents of the first ancestor at the time of the original gift. Thus, though everyone in the numaym may have access to particular resources said to be owned by the numaym, they do so only by virtue of their relationship to, and the largesse of, the numaym head.[4]

The process of food utilization reiterates the analogy of the numaym with a body. The chief functions as the mouth, the organ through which food enters the body from the spirit world, while the rest of the numaym acts as the stomach, which processes the food, and deals with all aspects of the disposal of undigested substance. The process is reversed when food is to be used to create new life at a potlatch or winter ceremonial, when the members of the numaym redirect the food from outside the

---

[4] If the Kwakiutl had not believed in an eternal cycle of reincarnation, then that original ancestor would have been considered dead, and the resources could then be held by either eldest sons, who inherit through rules of primogeniture, or by the numaym as a corporate group as equal recipients of his good fortune. But since the original ancestor is not only reincarnated, but is alive on the earth at all times (see Goldman, 1975: chap 3), the gift still belongs to him and to him alone, and the members of his numaym must, in fact, obtain from him the right to use those resources, either by direct request or by a standing arrangement in which the living ancestor is given a proportion of the catch.

We might look at the economic transaction in which a fisherman gives a part of his catch to the chief at whose collecting site the fish were caught, not as is traditionally done (see Goldman, 1937:181-82; Ruyle, 1973) as an act of redistribution, but as an act of reciprocity. For example, if the catching of the fish is considered the starting point of the interaction, the catch belongs to the fisherman, and his gift to the chief constitutes redistribution If, however, we realize that the Kwakiutl consider the productiveness of resources areas to be directly and primarily dependent on the chief's proper ritual performance, the starting point of the transaction is the chief's ritual "creation" of the presence of the fish that are later caught by the fisherman. Thus in creating, for example, one hundred fish that are caught, the chief is giving a gift of fish to the fisherman. If the fisherman keeps fifty of those fish, he has, in effect, received a gift of fifty fish from the chief; if he gives the other fifty fish to the chief, he has, in effect, reciprocated for the original gift of fifty. The transaction is, thus, not redistribution, but reciprocity. The entire process is a series of gifts of food.

inner body to the chief, who acts as the point from which food leaves the body and returns to the outer world. The chief's function in rituals is thus to remain in a permanent position in relation to the other chiefs to maintain the system of analogic social relations, a task he performs by "vomiting forth" (the metaphorical expression the Kwakiutl use to denote the giving of food gifts at a feast) both speeches and food.[5]

The numaym head controls food partly because only he can perform those rites that guarantee the maintenance of his ties to the spirits who have given the gift of food. Only as a result of the continued relationship of numaym head and spirits do the numaym's resources produce food at all. In addition, because the numaym head is the representative of the spirits among humans, there is a fundamentally sacramental character to the entire food collection and distribution process. And since the numaym head is the incarnation of the ancestor and the conduit through which food passes from spirits to humans, it is he who decides who can share his resources, how, and when. However, the proper performance of his moral duties in regard to both the resources and the members of his numaym requires him to give his wealth to others, to sacrifice his food to them as the spirits sacrificed themselves to the ancestors. He is expected to permit others subordinate to himself the use of his resources. Thus, every person is dependent on his numaym head for food in three ways: for gifts of food caught by other numaym members, for the gift of food he himself catches, and ultimately for the presence of food of any form whatsoever.

The relationship of human chief to spirit chief helps to alleviate the anxieties of the quest for food. The food-gathering process is full of worry, both the immediate worry of whether or not a fish will bite or will be landed successfully, and the long-range worry of whether there will be enough food to last the winter or to provision the round of necessary ceremonial activities. In addition, there are the deep anxieties over the real and imagined dangers of the food-getting quest. Will a canoe tip over as a man pulls a four-hundred-pound halibut into it; will he fall from the fishing weir into a raging river and be drowned; will sharks or killer whales overturn the canoe; will a storm arise, or enemy warriors appear suddenly; or, worst of all, will a sea monster surface from the deep to bring instant, incandescent death to all who see it?

People can help allay these fears with a few meek charms or with

---

[5] This is a perfect example of the way in which the ritual combination of analogy and action occur simultaneously at several levels. At the level of the numaym the chief provides the analogy while the other numaym members perform the action of the distributing (In no circumstances does a chief ever give something from his hands to another person; he always has a representative do the actual moving of the material.) At the level of the chief, who metaphorizes the numaym in relation to other numayms, the speeches he gives provide the analogy and the distribution of food the action.

power from the spirits. There are magical materials that will keep away monsters, and amulets and magical carvings containing small amounts of power that help influence the turn of events. A man may even try to oppose the power of the fish and the monsters with his own power, but the myths speak of the unfortunate ends to which these foolish, brazen men usually come (see Boas, 1910: passim). Instead, the best way to mitigate the dangers of food-gathering is both by direct alliance with the individual food-animal itself and through relationships to the chief of that species. Thus, a halibut is eased into the canoe to the accompaniment of a prayer both telling of the joy of the fisherman who has caught it and of the fact that the fisherman will perform the specific ceremonies needed in the halibut rituals (Boas, 1921:1320-27). At the same time,the fisherman has the right to fish for halibut only because the chief of his numaym has a covenant with the chief of the halibut-people. Since human commoners and animal commoners have a similar subordinate relationship to their chiefs, a covenant linking two chiefs analogically also analogically links the commoners who serve them.

The chiefs' ritual position is emphasized by proscriptions from such manual labor as the cutting of wood, the drawing of water, and the serving of food, as well as the acts of fishing, hunting, and butchering food. Instead, the chiefs must hire hunters, employ relatives to do the fishing, and have slaves to perform menial tasks. In order to appreciate the importance of the chief's ritual labor, we must remember that for the Kwakiutl the act of collecting food does not end with its eating, but that the most important aspect of providing food is maintaining correct relations with the supernaturals who supply humans. This responsibility is placed completely upon the chiefs, who must perform complicated and expensive rituals, keep ritually clean, abstain from sex, offer feasts and winter ceremonials in honor of the spirit beings, and ensure their underlings' ritual performances. Concern with the supernatural is considered to be a daily, lifelong concern of the chiefs, while the actual catching of food is merely a seasonal activity from which one is offered respite during the winter. The chief's labor is far more valuable if he is at home praying, or honoring the spirits with sacrificial meals, or planning a winter ceremonial that will please the spirits, or fasting to keep himself ritually ready at all times for interaction with the spirits. At the weir, in a canoe with hook and line in his hands, carrying water, or serving a meal, a chief would be equal to, and no more valuable than, a slave. But in his house (which, we must remember, is a ritual center of major significance) he is of far greater importance than all other humans combined, for he ensures that there will be food for all his subordinates.

Furthermore, we must remember that the chief is the incarnation of his ancestors and stands in relation to the chiefs of the animals by virtue of his interaction with them in ancient times, and that this places him in a peculiar relation to the rest of his numaym members. As an eternal individual, the chief's primary responsibilities are to the eternal items of Kwakiutl existence, the rivers and mountains, the houses, the masks, the names, the sacred boxes, and not to the temporary incarnations of souls in the form of individual animals. This latter is the domain of the commoners, those people who are themselves only the temporary individual incarnations of souls, and who supply food and new souls for the commoners among the animals. It should be remembered that the chief is allied to the heads of the spirits, and that these spirit-chiefs remain in their homes at the bottom of the sea, in the west and north ends of the world, underground, and so forth during the secular summer season. During that time, contact with them can be achieved only by magical communications, ritual words that travel to these remote places, and by spirit-messengers who bring back to their spirit-chiefs accounts of how well their animal brothers are being treated by the humans. Thus, while all humans have the responsibility of ritually treating all animals correctly, only the chief has the ritual power and purity to communicate directly with the head spirits of the animals. Therefore, it would be ritually and morally "incorrect" for a chief to deal in the killing of individual, commoner animals when he is capable of dealing with the head spirits with which he alone has a magic relationship.

Although chiefs may be given a large part of the food catch, this food is redistributed in meals, feasts, and ceremonies. All feasts and ceremonies, especially those given during the winter season, are important in that they provide—through the transformation of animal bones and skins changed by fire and by digestion into new matter—new forms that the future animal and human beings may inhabit. If humans do not provide bodily forms in winter, there will be no bodies available for the reincarnation of next year's fish and human infants, and thus, neither food-animals nor humans will be born. It is one of the chief's main responsibilities to ensure that enough food is saved, enough wealth is stored up, and enough material is available so that these feasts can be performed properly. It is therefore his chiefly task to ensure that large quantities of food are preserved and properly stored in magically empowered boxes, which keep the souls alive until the season when they will have to be sent back to their homes in the spirit world.

Although it is possible, therefore, that the chiefs have more food than commoners and are more likely to live through the winter season without going hungry, little of the food collected from commoners by chiefs is actually eaten by the chief and his relatives. The chief alone is not permitted to work. Thus, the bulk of his food supplies can be provided by the other members of his family rather than by other members of the village. Furthermore, chiefs are expected to share their food supplies with others after the end of the winter ceremonials, and to feed those people who helped them in tasks that benefited the group as a whole, such as building weirs, carving ceremonial objects, or constructing new houses. None of this work, then, was actually done for the chief himself, but was a collective activity aimed at improving the future welfare of the numaym and tribe. The food given to the chief forms the capital investment of bodies that will later be repaid, with interest, when the reincarnated food-animals return.

Since food is always owned and consequently must always be given, every human being stands in relation to every other in the single fundamental structural relationship of food-giver (superordinate) to food-receiver (subordinate). A single dyadic relationship, defined by food, its possession, and its bestowal, exists between chiefs to their related numaym members, husbands to wives (and sometimes wives to husbands), parents to children, hosts to guests, spirits to humans, and food-animals to humans. And since life itself is a gift that demands that one spirit sacrifice himself that another might eat of him and live, the gift of life itself, both this life and eternal life, places individuals in dyadic relationships of life-givers and life-receivers. Children are subordinate to their parents because they have been given life by those parents, but grandparents are subordinate to their grandchildren (see Codere, 1956:332) because the grandchildren give the gift of reincarnation to the grandparents. The gift of food is the gift of life.

Yet, even though the food- or soul-receiver is in one sense dependent on the gifts of his superordinate, that superordinate is also dependent for his reincarnation on the generosity of his subordinate. Salmon give humans life by giving up their own lives so that people might eat, but when they are eaten by people, they are granted the gift of eternal life because they can then be reincarnated in their own land at the bottom of the sea. Parents are dependent upon their children because if those children do not reproduce, there will never be grandchildren to be the reincarnations of their grandparents. And chiefs are dependent on their numaym comembers because only when all people work together to gather and distribute food can the rituals granting power and life operate correctly and efficiently. The entire Kwakiutl social world is locked in a web of food-based ritual relations.[6]

---

[6] The linkage between food-giver as superordinate and food-receiver as subordinate is clearly marked in all food exchanges. Perhaps its clearest delineation comes in potlatch feasts, where the food-giver is required to deliver formal speeches stating his guests' subordination. Only when he has done so, setting up a dyadic relationship with them analogous to his relationship with the spirits, can he complete the ritual by actually distributing the food (see Benedict, 1934: passim). The distribution of food at a potlatch, like all rituals, combines action with analogy.

The entire system of rules governing the ownership of resources is one of checks and counterbalances. No principle of ownership ever completely supplants another, even though at any given moment one principle may be deemed superordinate. The ownership of resources by the chief is counterbalanced by the rights other members of his numaym have by virtue of their having labored to obtain those resources, the right of the hunter or fisherman by the right of women to prepare food, the ownership rights of parents by the rights of children, the rights of mankind by the rights of the animals and spirits. Even within the numaym and within the nuclear family, food ownership is not freely shared.

The access of commoners to a foodstuff devolves upon them by virtue of their relationship to the chief.[7] Commoners perform all the labor of the food-gathering process, and hard work is considered to be an essential part of that process. However, hard work is not only the direct instrument of the collection of food-animals, but also an indication to the animals that the person working has the proper attitude toward them, and is willing to give of his own sweat and energy that they may be captured. This sacrifice indicates to the animals that they may depend upon that individual to later fulfill his role in the rituals ensuring them the rebirth they desire. However, hard work alone will never bring food into a person's hands, for it is only one small part of the ritual process—a necessary condition for the successful collection of food, but not in and of itself a sufficient condition.

Since the active part of food collection is totally the responsibility of the commoners, and the analogic part the responsibility of the chiefs, it is not surprising to read of a numaym whose members consider murdering their chief when food harvests are poor (Ruyle, 1973:610 [a Nootka example]), for they believe that if they perform their work correctly and serve the food correctly, the failure in the food-collecting process must be that the chief is not performing his ritual obligations. His death and replacement by a more responsible person are necessary if everyone else is to survive.

For the most part, the division of labor among commoners is based on sex, though there are some tasks, such as gathering firewood for the fires used to prepare certain foods, which may be done by members of either sex. Men do almost all the fishing (women are permitted to net certain

<hr/>

[7] A portion of all foodstuffs caught under the aegis of a chief is given to the chief, and commoners, whether members of the chief's numaym or other people temporarily benefiting from his largesse, can continue to exploit his resource areas only so long as they give a substantial part of their catch to him. The amount they have to give varies according to such circumstances as the scarcity of food, the character of the chief, his ability to enforce his demands, his plans and needs for ceremonies, and whether the food can be eaten by commoners at all. Even so, half the catch is considered the absolute limit that a chief can demand without definitely angering his numaym comembers (Boas, 1921:1333-34).

types of small fish), all the hunting, and the final preparation of foods that are sumptuary, such as cinquefoil roots. Women dig for molluscs (to serve as bait for the men to use or as human food in hard times), gather seaweed, and collect and do most of the preparation of vegetable foods. However, foods that are saved for winter feasts and ceremonial meals are prepared in part by men, in that they must be carried from the beach into the house by men, they must be cooked over fires prepared by men (e.g., men must build fires for salmon [Boas, 1921:232], though women build the fires for halibut [Boas, 1921:244]), or they may be gathered only upon the request of men (e.g., salmon, dogwood, and viburnum berries).

The sexual division of labor is a requirement placed upon humans by the animals, who like, and have the right, to be caught and prepared by certain people only. The Kwakiutl respond to these demands through specific ritual acts: men and women address different prayers to the same animals at different times in the collecting and/or preparing process; certain taboos are imposed upon the members of each sex, especially in hunting (Boas, 1921:637-44); and members of a particular sex may have total responsibility for a particular type of ritual. For example, it is the responsibility of women to see that all parts of a fish that are not eaten or prepared for food are taken back to the sea and thrown into the water. Thus, at a halibut feast (Boas, 1921:246) the woman sees not only that the offal is saved until after the feast, but that every bone, every piece of skin, every part of waste is collected on a mat and carried by her to the sea. Otherwise the halibut will be offended and will complain to his species comembers that he was not treated well and will not be reincarnated for future use because those parts of his body neither eaten (and therefore not magically transformed as food) nor thrown back into the sea (and thus not directly returned to his ancestral spirit home) will be missing, and he will be unable to reconstitute his form.

Within the family, rules for utilization, division of labor, and decorum also set up patterns of access to food. For example, women are not permitted to fish for salmon or halibut, yet they immediately assume ownership of the fleshy middle parts when the fish are brought to the village. The men own only the heads, tails, and fins of the fish, which are smoked dry and stored in easily accessible boxes for their snacks. Though feasts are given using the choicest parts of the fish, since these belong to the women, a man wishing to give a feast or potlatch has to request his wife's permission to do so (Boas, 1909:427-44, passim). Particular food-gathering and food-preparing tasks are strictly limited to people of a particular sex or age. Some foods have to be shared with one's spouse, some with one's spouse and children, some with one's relatives and housemates; but in all cases, the preparation of the food is assigned to specific people—husband, wife, hired help, or numaym comembers. All texts dealing with

1. Alert Bay, circa 1915. By this time the European influence on Kwakiutl culture is clearly discernible in Kwakiutl architecture.

2. A Northern Kwakiutl box, collected 1893, is typical of the elaborately carved boxes used to store items imbued with supernatural power. The carving on the front represents both Frog, giver of life, and Raven, bringer of death, as simultaneous manifestations of each other.

3. View of a house in Alert Bay, circa 1915. The raven's beak opens and is used as a ceremonial entrance; a secular entrance can be seen to its left. The soul of the house is represented by the small face at the top of the stairs.

4. Houseposts displayed outside a European style Kwakiutl house, Alert Bay, circa 1915. The imagery of coppers as the bodies of men and men as the souls of the spirits is clear. The Kwakiutl emphasis on orality is obvious in the carving of the bears' mouths and the eagles' beaks.

5. A shaman's raven rattle, a powerful image of the cycle of death and rebirth, depicts a raven carrying the corpse of a man whose soul, as it leaves his mouth, is captured by a frog that is being eaten by a crane. The raven carries the man's soul to the spirit world in its mouth; the raven's underside represents the soul in its own form, with a recurved beak symbolizing rebirth.

6. Nakoaktok man, photographed by E. S. Curtis. In front is a house dish in the shape of a sisiutl, to the rear a painted screen of the type used to set apart the sacred inner room at ceremonies. The dancers enter and exit through the mouth of the figure, whose hands are depicted in the upright gesture of shamanic curing.

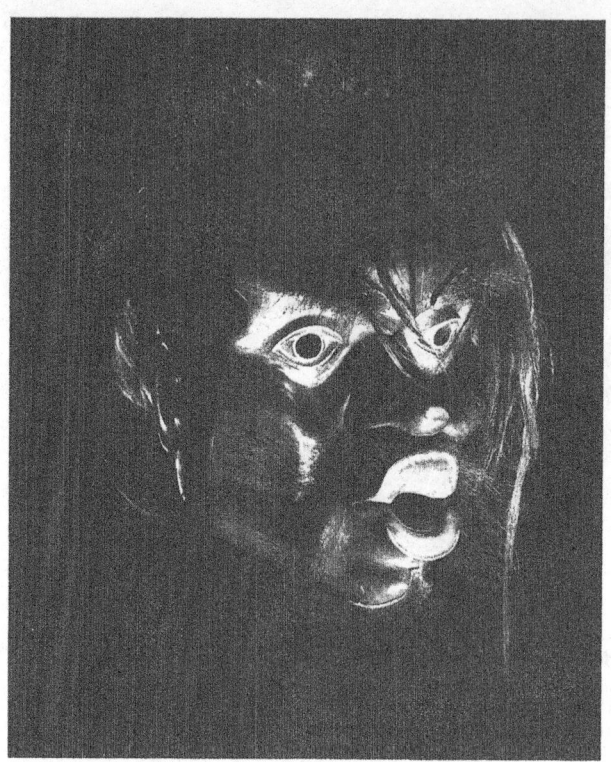

7. *Tsonoqua* mask. The *tsonoqua* were believed to be a race of mountain-dwelling man-eating giants, the females of which steal children and salmon from humans. Important figures in Kwakiutl myth and ritual, they represent hunger in its uncontrolled state: pervasive, potent, and wantonly destructive.

8. *Bukwis* mask. *Bukwis* lives in the forest where he eats rotted wood, lizards, toads, and the bodies of drowned people. The appearance of *bukwis* in human villages during the winter ceremonials indicates the beginning of the intrusion upon the human world of the voracious beings of the spirit world.

9. Thunderbird/*sisiutl* transformation mask. Transformation masks were used to illustrate the manifold and complementary components constituting the identity of a spirit being. Here the outer mask (above) opens to show Thunderbird, the inner mask (below) shows its prey, the *sisiutl*. The figure above the *sisiutl's* human face represents its soul.

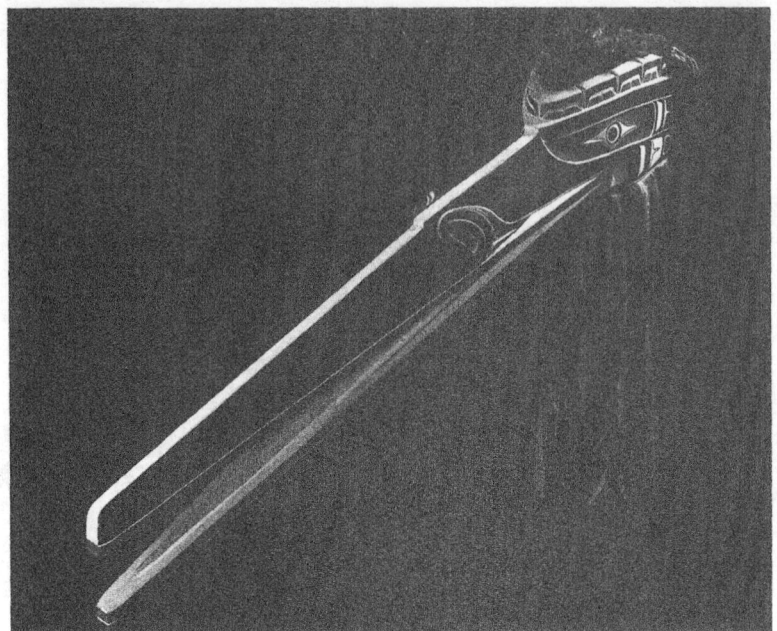

10. *Hohok* mask, a potent image of assimilation. One of the avian members of Man Eater's retinue, the *hohok* is a giant crane which kills men by cracking open their skulls and sucking out their brains.

11. This *hamatsa* multiheaded mask, carved by Mungo Martin in 1953, shows the three major avian associates of Man Eater: Cannibal Raven, *hohok*, and Crooked Beak of Heaven. These multiple masks were used to represent the appearance of Man Eater's cohorts as a corporate entity, as well as to show the inability of men to hide from beings who can see in all directions.

12. Dancing costume, photographed at the Field Columbian World Exposition, Chicago, 1894. A complex costume, it has movable parts representing a Thunderbird and the components of its identity: man, *sisiutl*, killer whale, sea lion, and human skulls, all linked together as predators and prey.

13. Diorama showing a *hamatsa* dancer entering a house through the screen that sets off the sacred inner room. The screen is painted in the image of a being with a large mouth, its soul visible beneath the *hamatsa* dancer. The drummers are playing on two types of ceremonial boxdrums, each of which represents a *sisiutl*. The costumes of the drummers symbolize their restraint, as contrasted to the *hamatsa*'s wildness. The eagle down, the visible manifestation of supernatural power, is an essential part of Kwakiutl ritual.

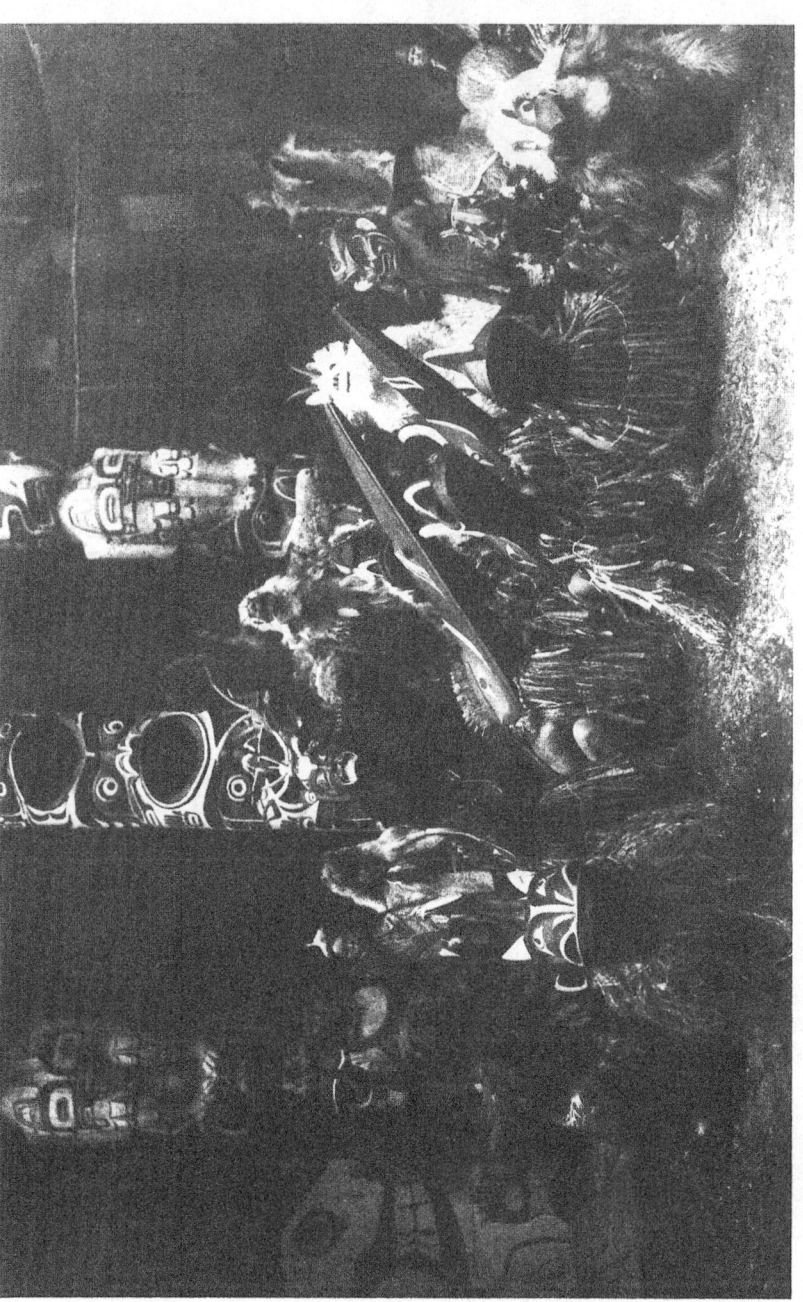

14. A wide assortment of masked dancers posed for a group portrait, photographed by E. S. Curtis. To the left is the screen leading to the sacred room, in the center area is the cannibal pole, through whose open mouths the *hamatsa* dancer enters and leaves the house. Among the dancers are a *hamatsa* (on the left), mountain goat, wasp, bear, Thunderbird, a spirit representing Weather, *bukwis*, octopus, wolf, deer, several *hohoks*, Crooked Beaks, and other beings associated with Man Eater. (Courtesy of the Provincial Archives of British Columbia.)

food preparation carefully point out who gathers the food, how far they carry it, to whom they give it, in what it is stored (baskets denoting women's ownership, boxes denoting men's ownership), and to whom and when it is served.

In some instances, the right to eat or distribute food belongs to the person who collects it. Thus, women automatically own all the vegetable foods, shellfish, and sea urchins that they gather. It is possible, however, for a man to hire women to gather berries; the food then belongs to him even though the women did the actual work. Men own all the seal, porpoise, and land mammals that they kill. The rule of ownership governing fish is slightly more complicated, however. Though in principle fish belong to the man who has caught them, once a fish is brought home and given to a woman to butcher, the middle (the most valuable, meaty part) of the fish becomes her property; only the head, backbone, tail and fins (i.e., those parts attached to the skeleton) belong to the man.[8]

However, the principle of ownership is not primarily determined by the actual work of gathering food. Instead, it is determined by who has the right to control the ritual process of turning living matter into dead. Thus, for example, even though a man may do the actual fishing or hunting, a proportion of his catch is owed to the chief because it is the chief alone who has the right to allow the fish or animal to be killed. Women receive the middle parts of the fish not because they are doing the butchering, but because it is their responsibility to ensure that during the butchering the essential rituals are performed so that the fish will be reborn in another life. And finally, the women who collect berries for a chief have no claim over those berries because he has not given them the right to process them into food. The denial of their ownership is reinforced by the fact that the women may not even remove the berries from their canoes. The

[8] There are symbolic reasons for this division of the internal from the external parts of the fish. The flesh of the salmon is red, a color associated with blood (especially menstrual blood), with coppers (which symbolize the souls of beings waiting to be reborn), and with the substance of human flesh. The skin, head, and backbones are analogues of men's ritual paraphernalia—masks and costumes (backbones representing the ladder by which the soul leaves the body). The structural opposition here, one that runs throughout all Northwest Coast societies, is that there is one group of people in control of the substance, or the material, of life and another in control of the processes by which substance is transformed and reincarnated. Only when these two groups work in concert can new life be created. In every Kwakiutl ritual these two opposing entities are brought together. For example, in the *hamatsa* dance, the *hamatsa* dancer controls the process (through his ties to Man Eater), whereas the rest of humanity controls the substance (their flesh) The very process of death is the combination of the two: humans have flesh, but only the spirits, especially ravens who are the representatives of Man Eater, know the mystery of how to process the flesh and release the soul so that it will make its journey to its new form. The obverse of human death, the food-collecting process, is itself an obverse ritual in which animals control substance and humans control process.

men of the numaym who hired them are the only ones who can remove the berries from the women's canoes and carry them up the beach into the house (Boas, 1921:211-12).

The woman's ownership of the valuable middle parts of the fish illustrates a fundamental postulate of Kwakiutl belief. Although we might think that a fish is dead once it has been speared and removed from the water, for the Kwakiutl this is only the first step in the process of death. Death may be reversed magically at this point, and the salmon can spring back to life. True death can be said to occur only when the woman has dismembered the body of the fish, which has the effect of releasing the soul of the fish from its carcass and allowing it to begin its journey to the land of the dead, where it will reside until it can be reborn. Thus, the true instrument of the fish's death is not the fisherman, but the woman, and her ownership of the choice parts of the fish is determined not because she has done some work in the fish preparation process, but because she has done the critical act of killing. Both the woman and the man say very similar prayers to the salmon in thanksgiving for the salmon's death, because both the man and the woman have contributed to that death (Boas, 1921:609; 1318).

The principle that death occurs only when the body is broken apart is critical in other areas of Kwakiutl life. We see it at work in the practice of tree burial, where it is the sacred task of the ravens to dismember the corpse, releasing the soul for its journey to the other world. We see it in warfare, where the Kwakiutl are careful to decapitate their victims. They do this not just for trophies, but because otherwise the spirits of the dead would not be released from the bodies, and they could spring back to life or, even worse, turn into zombies.[9] Finally, we see it at work in shamanism and the winter ceremonials, where death does not occur until the corpse begins to decay. Thus, the real horror of the Cannibal Dancer's ripping apart and devouring of a human corpse is not that he is actually eating human flesh, but that he is dismembering a corpse, and by doing so has become the direct instrument of an improper death for a human being, one of his own ancestors, and solely to satisfy his hunger.

In the food-producing process, the importance of the role played by the person who directly brings about the animal's death is validated by the distribution of the animal's body. In the case of seal and porpoise fishing, for example, ownership of the carcass first belongs to the man who does the killing. He divides the carcass into three portions—one for the steersman, one for himself, and one for the chief (Boas, 1921:447; 750).[10] The

[9] Decapitation severs the spinal and esophageal connections between mouth and stomach, thereby making it impossible for the soul to re-enter the body

[10] If more than one seal or porpoise is killed, all but one automatically belong to the chief.

steersman of the canoe is always given only a relatively small portion from the tail (the "rudder" of the fish) as his payment, despite the difficult work performed in guiding the canoe. The bulk of the carcass is divided by the two men most instrumental in transforming the living animal into food matter. The hunter gets his portion because he was directly instrumental in the death of the animal. The chief gets his portion because without his ritual support, no animal would have made itself available to be killed by the hunter.

The same pattern of distribution holds true for all food-gathering activities. The person who does the actual killing is entitled to a portion of the food; the people who help him but who do no actual killing are paid only a small amount; the person who performs the butchering gets a substantial portion, equal to that of the animal's killer; and the chiefs, though they do no actual physical labor, are paid a portion equal to that of the people who do the killing because of the fundamental importance of their ritual acts in the food-getting process.

Let us summarize Kwakiutl ideas of food ownership. Chiefs, through ritual action, convince food-animals to give up their bodies to humans for food. Commoners are dependent on the chiefs for the chiefs' continued ritual action, without which there would be no food since food-animals come only when they know that they are being collected by the right person, that is, the designated commoner representative of the chief with the proper jurisdiction. The chief is as dependent on his numaym for food as they are on him and the spirits, for the numaym members provide all the labor that completes the causal actions governing the ritual process of food collecting. No person has control over every step of the food-collecting and preparation process, and since the ownership of food changes as the food progresses through the various steps of that process, the Kwakiutl are inextricably linked in a complex web of shifting superordinate/subordinate relations based on a continuous cycle of gifts of food.

The collection of food is the first part of the cycle of food-related rituals. The second part involves the distribution of food at meals and feasts. Once again, the causal process of analogy and action operates, for the collecting part of the process acts to make the food-animal part of the human world, while the serving and eating of food provides the action by which the behavior of food-animals is controlled.

The religious principles informing the ownership of food-collecting rights are also at the foundation of all other behavior related to food, during both the processing activities and the actual eating of the food. At no point does the food material become simply edible matter. It is always the material representation of the eternal existence of the animal from which it has been taken. This awareness that food is obtained only by the grace of the animal being eaten and that the continuance of that grace is possible only if proper behavior toward the body of the animal is maintained permeates all aspects of Kwakiutl meals. Thus, meals are highly stylized and formalized procedures whose ritual aspects are endowed with great importance, since it is believed that failure to comply with ritual obligations would result in the loss of future food.[11]

Meals are not merely occasions for sociability; they are also ceremonies in the cycle of reincarnation. Since animals are graveboxes for human souls, containers of human spirit, the killing of an animal also involves the severing of a human soul from its animal flesh. Meals thereby act as funerals both for the animals and for the human souls within them, which must now find new bodily incarnations. The structure of a meal, whether it involves only two people or all the tribes, is the same. All meals and all feasts are funerals, all funerals are feasts. All ceremonies operate on the basis of the same processual principles; a potlatch differs from a family meal only in the amount of wealth of skins and souls being transferred, not in the nature of the distribution.

With few exceptions, Kwakiutl meals are times of social interaction between individuals and groups. Indeed, there are few foods whose collection does not inherently entail an immediate sharing with other people in other families, houses, or numayms. (Some foods are not shared immediately, but are saved for winter feasting; and some are eaten only by the family of the person who collects it because they are not acceptable foods for sharing.) Time after time the "recipes" in *The Ethnology of the Kwakiutl* (Boas, 1921) follow the pattern of the food collector's returning to the beach in front of his or her home and going immediately, or sending someone, to invite friends, relatives, or neighbors to join in the eating, and occasionally the preparation, of the food that has been brought back.

Though the sharing of food is a critical part of Kwakiutl meals, it is impossible to tell whether there is an emphasis among the Kwakiutl, as Wilson reports for the Nyakyusa (1951), on being invited to meals at other people's homes, of good company and camaraderie at meals as the basis for social relationships, and of emotional relationships or friendships expressed through the medium of food sharing. There seems to be little information for the Kwakiutl on whether they are concerned about being invited to other people's feasts. Instead, it seems as if invitations to feasts

---

[11] We have already seen that a great deal of interpersonal hostility potentially surrounds the ownership of food resources (see Drucker and Heizer, 1967:98-124), and we can argue that the prepared food itself (a metaphorical extension of those resources) is also a possible source of antagonism between people. The ritualization of all aspects of food-related behavior serves to minimize the possible hostility resulting from individual greediness or stinginess, for the distribution, preparation, serving, and sharing of food is completely predetermined by religious dictate.

are almost completely based on group co-affiliation, especially membership in the same clan or numaym, and on friendships and alliances between people of similar status. We can get no idea from the texts of how
many meals are eaten by the nuclear family alone and how many are
shared by all the families living in a single house. It does seem likely,
however, that except for food preserved and stored in boxes for some
time (which is served during the winter by a woman to her own family),
and except for a supply all women in a house would have, food, especially that which is fresh, is normally shared with whoever is present,
whether kinsman or not.

The most notable characteristic of Kwakiutl meals is their orderliness.
The same careful attention to organization, planning, and detail that Codere reports for technical tasks (Codere, 1950:18) is observable in the accounts of all aspects of the food-gathering and preparing processes. The
emphasis on etiquette and formality is noticeably present in every account. Strict rules govern almost every aspect of the meal, including the
placement of the utensils, the point when guests must be called to sit
down, the size of the containers used to bring and serve water, whether
napkins must be provided, and what type of prayers must be recited.

While Codere (1956) reports great conviviality at meals, and a story
about Boas and his Kwakiutl friends (Boas, 1966:xxvii) indicates some
levity at dinners, there is no evidence in the description of feasts in the
texts of any but the most formal behavior. Ritual singing, primarily of
feast songs (which, as we have seen, are really prayers), is often an
important part of a meal, especially any meal involving four or more
men. Meals are times of serious learning, for it is then that the young
people hear the songs, the myths, the social charter of their group; it is
then that they learn the stories of their ancestors. There is no report of
conversation during the eating of any meal, though it reportedly occurs
during the preparation of various foods, for example, salmon cheeks
(Boas, 1921:233), involving large numbers of people. It seems that the
guests at a meal sit quietly, both while the food is being cooked and
served and after it is eaten. In many cases it is reported that guests wash
and leave immediately after they finish eating. In other cases, it seems
that after they wash and the dishes are removed and cleaned, they may
remain for after-dinner conversation. Even at feasts, which we associate
in our own minds with some sybaritic ribaldry and loquaciousness, only
the holder of the speaker's staff may speak, and other people sit quietly
or talk in hushed tones.[12] Nor can we find much in the potlatch that
indicates fun and frolicking. Indeed, the so-called play potlatch is re-

[12] Graphic evidence of this are films of potlatches (e.g., *Crooked Beak of Heaven* and
Potlatch . . . A Strict Law Bids Us Dance), which show people sitting quietly while awaiting
the distribution of food and gifts.

ported only for women (Codere, 1956), who are excluded from many ritual feasts, and it can be viewed as a measure of hostility towards husbands who keep their wives from participating equally in the feast rites.

This seriousness at meals may be a measure of hostility, anxiety, and antagonism between individuals, but we can only speculate about this. What is easier to appreciate is that Kwakiutl meals are religious convocations, that they share the same sacredness as do all religious occasions, that they are clearly defined by ritual acts as sacred occasions, and that proper decorum is required not as a responsibility of one human to another, but as the requirement of a human to the animal whose corpse he is about to ingest in food form. All meals are localized states of sacredness, created by the ritual drinking of water and singing of sacred songs, by the ritualization of food serving and eating practices, and by the exclusion of secular behavior. The relationship of human to food animals demands a lack of levity and a denial of hedonism, greediness, antagonism, and human sinfulness. Silence, or at least decorous quiet, is therefore commensurate with man's subordination to his superiors—the food-giving spirits.

It can be argued that there is a great deal of indifference to the rituals, the dances, and the myths. Codere reports that children pay only partial attention to their grandfathers' retelling of the tales of Mink (Codere, 1956:336-37); other people report that there is indifference even during the sacred winter dances themselves (Drucker and Heizer, 1967). The first example may be countered by the argument that the telling of the myth is not itself a sacred event, but can become a sacred event only when a localized state of sacredness exists. The myth thereby becomes a recreation of the actual event, in this case recreated through dance and song. The second example may be countered by the argument that the ritual performance itself causes powers to work, and, as with shamanism, the attitudes of auxiliary spectators are not important. In addition, sacred obligations do not fall equally on the shoulders of all people because most commoners, women, children, and guests of less-than-the-highest ranks are dependent only indirectly on the beneficence of the spirits. The chiefs and the seat-holders, who are directly tied to the spirits, maintain silence and pay intense attention to the dances. Indeed, their lack of interest is considered a supreme insult and may start a rivalry battle (see Boas and Hunt, 1905).

Thus, though there are aspects of sociability in Kwakiutl meals, the determining force in the nature of etiquette is the fact that meals express the relationship of humans to the spirit world, and that they reinforce the hierarchy of society only as a byproduct of reaffirming the interrelated destinies of food and humans, reified in hereditary rights. Proper etiquette is only one form of religious act.

Information on meals is concentrated in two places: in *The Kwakiutl of Vancouver Island* (Boas, 1909:427-43) in a section on meal behavior, and in *The Ethnology of the Kwakiutl* (Boas, 1921) in the recipes (305-601) and a short but critical section on feasts (750-76). However, other materials on meals, eating behavior, and food customs and taboos are scattered throughout the rest of the corpus of Boasian texts. Almost every family history, description of ritual, ceremonial, myth, and song has embedded in its retelling some information about food, the eating of food, and the symbolic relationship of humans and food.

The more than three hundred pages of recipes in *The Ethnology of the Kwakiutl* (Boas, 1921) have often been singled out by anthropologists as an example of how Boas's particularist bias forced him to collect trivial, useless material. However, in those pages of recipes lies the key to the entire organization of Kwakiutl social and mental life. The so-called recipes are not recipes in our sense of the word, but rather accounts of the social events that comprise the preparation, preservation, cooking, serving, and eating of food at meals. The accounts include such important data as when the food is eaten, by whom, whether guests may be invited or indeed must be invited; how rules of ownership, the division of labor, and social rank affect food distribution; the patterns of interaction between members of the family, household, numaym, and tribe; and the ritual relationships between mankind and the spirit beings who provide humans with sustenance. Since Kwakiutl social and intellectual life centers around the entire gestalt of eating and assimilation, these pages of descriptions of rites concerning food are the most important data we could hope for.

Even the various customs in the preparation, cooking, and eating of foods are considered to have direct causal effects on the ability of hunters and fishermen to catch food in the future. For example, rather than being scraped off, seal hair must be burned off and the residue knocked off with sticks (Boas, 1921:607-8), for otherwise, in the future the seals will be able to escape from the hunter; the first silver salmon of the season must be completely eaten on the same night as they are caught or no others will ever again be caught (Boas, 1921:611). It must be emphasized that these are not merely examples of a handful of rituals involving food. Rather, they display the basic Kwakiutl attitudes toward food and man's ability to obtain it.

The Kwakiutl eat three meals a day—breakfast, which is generally limited to family and household members, though friends and relatives can be invited to share some types of food, lunch, and dinner, both of which are structurally similar in their organizational principles (social and culinary), and both of which are generally eaten in groups larger than nuclear family size. The times when these meals are eaten are governed by the events of the day: when a person may return from his work, which he does only when it is finished, whether guests are to be invited to join in, and so forth. Wives are expected to awaken before their husbands in the morning to begin the stoking of the fire and initial food preparation necessary for readying breakfast, but the time of this meal varies, depending on how diligent both wife and husband are. Diligent workers will eat breakfast early, but not hastily, so that they can begin their daily chores.

Meals are eaten on the floor adjacent to the family's fire. The housewife sits on one side of the fire, her cooking utensils on her left. For some ceremonial meals she moves away from the eating area after the food is served and sits quietly until the end of the meal, when she must take the dishes to the beach and clean them by the water's edge. During family meals husband, wife, and children eat at the same time, but when guests come, the wife and children eat separately after the guests have left. When guests are present, the host eats only after his guests have been served and have begun eating.

Food is served on woven cedar-bark mats, which are spread in front of the fire. The age and quality of the mats is prescribed according to the food being eaten: some foods must be cooked and served on old mats, some on new. Several people sit by a single mat. Dry food is placed directly on the mats, but liquid, mushy, or piecemeal foods are served in food trays. A special section of each tray is reserved for a container of oulachen (candlefish) oil, which is eaten with foods that either have become dry or tough as a result of the preserving process or that are naturally irritating to the throat. The oulachen oil is placed on the side of the tray nearest the fire, across the tray from the person using that tray, so that food already dipped in oil is brought to the mouth over the rest of the dry food.

Posture at meals is limited to two positions. In addition, blankets are worn at all meals by every adult. The most frequent, decorous, formal position is squatting, with the right elbow resting on the right knee, the left arm concealed beneath the blanket. The second posture, less formal, consists of sitting with the knees together, flexed and to one side, but still hidden beneath one's blanket, and still with the left hand concealed beneath the blanket.

Food is eaten either with the fingers or with a spoon.[13] In either case, only the right hand can be used. When spoons are used, the only acceptable position is squatting. In part, this is because the types of foods requiring spoons are served in large bowls that are shared by several people. Squatting allows more people to use the common bowl than does the less formal, sitting, posture. Food is taken up with only the point of the spoon

[13] Some special foods, such as whipped soapberries, are eaten with specially shaped utensils.

and sipped as noiselessly as possible. To prevent the use of the spoon in witchcraft, people dip their spoons into water that is always passed around for that purpose alone at the end of every meal requiring spoons (Boas, 1909:427).

The amount of food eaten is generally small. In accounts of feasts (Boas, 1909) the amount of food prepared is astonishingly meager—for example, two salmon backbones (removed during the preservation process and containing little flesh) per person. Only a few foods are consumed in quantities large enough to be satisfying, and then only at some of the most important tribal-wide feasts. Yet, however little food is served, it is still incumbent on people not to finish everything in their dishes. Noblemen and noblewomen are particularly careful to observe restraint while eating (Boas, 1909:427). They hardly open their mouths, chew their food slowly and at great length, are not permitted to show their teeth while chewing, and use spoons with specially pointed narrow tips that enable them to sip without having to open their mouths very much. Food to be dipped in oil is rolled up, and only a small corner, which is to be bitten off and chewed slowly, is dipped into the oil. Second helpings are never served; whatever food is left over is distributed among the guests to be taken home and given to their own families. Loud or noticeable chewing and swallowing are considered disgusting; eructation and flatulence are considered indicative of having eaten too fast, and thus incorrectly. Jokes made about flatulence are regarded as insults and the flatulent offender, shamed by his lack of self-control, is required to erase his shame with a ritual feast.

The drinking of water has an important part in many magical rituals, including meals. It is believed that failure to drink water at the proper time will cause the body to rot inside, a symptom of spiritual impurity (Boas, 1966:148-55; 376-88). The drinking of water is used to differentiate symbolically between two states of existence. Thus, for example, people rinse their mouths in the morning to end the state of sleep and begin the state of wakefulness. Every breakfast has to be preceded by this ritual cleansing. The beginning of a meal is always marked by a drink of water before which no food can be eaten and after which strict rules of etiquette are held to be in effect. The number of sips of water taken before and after a meal is regulated according to the food being eaten and the relationships of the guests present, but it is usually limited to a single, small ladleful. During the meal water is served only when a course is finished, thereby indicating the end of the ritual activity associated with that particular food. Chiefs who are in intimate magical relationship with the food-giving spirits are careful never to eat foods that might require them to drink water except at the end of a course.

The end of each meal is also marked by a ritual drink, after which the

guests are required to return immediately to their own homes. This signifies the end of the ritual gathering of the food sharers. There are excep-
tional cases in which the eating of certain foods cannot be followed by
this ritual drink. Instead, the guests are required to return to their own
homes before they next drink water. In these instances the magical power
involved in the meal is carried back to the homes of the guests to be
shared with their respective households.

Family meals usually consist of a single course. Feasts, that is meals
when guests from outside the household are invited, may contain a second
course, if the first course is not a food after which second courses are
forbidden. Generally, the first course at two-course meals is a fish-based
food, and the second course is a vegetable food. Even at great feasts, few
varieties of food are served. For example, at a crabapple feast, only crabapples are served, and the feast ends as soon as the crabapples are finished
(Boas, 1921:762).

The particular organizational pattern of a given meal is determined by
a large number of interrelated factors: by the type of food being served,
whether the food is available, who in the family owns and has the right
to serve it, the season of the year, the time of the day, the number of
guests arriving, their ages and statuses, and whether the serving of the
food is a special sumptuary prerogative or a more universal right. Each
type of food has its own formal relationship to people, which encompasses every aspect of its collection, preparation, serving, and eating. Thus,
the meal itself is merely a point in the longer ritual process, not, as it is
in our culture, the endpoint of that process, for the relationship of human
to food continues even after the food has been eaten.

Each particular type of food, different sections of the same animal, or
the same section of animals caught in different places or by different
methods have their own rituals of preparation and affect the organization
of the meal. The two culinary characteristics of the food most critical to
the organization of the meal are whether the food is oily enough to be
eaten without irritating the throat, and whether it must be served dry or
in a broth.

The difference between oily and nonoily fish is symbolic of the differences between nobles and commoners, since oily fish is preferred to dry
fish, and since the Kwakiutl are always aware of the social distinctions
inherent in who is permitted to eat the preferred foods.[14] Indeed, people
of high status often will not eat dry foods but only foods that are tender,
mushy or oily enough to be eaten without irritating the throat and causing
embarrassing fits of coughing. Dry food is usually not served to nobles,

---

[14] Oily foods are never eaten for breakfast, for it is believed that eating them will make
one sleepy, lazy, and fat.

but when it is, it is first soaked for a long time in water, and served with copious quantities of oil. Even so, the proper host is careful to remind his guests that the food they are eating may be tough and scratchy or contain small bones. Those foods that are irritating, but which cannot be softened by soaking in oil—some of which, such as roasted salmon backs, are considered to be great delicacies—are not eaten by people of high status. They are eaten only by young men, "those who do not have a man's mind" (Boas, 1909:428), that is, those who are still unaware of their responsibility to maintain the rituals of etiquette and decorum.

The second culinary distinction between food types is the manner of its cooking and serving—whether it is dry or in a broth. While this distinction might, at first, seem to be dictated by the texture of the food, there are actually two important symbolic reasons for the presentation of food in a particular medium. The first concerns the preservation process, for if fish is preserved for future use as a dry dish, then the bones are removed during that process and discarded in an important magical rite (Boas, 1921:247). If the food is prepared for later use in a broth, however, the bones are left intact, for they are an important thickening agent for the broth. In such a case, the server of the food is required to ritually collect all the bones that have not been eaten by his guests and to dispose of them in another important ritual. The second reason concerns the fact that fish served dry is both preserved and reheated through direct contact with fire, while food prepared for use in broth never comes into contact with fire. Since, as we have seen, fire is the primary means of transubstantiating present food into future food animals, special ritual provisions must be made at meals where broth is served to see that the bony remains do come into ritual contact with fire.

The second major factor that influences the structure of meals is the number of men present. Here the number four is the critical dividing point. If fewer than four men are present, the singing of sacred ancestral songs and feast songs is not permitted, but if four or more men are present, the singing of sacred and feast songs is required (Boas, 1909:430-43 passim). Meals with fewer than four men are informal, since the men will all sit around a single dish, and thus, there is no strict seating according to rank. This is not true when more are present, for in that case, the man of highest rank sits in the center of the row, and the others, according to their ranks, alternately at his right and left sides. A drum is handed to the guest who is on the right hand end of the row of guests, and he plays it, accompanied by the handclapping of the others, while the company sings sacred songs. The number of songs sung is prescribed by the number of guests present, and is carefully noted in the account of each meal (Boas, 1909:427-43). The food is served only when the ritual songs are finished.

Food is considered to be symbolic of social status. Certain foods can be eaten only by people of high rank and never by commoners. For example, chiefs have sumptuary rights over halibut skins, salal berries, winkles, salmon cheeks, a mixture of currants and salal berries, the insides of seals, and long cinquefoil roots (Boas, 1921: passim). Commoners are permitted to eat only the tougher, less tasty cinquefoil roots. At feasts where both commoners and chiefs are present, these discriminatory practices are considered to teach the common people their station. Other foods are considered to be indicative of the low status, poverty, or unfortunate circumstances of the people who eat them. For example, fern roots are considered food for poor people exclusively (Boas, 1921:196), lupine roots are eaten only in the early spring when food is scarce, and chitons and various fish parts (e.g., holed skin and dried halibut heads and stomachs) are reserved for either old or poor people or for use in meals to which no guest may be invited (see Boas, 1921).

Social status plays two important roles in the structuring of meals. First, while there are meals at which a commoner will have some role in the preparation of the food as well as in the eating of it, this is never the case for chiefs. The role of a chief is not to prepare or serve food, but to act as the recipient of food. Second, the manner of serving chiefs food is different from that of serving commoners. Indeed, rivalries may begin when one chief serves another in a manner not befitting his status, either by serving him a piece of food designated for commoners only, by serving him his food out of the correct order as established by his social standing (especially by serving him after someone of lower status has been served), or by serving the food in a messy or careless manner (cf., Hunt, 1906; Drucker and Heizer, 1967:98-118).

Although it has been traditional to see the anger of chiefs, who have been mistreated at meals, as the result of their pridefulness (Boas, Benedict, and Codere all hold this position), it is in fact not necessarily individual pride or egotism at the root of this reaction. Instead, we can trace the foundation of the insult to the fact that chiefs stand in a particular relationship to food in that it is only by virtue of their social position and religious action that any food whatsoever is obtained by their numayms. Thus, to treat a chief in a manner not in accordance with his ritual status is to belittle him not just as an individual but as the head of his entire group, as the representative on earth of an ancestor, and as the recipient of gifts from the supernaturals. Therefore, an insult to an individual chief is actually an insult to his entire claim to supernatural power. The incredible amounts of wealth that go into the so-called wiping out of that shame actually act to prove incontrovertibly, by overwhelming material evidence, that the chief does hold that power, that he is a rightful inheritor of his social and ritual position, and that he can lead his group in a successful attempt to collect food.[15] The participation of his numaym comembers is not, then, dependent simply on a chief's individual charisma, but on the fact that the ritual status of the entire numaym is impugned when that of their chief is impugned.

We have seen that the religious basis of meals is well illustrated throughout the entire corpus; and we have already spoken about the ritual handwashing and mouth rinsing, rituals of table setting and food presentation, and most important, the singing of sacred feast songs that make each meal a temporally and spatially localized situation of sacredness. The creation of this sacred state places a moral responsibility on the diners not to act in a way that may have disasterous repercussions. For example, fast eating and noticeable chewing will bring about the destruction of the world more quickly by increasing the aggressiveness of the world; eating large quantities will reinforce the process of eating, which will make people hungrier and greedier, and make food scarcer as a result; failure to dispose ritually of the remains of a meal will reinforce the presence of offal in the world until there is nothing but offal. The sacredness of the meal ends only with the ceremonial cleansing of the hands and face and of the dishes in which the food was served. These acts set the meal apart as a ritual entity with magical significance, creating the boundaries of the ritual occasion, and raising the meal to a transcendent level.

In summary, the web of social relations is, both in nature and function, a web of analogic food-based relations, every detail of which is sacramental because every part is a synechdochic realization of the whole. Human interrelations are metaphorized and delineated through the humans' responsibilities toward food-animals. Humans organize the internal nature of their society by relating themselves in a coherent way to those universal elements that lie outside their society; the rituals of food collec-

[15] This dependence on spirits for success is so essential that it is believed that few human actions can be completed successfully without aid from the spirits (Boas, 1966:155-65) One historical case, the well-known incident of the rival chiefs (Hunt, 1906), has been repeatedly misinterpreted because of scholars' failure to understand the underlying importance of spirit aid as a validation of position and power. In this case, two friends begin a rivalry that eventually leads to the impoverishment of one of them, who then goes off to war, where he and his war party are ambushed and killed Benedict (1934.197-99) interpreted this act as a suicidal response by the defeated chief to the shaming he had received in the rivalry potlatches, and other scholars have echoed her views. The implication they make is that the Kwakiutl tell of the death of the defeated chief as an object lesson in how little value life has for the low-status person However, another interpretation, more consonant with Kwakiutl ideas than this one, is that the defeated chief's lack of spirit-power, already proved by his inability to obtain wealth with which to best his rival, prevents him from successfully raiding the enemy. His death, especially by ambush, is a clear indication that he did not possess the power that he needs to be a great chief Both his defeat in the rivalry and his death in war exemplify the foolishness of trying to act without the proper aid from the spirits

tion and distribution provide a matrix for an indigenous sociology, social roles and ritual responsibilities analogizing and defining each other. The hierarchical distinctions drawn between humans are possible only because all humans are subordinate to the spirits, the ultimate food-givers. Humans are able to exist only because animals are willing to sacrifice themselves for human welfare, and they can coexist only because they are willing to sacrifice themselves for the benefit of others. Humans focus their attention on the proper acting out of their role as predator upon animals; only then can they ensure the proper acting out of their role as predator upon other humans. The treatment of food, as a detail in the ritual of human existence, analogizes and embodies the whole sacrament of social and, ultimately, cosmic existence.

THREE

Animals as Metaphors
of Morality

... depuis l'huître jusqu'à l'aigle, depuis le
porc jusqu'au tigre, tous les animaux sont
dans l'homme. . . . Les animaux ne sont
autre chose que les figures de nos vertus et
de nos vices, errantes devant nos yeux, les
fantômes visibles de nos âmes.
—Hugo, *Les Misérables*

ANIMALS PLAY a critical metaphorical role for the Kwakiutl. Their bodily forms are seen as symbols of their characters, their postures as representations of their actions, their behavior simultaneously as models for human behavior and as reinforcing repetitive images of human behavior. Animals act as nexi for constellations of symbols and metaphors. They are living examples of the active manifestation of the forces and characteristics that constitute the cosmos.

Animal characteristics play a direct role in the structuring of myths in both our own and Indian cultures. For example, the famous tale of the race between the tortoise and the hare is based on the fact that a hare's normal pattern of movement is one in which a brief period of fast running will be followed by a long period of complete motionlessness and then another period of motion, but in another direction—a trait that helps them escape from predators. Tortoises, however, move slowly but without stopping, for their defense against predators does not lie primarily in their means of locomotion. Similarly, in the Crow myth of Old-Man-Coyote and the Berrying Girls (Lowie, 1918:43-45), in which the culture hero tries to take sexual advantage of some women by hiding in a patch of wild strawberries, the point of the myth is lost unless one realizes that the glans of a coyote's penis, unlike man's, is strawberry red in color and conical in shape, that the fruit of the strawberry plant is difficult to see through the thick foliage, and that it takes some effort to remove strawberries attached to the plant.

Thus, the choice of a particular animal to metaphorize a motivation, belief, or behavior is not random. Instead, the creator of the story chooses a particular trait of a particular animal and extrapolates from that trait to reach a symbolic statement of a human behavior (cf., Boas, 1938: chap. 13; Willis, 1974). It is therefore impossible for us to understand the structural and metaphorical character of Kwakiutl myths without understanding the empirical data of natural history that forms the foundation of those myths. It is impossible to understand why sparrows are considered the messengers of the spirits, why the Bear Dancers are the holders of spirit-force, and why the Seal Society has its particular functions as ritual leaders without understanding the interpretations the Kwakiutl attribute to the behavior of the actual animals involved, and thus understanding how the animals and humans are related by anatomical, behavioral, and motivational similarities.

For the Kwakiutl the animal world, like the human world, is predicated on two opposing principles: the principle of hunger—the need and desire for food, which drives humans and animals alike to kill—and the principle of sociality—the principle by which humans and animals consciously suppress their hunger for the benefit of their associates. Just as humans share food at feasts, so do the animals share food with their conspecifics: parent birds regurgitate food for their nestlings, gregarious scavengers congregate at a kill site to share a carcass, raccoons kill crayfish for their young, wolves bring food to their dens for those members of the pack who did not hunt that day.

Indeed, food is the medium for marking and maintaining all relations between humans and animals. There is more than ample evidence that for animals, as well as for humans, the power of hunger is great enough to overcome the force of wisdom and reason. Crows and ravens, both highly intelligent birds, will be drawn to traps by the presence of food and will squabble noisily over carrion. In the winter when they become hungry, wolves lose their normal wariness of humans and walk into the midst of villages. We need only remind ourselves that the normal method of trapping a carnivorous animal is to bait a trap with food to realize that the power of hunger alone can be sufficient to draw those animals to their deaths.

Thus, food used as bait becomes the means by which a human destroys the animals around him and by which he unites himself with them in a bond of life and death. This is why there are different rituals for salmon caught by hook and line and salmon caught in nets and trolling weirs, for in the latter case, no bait is involved, while in the former, the very presence of food causes the willingness of the salmon to die for humans. In short, food is the method, the model, the medium, and the metaphor, by which humans and the animals are united.

Of all the possible ways in which the Kwakiutl might organize animals into a coherent system of natural history, the one they choose is based primarily on the oral characteristics of the animals: the shape of the head and mouth, the fervor with which food is eaten, whether the animal is carnivorous (which includes scavengers) or herbivorous, whether teeth are present, whether the animal makes varied and frequent vocalizations, and all behaviors associated with the catching and killing of prey. Color, body shape, distinctive markings, and internal anatomical differences—the foundation of Western taxonomy and natural history—play a vastly subordinate role in the Kwakiutl characterization and metaphorization of animal behavior and motivation.

It is these oral characteristics that are used to delineate and represent the animals in myth and in everyday thought. The long beak of the heron, its slow stalk through the water, and its lightning strike followed by the animated swallowing down its long throat of its struggling prey are the characteristics that bring power and meaning to the myth of the origin of herons (Boas, 1935b:6-7). The busy, constant pecking of the woodpecker, its insatiable hunger and continual need for satisfaction are the traits that delineate woodpeckers. The huge maw of the killer whale as it swims through the water snatching prey from the deep, all the while making fantastic vocalizations with its blowhole, the gluttony of the mink, the carrion-eating of ravens, the divebombing of eagles as they swoop upon salmon, and the darting tongues of lizards are characteristics the Kwakiutl see as the critical aspects of animal behavior.

The Kwakiutl have a constellation of beliefs about the nature of animals that is found throughout most of aboriginal North America. While we believe that animals act primarily by instinct and humans by cultural conditioning, the Native Americans believe that humans and animals are equally instinctual, equally cultural, motivated by the same universal desires. Humans and animals have the same capacities for reason, for speech, for consciousness, for understanding, for moral choice. Yet, each species also has its own special, particular place in the world, its own sense of being, its own special insights, perceptions, and awarenesses. Henry Beston, though not referring to Native American thought about animals, came very close to capturing its essence:

> In a world older and more complete than ours they move finished and complete, gifted with extensions of the senses we have lost or never attained, living by voices we shall never hear. They are not brethren, they are not underlings; they are other nations, caught with ourselves in the net of life and time, fellow prisoners of the splendor and travail of the earth. (1928:25)

It is impossible to understand Kwakiutl art and myth without realizing that the power behind them comes from the peculiar oral behavior of the animals involved; and it is impossible to understand Kwakiutl life without seeing how the Kwakiutl themselves envision the animal world, which—in terms of the constant struggle for food, for death and life, for visceral satisfaction—is not so much around them as a part of them. The Kwakiutl see in animals, and extrapolate from them, new dimensions for the ideas and emotions they themselves feel to be the prime movers of human behavior.

This numinous feeling extends to their relations with animals and to their interpretations of animal behavior. Kwakiutl ideas of natural history, of the motivating forces acting on animals as well as humans, and of the cosmic principles that create and direct all animate beings are as firmly based in metaphors of orality as is their metaphorization of human behavior. This is hardly surprising, since ultimately humans and animals are serial incarnations of the same souls, each dying so that the other may be reborn. The Kwakiutl model their own behavior, indeed their own society, on the behavior they observe among animals. This reflexive metaphorization, in which animal behavior provides an empirical basis for the structuring of human behavior and in which the structure of human society provides a metaphor for the structure of animal societies, gains tremendous importance for the Kwakiutl, for it is a self-contained, self-reinforcing mechanism.

The Kwakiutl world is one where countless varieties of animals all kill and destroy to satisfy their hunger, united in a common bond of becoming food for each other, all active participants in an intricately interdependent system of resurrection. It is a world filled with the gaping maws of killer whales, the fearsome teeth of wolves, bears, seals, and spawning salmon, the tearing beaks of eagles, ravens, owls, and hawks, and the unending voraciousness of rodents, lizards, frogs, and snakes. It is a world filled with images of mouths, and of the death they bring to the creatures of the world.

In this world, oral desires form the prime movers for all creatures, and their oral behavior indicates their continuing search for food, for death, and ultimately resurrection. The plentitude of animal species is not only a wonder of evolution, but becomes graphic proof of the many different forms hunger can take, the many ways death may be brought about, and the diversity of manners in which the world has been organized so that humans might never forget how potent a force hunger is. No matter what outward form an animal may have, its actions are always ultimately determined by its desire for food, for the death of some other animal.

The oral peculiarities of animals play an important role in myths, rituals, artistic iconography, and social identification. Animals used for primary crest identification (which means animals with whom man has a special link through eons back to the days when humans first walked the earth)—beaver, bear, eagle, wolf, raven, and killer whale—have a cluster

of four similar traits distinguishing them from all other animals: they are
social, they are noticeably voracious, they make a large number of vocalizations, and they are carnivorous.[1] Mythical extensions of animals—
such as the Cannibal Bird that cracks open men's skulls and sucks out
their brains, the Thunderbird, *tsonoqua*, *bukwis*, sea wolf, sea bear, and
sisiutl—are always carnivorous. In myths, the actual behavior of animals,
a mink's gluttony, a heron's incessant searching for fish, a whale's incredible appetite, an eagle's swooping descent upon a salmon, forms an
important part of their characterization. And the behavior of actual animals forms the basis of that of mythical animals: the Thunderbird swoops
upon whales as the eagle does upon salmon; the sea wolf hunts in packs
for seals and salmon as the wolves of the land do for their prey; the
Cannibal Birds kill humans to get the flesh from their corpses as their
relatives the ravens pick the flesh from corpses; the double-headedness
and lightning swiftness of the *sisiutl* mimic that of terrestrial snakes.

The Kwakiutl stand in a special relationship to one class of animal in
particular, the predator, especially those predators who, in some way,
feast off either humans or salmon. It should be remembered that humans
and salmon are inextricably intertwined in a web of resurrection-oriented
rituals, and that salmon are the mirror images of humans. Thus, all animals that eat salmon must perform the rituals that make the salmon want
to die, the rituals that promise them resurrection. But even more important, since salmon are humans, and humans eat salmon, by analogy humans eat humans—and are thus cannibals. Furthermore, crest animals
that eat salmon are themselves de facto man eaters. In point of fact, most
crest animals actually do eat humans, either live humans (killer whales,
wolves, and bears) or dead humans (eagles and ravens). Thus, because
these animals are all direct links in the cycle of resurrection for both
humans and salmon, they are themselves by definition humans. Like all
animals, they are considered to be humans who have donned magical
masks and blankets (skins), which transform them into the animals seen
in daily life. All those animals whose food is in some way related to that
of humans are a part of the same system of transubstantiation and metempsychosis as are humans and salmon, and thus must be dealt with in
a manner consistent with the highly sacred character of man's role in the
chain of being.

The special character of this human/predator relationship is codified in
the system of totemic identification, for all those animals with whom man
shares responsibility for the successful maintenance of world order are
conjoined with him totemically. In the Kwakiutl case, this identification
is thought to have originated at the beginning of time, when the spirit

---

[1] For the explanation of why the Kwakiutl think beaver are carnivorous see below p. 117

chiefs of the animals became involved with the ancestors of the present human population. Through various magical acts, recorded in each group's origin myths, the ancestors were able to coerce the spirit chiefs of the animals into agreeing to contract an eternal relationship with them and their descendants for the mutual benefit of both human and animal groups. It is only by virtue of these eternal covenants that humans today are able to obtain food, and that the animals are able to live in harmony with humans, for otherwise, humans and animals would be in open competition for the same food resources, and thus, the same souls represented by that food.

These sacred covenants are recorded in two ways: orally through myths and visually through carved objects. The Kwakiutl spend a great deal of time recounting their myths, retelling their sacred histories, and performing those rites that have their foundations in oral tradition. Meals are an important sacred event if only because they form a regular and universal occasion for the learning of group traditions. The singing of holy songs commemorating the covenant between one's chief and a particular spirit animal's, the instruction of the young in the learning of the myths, and discussions of the fine points of interpretation of these myths form an important part of formal dining behavior (Boas, 1909:432). Many other rituals incorporate the retelling of these ancestral myths as part of their structure. Marriages, births, winter ceremonials, potlatches, the formation of war parties, and indeed almost all other types of Kwakiutl group endeavor require the recitation of the myth itself, in whole or in part, or a reference to the myth, either directly or as part of a song.

Although the importance of these ancestral myths has been emphasized by many Kwakiutl scholars, little thought has been addressed to the question of how these myths formed a basis for the symbolic identification of the individual with a group. For example, although traditional definitions of the numaym have focused on common kinship, common residence, or group cooperation as the basis of numaym organization, none of these characteristics has provided a satisfactory explanation why a particular Kwakiutl would identify with a particular locale, kin, or labor group. The key to Kwakiutl social organization is that members of a single numaym share the same set of structural relationships to the animal-spirit world, and that these relationships are expressed on a map by the sharing of resources, which, since they are localized, create a general pattern of local identification. Because the relationships are inherited through kinship lines, this provides both an illusion of kinship relation as the basis for organization and, since only people who have the ritual right to harvest a particular food resource at a particular spot can do so without fearing death through secular or magical retribution, the aura of group cooperation. Thus, neither kinship, nor coresidence, nor cooperation is the basis for Kwakiutl numaym organization. These are only the results of the sharing of a particular set of mythic rights and responsibilities toward the world of animals and spirits.

Indeed, those actions in which the numaym forms a corporate group are all directly related to these mythic food-related rites and their extensions into the realm of metempsychosis: numaym members cooperate to procure, produce, and serve food, to produce the winter ceremonials, for which the potlatch is only the ritual preparation, and to form raiding parties, the function of which is to restore the equilibrium of the system of soul exchange when it begins to break down.

The second way in which the covenants of human and animal are reinforced is through the presence of tangible objects representing that covenant. The most famous of these objects are totem poles and house posts, but three other objects have great importance also: boxes, feast dishes, and masks. It is important to remember that all these objects, and indeed even the right to make them, exist only where the spirits have given to humans the magical power that invests these objects with their own power. All these objects have names, which are considered to exist eternally. These names represent the souls of the objects, so that even when there is no visible manifestation of the object, the object still exists in an anticipatory form, waiting to inhabit its next body. House posts especially are reinforcers of the ancestral identity. Not only are they visibly present, and not only do they dominate the atmosphere of the house, but they are in actuality, as in metaphor, the foundation upon which the house itself, and thus the numaym inhabiting that house, stands. Indeed, during the winter it is believed that the spirits with whom man is allied come to live in the villages of humans. No scholar has yet asked where these spirits reside. Do they just hover in the air, or do they take possession of peoples' or animals' bodies? The only obvious answer is that they come to reside in the house posts themselves, which become their gateway to the world of humans in the same way that the posts are the gateway for humans to the world of the spirits. And during the winter ceremonials, the spirits leave the posts and inhabit the wearers of the costumes who impersonate, embody, and thus become them.

The three primary characteristics of Kwakiutl totemic animals are those that make them peculiarly human in their behavior: first, they are carnivorous (they live off the flesh of other animals, surviving only on the dead flesh of the beings they kill, and are motivated by the same hunger as humans); second, they make a large number of vocalizations (they speak, as humans speak, and in the act of speaking, set up automatically a formal relationship among themselves and with humans in the same way that prayers by humans set up formal relationships among themselves and with the animals); and third, they are all social (they live in a society that demands the temperance of carnal desires for the mutual benefit of all members of the group).

One other characteristic common to all totemic animals, though not exclusive to them, is that they all produce multiple offspring. Therefore, the birth of human twins is considered to be an especially powerful gift from the salmon because twins are considered to be direct emissaries of the salmon who come to live with humans as liaisons with the spirit world (Boas, 1966:365-68). Special rites surround the lives and deaths of twins, and twins play a critical role in many types of ritual. The birth of multiple offspring among animals represents to the Kwakiutl a highly cogent statement of the strength of the animals' relationship with the spirit world. Since the animals are often given the gift of twins, indeed, since multiple births are the rule, the belief is that they must be discharging their responsibilities towards those offspring so well that the spirit world is willing to keep providing twins with great frequency.[2]

For two reasons, the animals' ability to produce twins is another facet of their orality. First, since the Kwakiutl believe that pregnancy is created through ritual oral acts, the ability to produce multiple offspring is indicative of the animals' care in performing the proper oral impregnating acts. Second, since twins are direct links to the salmon-people, they provide direct access to food and represent the animals' ability to control food. Indeed, the animals' ability to find food easily is often a part of a Kwakiutl's metaphorization of their characteristics in prayers (e.g., Boas, 1930:193).

The relationship between humans and their totemic animals is manifested through the medium of totem poles. These poles relate in graphic form the events of a particular myth specific to the history of the numaym and thus they encapsulate the collective identity of the numaym. Poles are often raised to commemorate important events, but this commemoration is reflexive—the event validates the continuing relevance and power of the numaym's myths, which in turn give meaning and power to historic events.

Indeed, the erection of totem poles is required at certain key events in ritual transactions involving the spirits: the selling of coppers, marriages between two chiefly lines, or the building of a house, for example. Here the poles are erected because each of these events is intimately connected with the eternal relationship of humans and animals, a relationship that exists for their mutual benefit in fostering reincarnation, and each event can occur only with the blessings of the spirits. The erection of a pole at these events thus commemorates not the event, but the eternal relationship

---

[2] In a sense, then, all animals are in one way superior to humans. They have the ability to produce twins and to take care of them far more readily than do humans, for whom the birth of twins is a relatively rare event.

itself. It is a statement that the relationship still holds firm even though an important social change has occurred, such as a new person becoming chief, or the numaym living in a different place.

At the end of the nineteenth century, a time when many Kwakiutl had abandoned their ancestral villages and relocated at settlements such as Alert Bay and Fort Rupert, there was a great increase in the number of poles being erected. While this increase was made possible by Kwakiutl prosperity, it was made necessary by the dictates of Kwakiutl religion. Although the spirits would have had identification with the local geographical features of the ancestral villages, they would have had little identification with those of the new settlements. The construction and decoration of houses and poles created a local environment that recapitulated the ancestral village, thereby permitting continued contact between humans and spirits.[3]

Let us examine more closely the characteristics and behavior of some specific totemic animals, which constitute the fundamental material through which the Kwakiutl comprehend their world.

The most structurally direct relationship between humans and animals is that between man and the salmon. Salmon are considered to be people who live in houses like humans do, in villages at the bottom of the sea in the west. They are organized into numayms, and have chiefs, commoners, and slaves, winter ceremonials, initiations, marriages, and engage in all other human activities. Most importantly, salmon own masks and ceremonial blankets, which they don, transforming their outward form from human to piscine. In this guise, they gather at the river mouths each spring and swim upriver.

A number of the characteristics of salmon reinforce the Kwakiutl metaphorization of their behavior. First, the skin of a salmon is easily removed from the flesh, as is a blanket from a person. The head and cheeks are of hard, chitinous material that is easily thought of as masklike, especially as it can be removed in its entirety from the body of the salmon with little difficulty. The striking changes of form that salmon undergo in their upriver swim to the spawning grounds are also visually and symbolically important: as the fish progress upriver, they become thinner; their skin color changes from greenish gray to red, with green on the head, a color combination that looks artificial, almost painted on; their jaws enlarge greatly and a rather fearsome row of teeth grows up along the

[3] In much the same way, the ancient Egyptians provided statues that were accurate images of dead Pharaohs so that if the Pharaoh's body, the true resting place of his soul, were destroyed, the soul would be able to find another site where it could rest (McQuitty, 1976:72)

jaw; though the salmon cease to feed, their jaws move actively and powerfully.[4]

The salmon life cycle is the structural equivalent of the human life cycle. Salmon are considered to live in villages at the bottom of the sea for the sacred winter season, during which time they perform winter ceremonial dances. They leave these villages in the summer to return to those rivers where they will be caught by men. Those who escape swim upriver, getting less fatty and more fearsomely toothy as they progress farther. Finally, just as men's lives come to an end as they reproduce and pass on their names, privileges, powers, and eventually even their souls to their children, so do the salmon die, exhausted and emaciated after they have spawned and have passed on their power to their progeny. The salmons' souls are then transformed and released through magical rites carried out by humans and other animals, and they return to their homes in the sea. In a sense, both man's and the salmon's entire life is devoted to the continuance of the species, and man is reminded of this every year as the bodies of the salmon, their spawning completed, wash downstream.

Part of the salmon life cycle, the replenishing of the species through the growth of eggs into fry, is invisible to the Kwakiutl. No mention is made in the texts of this critical stage, and indeed, it seems in keeping with Kwakiutl ideas of rebirth for them to imagine that the salmon spawn is merely an excrescence of old salmon rather than the seeds of the new generation. The Kwakiutl, presented with an important gap in their knowledge of the spawning process, that is, how the full grown salmon reappear year after year when they never seem to travel downriver, create an idea of soul migration. Salmon must reproduce magically since they do not reproduce by visible means.

Eagles, too, have an important place in the Kwakiutl metaphorization of their world, and the characteristics of eagle behavior provide a direct analogy to the behavioral and motivational principles of human action.

The eagle that dominates the Northwest Coast biome is the Bald Eagle (*Haliaeetus leucocephalus*). Though Golden Eagles do sometimes appear, the Kwakiutl do not seem to distinguish between them and immature Bald Eagles. Thus, though the behavior of Bald and Golden Eagles is quite different, it is that of the Bald Eagle that provides the empirical basis of Kwakiutl metaphorizations, and some of this behavior relates directly to that of humans. Eagles and humans frequent the same types of beaches, those with a rocky shore facing onto a cove or a narrow strait between two islands. These are the areas where fish congregate and where their bodies are washed up on shore. Also, eagles, like humans, build perma-

---

[4] The striking physical changes that salmon undergo between the early stages of their migration and the later stages can be observed by comparing pictures of salmon found in Hewlett and Hewlett (1976:139) with those in Sutton and Sutton (1973) and Chasan (1975).

nent wooden dwellings, nests, which they inhabit year after year, except for brief periods during the summer months, for their entire lives (Platt, 1976:783-88).

Bald Eagles are actually sea eagles. Their primary food is salmon, which they catch live by swooping down upon them from great heights and plucking them from the water with their talons, or whose dead bodies they eat when they are cast up onto the beach. Eagles are also notorious for stealing the food of other animals—ospreys, hawks, ravens, crows, and even smaller Bald Eagles—and for aggressively chasing other animals away from scavenging sites.

For the Kwakiutl the aggressiveness of eagles is their most important characteristic. Among the animals, eagles are considered to be the most energetic pursuers of their goals, and the term "Eagle" is applied to the group of twelve people who, near the end of the nineteenth century, took over the position of being the first people to be given their gifts at potlatches. These people were all nouveaux riches, and none of them were rightful owners of the hereditary privilege of being served first. Indeed, since the prerogative of receiving the first gift (an equivalent of food) was being taken from its rightful owners (the hereditary chiefs) and given to these men who had stolen that prerogative from them by amassing wealth at the expense of others, the term "Eagle" is a double-edged metaphor for one who comes first, but not by his own rights. The Eagles stole their position just as real eagles sometimes steal their food from other birds. Furthermore, since the position of Eagle became established only when the Kwakiutl death rate created a situation in which hereditary prerogatives fell into disuse, the Eagles gained their position by scavenging among the no-longer-held privileges, just as eagles scavenge among the remains of the corpses of dead fish on the beach. The Eagles took their position by commandeering the positions of those people who had no rightful heirs and no relatives to bury them. It is a terrible fate for the dead to have no children who will provide them with grandchildren into whose bodies they can be reborn. They die then without hope of reincarnation. Similarly, those salmon that are killed and eaten by humans are reborn through the ritual process, but those who die and lie unburied on the beach like their human counterparts have no hope of reincarnation. Their eternal existence continues only because the eagles have ingested, and thus incorporated into themselves, part of the fish's characteristic essence. Similarly, the Eagles provide a mechanism for the eternal continuation of the life of the hereditary chiefs they replace by incorporating as a part of themselves those ritual privileges and responsibilities that lay at the foundation of the chief's self.

The eagle's habit of sitting at the top of a tree may explain its frequent positioning, facing forward over the beach and out across the water, at the top of Kwakiutl totem poles. (Illustrations of this can be found in Keithahn, 1963.) Here it is supposed to be watching for prey. The carved eagle represents not the bird, but the eagle-spirit, and its prey is human, not fish. However, since humans and salmon are thought to be analogous to each other, real eagles are consequently considered the destroyers of humans in salmon form.

In fact, it is the eagle's catching of salmon by swooping through the air that is the most metaphorically powerful conception of the Kwakiutl, for they extend the power of the individual eagle to bring swift, sudden death from the sky to an unsuspecting salmon to the awesome power of the Thunderbird (graphically represented in carving in the same form as an eagle except for the two "horns" of its supernatural power, which come from the top of its head) to drop from the sky bringing instantaneous death to unsuspecting whales and men who lie at the surface of the water, whales in the water and men in their canoes.

The final metaphorically important behavior of eagles is their vociferousness when feeding at a beachside scavenging site. This vociferousness can be seen as indicative of the lack of control that the desire to eat dead flesh exerts on animals, for the speech of the eagle is normally quiet and well spaced, but the power of hunger makes it loud and raucous and screaming—dissocialized. So was the pushiness of the Eagles, who constantly asserted their right to be served first at the potlatch, indicative of their dissocialization, their bestiality.

Grizzly bears (*Ursus horribilis*) are the only other animals besides eagles and humans that habitually feed on live salmon, and they are thus inextricably linked to the cycle of resurrection directly affecting humans and their salmon analogues. This linking makes bears, like eagles and their mythical relatives, an essential part of the winter ceremonials. Eagles, bears, and humans are all dependent on the salmon for their survival, and thus the rites affecting the fecundity of the salmon must, of necessity, involve all these species acting cooperatively.

The actual behavior of bears reinforces their structural similarity with humans in several ways. First, they are omnivorous—the only other animal on the Northwest Coast besides man that is—and thus, they become competitors with humans and analogous to humans because they stand in the same structural relation to all foodstuffs. Second, like human hunters, bears hunt alone, except in the summer when they congregate at salmon streams to fish (Bledsoe, 1975). Third, bears spend the winters in their underground dens as humans spend the winters in their homes. Fourth, bears stand on their hind legs and may even walk on two feet for brief periods. (This similarity to humans is intensified by the fact that the prints of the hind feet of bears look like human footprints (Murie, 1954:25-36). Indeed, though Bear Dancers in costume at the winter ceremonials wear claws on their hands, they go barefoot.) Finally, bears' restlessness, their ferocity, and their untempered voraciousness makes them a cogent metaphor for the terrible ferocity that man can be driven to if he does not control his hunger. This connection between a human's hunger and a bear's accounts for the close association of *hamatsa* dancers with Bear Dancers in the winter ceremonials.

The carefully balanced mutual dependence of humans, eagles, and bears is an essential aspect of the cycle of food-getting and resurrection. It can succeed only when all three spirits cooperate, and must fail when they compete. But even when they do cooperate, one species of animal more feared than any other, the wolf (*Canis lupus*), is at work trying to bring destruction to them and their carefully planned rituals. Kwakiutl myths (see Boas, 1935:154-57) portray wolves as the enemies of all other animals (their very smell and the smell of their dung frightens the other animals). They wage war against the other animals, steal their salmon, and even destroy them by stealing their corpses for winter food. In fact, it is believed that they climb upon one another's backs to reach the corpses of humans placed high in tree burials (Boas, 1935:155). It is thought that any initiate who travels to the spirit country and enters the house of the wolves is first bitten and then greedily devoured by the hungry wolves, who then feel guilt for what they have done and revive him (Boas, 1935:156). Wolves are considered to be a primary source for humans of spirit-power, both beneficent quartz crystal power (which they vomit up) and death-bringing power.

The behavior of real wolves reinforces these mythic traits. Social animals, living and hunting in packs of up to two dozen members with an obvious status hierarchy, wolves are skilled and relentless hunters of a variety of animals, as well as efficient scavengers. Wolves often live in clusters of underground dens. At kill sites they feed in an orderly fashion determined by each animal's position in the status hierarchy. They have very noticeable teeth and tongues and are vociferous. Though intraspecific fights do break out, normally wolves are gentle, friendly animals when they are not hunting. Wolves share food in that pack members returning from a hunt frequently vomit up partially digested food for those members that stayed behind. But even more important, wolves are related to dogs, and dogs are the companions of men, both species thus forming a dialectic contrast. As dogs are the helpers and companions of men, wolves are the destroyers and enemies of men; as domesticated dogs represent the force of hunger repressed and socialized, wild wolves represent the primal destructive force of hunger; as dogs represent the ability to live together peacefully when hunger is repressed for the social good, wolves represent the true, awesome power of hunger to destroy the fragile bonds of sociality. Wolves, then, are so fearsome partly because they represent what can happen to perfectly socialized beings when hunger overcomes their self-control. They are the living image of voraciousness out of control, and the fact that they are social only reinforces the terribleness of this destructiveness.

Thus, wolves are the enemies of mankind because man, to survive, must repress his desire to feed, and wolves display not a trace of that repression. Wolves, then, are the animal representation of man's unconscious bestial desires, and as those desires threaten to destroy the psychic harmony, the integrity, of the self, so then wolves threaten to destroy the harmony, the integrity, of the ritual of interspecies salmon sharing.

The importance of ravens (*Corvus corax*) in Kwakiutl thought and ceremony stems from the fact that they are the only birds on the Northwest Coast who eat human carrion. (None of the other raptorial birds of the Northwest Coast feed on human corpses: eagles eat fish, hawks specialize in small prey, and turkey vultures only rarely approach human living areas.) By consuming corpses, ravens perform two tasks: first, they dismember the corpse, thus causing its true death and releasing its soul; and second, by digesting the flesh, they transform it from matter in this world into matter in the spirit world. Thus, ravens are the animals who ensure the transfiguration of human flesh, and without them no human could truly die.[5] As the eaters of human flesh from tree-burial and platform-burial sites, and of the offal and carrion that is the ubiquitous symbol of death, ravens are ultimately the animals most associated with death.

The ravens' involvement with death, their critical role in the transformation of life into death, is considered to give them an intimate knowledge of death, and thus they act as harbingers and prophets of death. Their cries are thought to herald impending disaster, and the ability to understand the cries of the ravens is an exceptionally rare gift, imparted to one only if the ravens are allowed to eat the afterbirth of that individual soon after he is born.

Normally the afterbirth of a child, which is considered a part of its living flesh, is ritually treated to prevent sorcerers from using it to bewitch the child. It is then buried at the foot of a live cedar tree, where its substance is absorbed into the tree. This ritual is believed to ensure the longevity of the child in three ways: first, the tree becomes the guardian of the child; second, just as the tree lives a long time, so too will the child; and third, since children are considered to have a very tenuous link to this world until they have been given their first name (at ten months), the absorption of their living substance into that of the tree helps establish a firmer link to life. However, a very few parents take the risk of fore-

---

[5] This belief is represented on raven rattles, which depict a human corpse on the back of a raven.

going this ritual protection and place the afterbirth of their newborn child on the beach, where the ravens eat it. This is a difficult decision for a parent to make, for he endangers his child's life by so doing. Not only does he forego the guardianship of the tree for his child, and not only does he fail to establish that link with life that will keep his child from dying, but he actually increases the risk of that child's immediate death. Since ravens transform living matter into dead, and since they will eventually eat the entire corpse of the child whenever he dies, their eating of his afterbirth is, in effect, an act of bringing a partial death to the child, of starting the process of his death. In addition, the eating of his afterbirth links the child with death, decreasing his interest in life, and makes it more likely that, perhaps because his raven mentors give him glimpses of the world of the dead, he will want to return to the spirit world from which he has just come. Thus, it is because the child is in part dead that he gains the special ability to know death as the ravens do. It takes an exceptionally brave parent to risk the death of his child by feeding its afterbirth to the ravens. Not only might the child die, but if it does, the father's hope for immortality is also threatened, or even completely destroyed, since he can be reborn only if his children survive to have children of their own.

The Kwakiutl believe the cries of the raven foretell death, yet in the list of these cries Boas provides (1921:606-7) few of them seem to indicate death. Several of them foretell good fortune in catching food, propitious weather, or even the visit of a stranger. Yet, although at first it might seem that only a few of these cries relate directly to death, if we remember that the Kwakiutl consider the eating of food as structurally equivalent to some kind of death because it involves the dismemberment and material transformation of animal bodies, we can see that all cries forebode death. The ravens' prediction of a good food catch are predictions of death not for humans, but for animals. Similarly, food-gathering success is dependent on the state of the weather, and propitious weather implies good hunting and death for those animals caught. The one cry (*wax wax wax*) that seems least concerned with the prophecy of death means a stranger will arrive on a visit, and is actually fatal in import, for during the last half of the nineteenth century, strangers often brought with them disease, conflict, and trouble, especially as the Kwakiutl were among the last tribes of the area to be acculturated. Strangers also brought with them white ideas and Christian beliefs—sure signs of moral decay.

The ravens' cries are important not only because these animals are symbolically and behaviorally eaters-of-life, but also because the belief that their cries foretell the future is an example of one of the Kwakiutl's most important and pervasive ideas—that the future is determined, and that the spirits will give hints to humans about its direction if the proper rites are performed. The magic link to the world of spirit-power is established through the messages of the spirits, spoken in visions, myths, dreams, and the vocalizations of living animals. The entire world speaks to the Kwakiutl, especially of the all-important knowledge of how to kill and how to survive—the basic forces of the cosmos. Ravens, vocal and intelligent, have the characteristics that make them the rightful repositories and distributors of this knowledge.

For the Kwakiutl, owls have a peculiar symbolic relationship to humans: in some local areas they are considered to be the spirit-doubles of humans (Boas, 1930:257). The Saw-whet Owl (*Aegolius acadicus*, formerly *Nyctala acadica*) is of special importance (Boas, 1930:208) because it is very tame and occasionally frequents human habitations.[6] It still-

---

[6] Identifying from the Boas texts the particular species of owl the Kwakiutl consider to be their spirit-double is a very difficult task. In the Kwakiutl text (1930b:202), Boas records the word *bEkwà*, which he translates elsewhere both as "small owl" (1921:1454) and also as "*Nyctala acadica* (soul, ghost)" (1892:40). Thus, the Saw-whet Owl is apparently the spirit-double species, and its behavior and characteristics (cf., Karalus and Eckert, 1974:56-64) fit with those described in Boas, 1930:208, in which the spirit-double owl is noted as being very tame and is called "the smallest owl which is hardly larger than a sparrow," which flies about "as soon as it gets toward evening." However, the Saw-whet Owl is neither the smallest owl in the area, nor, though it is very tame, is it often seen (Harrison, 1975:102), for it is a shy, secretive crepuscular and nocturnal hunter of the deep woods (Burton, 1973:173-74). Instead, the smallest owl in the Kwakiutl area, also a species that is renowned for its sedentary habits, its frequenting of human habitations, and its tameness, is the Vancouver Pygmy Owl (*Glaucidium gnoma swarthi* Grinnell), which is slightly more diurnal and less secretive in its behavior than the Saw-whet Owl (Karalus and Eckert, 1974:214). Since most of the behavior of these two species is similar (Karalus and Eckert, 1974), it is impossible to tell which one of them could be correctly identified as the spirit-double species; yet, since in coloring and postural attitudes the two species differ greatly, it is impossible to draw more detailed and specific conclusions than I have here about Kwakiutl metaphorization of the soul in its owl form.

The situation is further complicated by the fact that elsewhere (1932:221) Boas identifies the spirit-double species as the Screech Owl (cf., Goldman, 1975:241). However, neither the physical traits nor the behavior of Screech Owls coincide in the least with the description given in 1930 (p. 208). Nor does the vocabulary of Kwakiutl owl terminology clarify matters. The word *bEkwä*, translated as Saw-whet Owl in 1892 (p. 40), is translated as "small owl" in 1921 (p. 1454). There is no way of determining whether, in the later work: Boas rescinded his earlier positive association of Saw-whet Owls with spirit-doubles and is stating that some undiscerned species of small owl (Pygmy, Screech, Saw-whet, or Boreal) is the spirit-double; that, as small owls, Saw-whet Owls are the correct "small" owls; or that all small owls are called by a single generic term. The term *HôpHôp*, which Boas translates as "screech owl" in 1892, is translated only as "owl" in 1921, a gloss far too vague to indicate whether the word is generic or specific. In any case, if we take the word *HôpHôp* to mean Screech Owl, then does the word *bEkwä* also indicate Screech Owl, but in a spirit-form, and contrary to its first definition in 1892? The confusion over vocabulary is intensified by the fact that the long textual passage about owls and spirit-doubles (Boas, 1930:257-60), which is the basic material on spirit-doubles and owls, uses the term *DE'xdExELil*, a term for which Boas gives no translation in the 1921 English-Kwakiutl vocabulary (p. 1454),

hunts from a low perch from which it surveys the surrounding area, a behavior we have already seen forming an important facet of the Kwakiutl metaphorization of eagles. The Indians envision this searching to be the quest of the owl not for food, but for something more particular—the individual who is the owl's spirit-double. They maintain that when the owl spots the correct individual, it will drop from its perch onto the head of that person, who then captures the owl, paints it with red ochre, and says a prayer to it before releasing it again. The only living creatures that are painted with red ochre are owls and people. Since people are painted red only twice in their lives, when they are ten months old and receive their first name (their first self) and when they die, the painting of the owl reinforces the metaphorical equivalence of its existence and that of its human double. As with other animals whose existence directly affects human life and reincarnation, these owls are called Long-Life-Makers, for only through them can man hope to be reborn.

Of the many species of owls found in Kwakiutl territory, the most ferocious and voracious is unquestionably the Great Horned Owl, represented by the subspecies Dusky Horned Owl (*Bubo virginianus saturatus* Ridgway), the largest of the subspecies of Horned Owls. Horned Owls eat a large number of a wide variety of small birds and mammals, reptiles, other owls, and even fish. Their normal method of hunting is to still-hunt, dropping upon unsuspecting prey from above, but they also hunt by cruising and by walking about on the ground, trying to flush prey from hiding (Karalus and Eckert, 1974:234), a habit linking them to men, who also hunt by walking about. The still-hunting habit links owls to eagles, hawks, and Thunderbirds, all of whom still-hunt as well. Indeed, because of the similarities between their hunting methods, and the fact that both Horned Owls[7] and Thunderbirds have horns, we might consider the Horned Owl to be the Thunderbird vis-à-vis the world of small animals, for it stands in relationship to them as the Thunderbird does to man and his world—an agent of silent, sudden, and terrible destruction.[8]

---

and translates simply as "owl" in the Kwakiutl-English vocabulary (1921:1406). Since terms for Great Horned, Snowy, Screech, and Saw-whet Owls listed in 1892 (p. 40) bear no apparent lexical relationship to this word, it is impossible to tell even whether *DE'xdExELil* is a generic or a specific term.

[7] While there is no direct textual evidence to support the idea, we might envision the Kwakiutls' idea of the relationship between Horned and Screech Owls to be the same as the relationship of Thunderbirds to eagles, that is, chief: commoner It does not stretch credibility very far to imagine Screech Owls as miniature Horned Owls The association of Horned Owls with chiefs is further reinforced by the variety of foods they eat, since chiefs have sumptuary rights over varieties of food forbidden to commoners.

[8] Of course, as men are the prey of Thunderbirds, and owls are Thunderbirds vis-à-vis small animals, their prey become equivalent to men. This may help to explain the importance of Mouse as a figure in Kwakiutl myth (Boas, 1935.162), where she frequently helps humans

Interestingly, the owls of Vancouver Island differ in their vocal habits from those of the subspecies of other areas. For example, both the Vancouver Pygmy Owl and the Dusky Horned Owl are more vocal in the autumn than in the spring or summer (Karalus and Eckert, 1974:215), so that they become associated more with the oncoming sacred winter season than with the secular summer season.

Though George Hunt states that all the Kwakiutl tribes believe that men have owl masks and are incarnated as owls after their deaths (Boas, 1930:260), he appends this statement to an account of getting himself into trouble by shooting an owl on the instructions of a man who did not believe that men and owls were related, and who died very soon after (Boas, 1930:257-60). The other Indians involved took this as proof that all humans indeed had owl masks, and that George Hunt had killed the owl that was the spirit-double of the man who instructed him to shoot it.

Owls, like all other birds of prey, have one other behavioral trait that gives them a special metaphorical essence for the Kwakiutl: they regurgitate in the form of dried pellets the indigestible portions of the animals they eat. Since these pellets consist of the skins, hair, and bones of the mammals, and the feathers and bones of the birds the owls eat, and since the pellets are dry, they are structurally equivalent to the mummified corpses of humans left behind after they have been scavenged by ravens and eagles. Furthermore, since skin and bones are the parts of animal anatomy associated with their masks and dance costumes, the owls' regurgitation of these body parts indicates that they have eaten the human aspect of the animals they kill and have recycled the animal aspects that reside in the skin and bones. Owls, then, like eagles, are cannibals, for they eat humans.

There is one other piece of evidence linking owls with cannibalism. The cry of the *hohok*, or Cannibal Bird ("hoho hohok," in the rhythm ♩ ♫ ♩, or "ho hohok," in the rhythm ♫ ♩), is a rendition of the booming calls of the Barred Owl (*Strix varia*). The Barred Owl occurs only very rarely on Vancouver Island, and then only in the winter season. Perhaps its rarity and its association solely with winter give it a mystical quality in Kwakiutl thought that makes its calls appropriate for adoption as those of the *hohok*.

Other calls and noises made by owls and other raptors find their way into Kwakiutl rituals. The shrill pipings of sacred whistles sound similar to the calls of eagles and of the Short-eared, Snowy, Hawk, Boreal, and

In addition, animals that are the prey of owls have a special relationship to men, who are both the prey of Thunderbirds as well as owls themselves. Mice, which tunnel downward, act as the messengers from the spirits to men (Boas, 1935:162). Two songbirds that fly upwards, wrens and sparrows, both also common prey of owls, carry messages (songs) from humans to the spirits.

Saw-whet Owls, while various bird dancers make explosive sounds that are close to the calls of the Great Grey, Barred, Spotted, and Pygmy Owls. Even more noticeable, however, are the beak clicking and snapping, which are essential parts of Kwakiutl bird masks and dances. Beak clicking is found as an aggressive act among all the raptors, and is accompanied by a fluffing of the feathers, notably the feathers on the head; if the intruder does not back away immediately, the bird will attack. The presence of beak clicking in Kwakiutl dances, then, symbolically expresses the imminent destruction that the bird-spirit is about to wreak. Furthermore, representations of birds in Kwakiutl art often show the head and wing feathers raised and separated in a way that captures the fluffing behavior preceding an attack, a behavior that can also be observed in dances (e.g., the Eagle Dance in Curtis's film, *In the Land of the War Canoes* [1914]). The aggressiveness of the raptors is also an essential part of the songs accompanying their dances (Boas, 1897:476).

Finally, we should note that the nests of all the large raptors—eagles, ravens, hawks, and owls—are basically similar in form, so much so that birds of one species often use nests made by birds of another. All these nests are platform nests made of sticks and twigs piled together high in a sturdy tree or on a cliff face. Thus, they possess the same form and placement as the tree and cave burial sites of humans, which are either platforms made of sticks placed high in sturdy trees or cave burials in the sides of cliffs. (It is conceivable that these birds might even use the remains of human burial platforms once the corpse's flesh had rotted away.) The association of the death of humans and the subsequent birth of raptorial birds from the eating of that dead human flesh is thus strengthened by the close similarity between nest and burial sites.

The Kwakiutl differ from most of the other Northwest Coast tribes in identifying their mythic culture hero / Trickster figure not as Raven, but Mink.[9] Minks (*Mustela vison*) have a number of characteristics that might account for the Kwakiutls' interest in them and for their use as a Trickster figure. First, they are very aggressive animals, far more ferocious than one would expect an animal of their small size would be. Second, they are noisy, active animals, full of energy and often playful. Third, they are amazingly voracious animals, attacking and killing a wide variety of prey (Burris and Burris, 1974:36-37), sometimes killing far more than they can eat and leaving the rest of the food scattered about. (Sometimes mink eat so much that their bellies hang to the ground and they can no longer move.) Fourth, minks represent the independent spirit of men, for

---

[9] There is a culture hero/creator figure, but not a Trickster, *Oemal*, whose inchoate identity is associated with Raven by some scholars but is never specified in the myths.

though they are family animals, the males range freely away from the family for much of the time.

It is for another reason, however, that the Kwakiutl choose mink. As has been long recognized in anthropology, Trickster figures perform an important role as mediators between the human and the spirit world, and between acceptable and unacceptable behaviors. They can perform acts that everyone else would like to perform but, because of social custom, cannot. They are simultaneously semihuman and semidivine. No animal on the Northwest Coast embodies this dual nature better than the mink: it is one of the few creatures whose life transcends the normal boundaries of existence; it is nocturnal, free, and active when other species are forced to curtail their activities because of the dangers of the night, yet it is also able to move and hunt during the day; it is a family animal, yet it is also an individual; it is a playful, fun-loving creature, yet it can quickly turn into a ferocious and deadly killer; it is a small animal, yet it can eat more than its weight in food; and most importantly, it is the only creature on the Northwest Coast at home equally on the land or in the water. Thus, mink as the mediator of night and day, of land and water, of sociality and individuality, represents more than any other creature the duality of human nature, and especially of the ideal person—the individual who is both socially well adapted and yet has the power to transcend the boundaries placed upon the average person. Finally, minks are considered to mediate between the most disparate categories of all, those of life and death. Because their skins are so loosely attached to their bodies that they are very easy to remove, minks are closely associated with the process of taking off and putting on skins, the process whereby humans, spirits, and animals interchange identities.

The life cycle and behavior of the beaver (*Castor canadensis*) is considered to be closely analogous to that of humans. Beavers live in lodges along the water's edge. They are industrious, obviously familial in their social organization, and permanent in their residency. They build dams as men build weirs, and they spend the winter in their lodges, from which the vapor of their breaths emerges looking like smoke (von Frisch, 1974:273) and from which a steady and varied chatter arises. In addition, beavers leave tracks very similar to miniature human footprints and often sit up on their hind legs, holding their front paws like human hands in a shamanic gesture.

The most critical similarity is that both beavers and humans—and only those two species—cut down trees. The Kwakiutl see trees, especially cedars, as living beings with faces, arms, legs, and souls. Like all other living beings, trees are dependent on other beings to perform those rituals that will enable them to be reborn. This funerary responsibility is a prime aspect of the woodworker's art, for he must perform extensive rituals to ensure the proper release of the soul of the tree he cuts down and upon whose woody flesh he works. The beaver's habit of chewing a stick while sitting up is thus a visually powerful representation of the beaver's crucial role in tree resurrection, for the beaver's stripping of the bark releases the soul of the tree, his chewing transforms the tree into soul form through the eating of its flesh, and his display of the palms of his hands proves his magical-sacred intent in the acts involved, for it sets up the sacred state so essential to the transmigration of souls. Thus, beavers and men are one, not just because they both use wood to build their homes, but because they alone can ensure the survival of the forest.

One other point must be made about beavers here. They are, in the Kwakiutl metaphorization, carnivorous. Since beavers kill and eat trees, which are living beings, they are by definition flesh-eaters. Thus, beavers, like other crest animals, are carnivorous.

Reptiles and amphibians play a very important role in Kwakiutl rituals, especially those directly affecting birth (including both love and pregnancy magic) and death. The oral characteristics of reptiles and amphibians account in great part for their magical potency, for although frogs, salamanders, and snakes are not dangerous to man, their vociferousness, the constant motions of their tongues, their ability to strike so rapidly that the human eye cannot follow the motion of the strike, their aggressiveness, their voraciousness, and their ability to eat large prey are easily transmuted into the idea of their life- and death-bringing powers.

The heads of reptiles and amphibians are essential to the action of Kwakiutl rituals meant to cause pregnancy: a woman must squat at a place where a frog had been sitting for a long time (Boas, 1966:358) or must eat a potion made from the heads of lizards (Boas, 1921:644-48). Frogs play a particularly large part in impregnation rituals perhaps because, with their large mouths and long tongues with bulbous tips, they reproduce both phallic and vaginal images.

Since the wet piles of rotting wood in Kwakiutl villages sustaining abundant insect life form a perfect habitat for toads, salamanders, and snakes, these animals are also specially related to humans by virtue of the fact that they live in direct contact with them. Thus, unlike other animals, which do not reside in the village but obviously come to visit, such as birds that fly away, fish that migrate, or deer and bear that live in the distant forest, toads, snakes, and salamanders are an integral part of the life of a Kwakiutl village. Although these animals may not always be visible, because they hide beneath logs, in clumps of vetch, or even in humans' houses, the Kwakiutl are certainly aware that they are always nearby, killing and eating.

Insects that prey on man, especially mosquitos, lice, and wasps, each of which draws blood, and is therefore a man-eater, also have symbolic importance to the Kwakiutl. Wasps are the insect man-eaters of the air, lice of the body, and mosquitos of the woods.[10] While lice are the predators of humans, other animals may be considered to be the lice of supernatural beings. (For example, eagles are considered the lice of the Thunderbird.) Small and insignificant in themselves, these bloodsuckers gain their power through the direct incorporation of the life force, the blood, of other animals.

The equivalence between humans and wasps (called wasps in the texts, but probably hornets) is drawn on several levels. First, wasps are social beings who live in houses (nests). Second, they disappear in the winter, a fact linking them to other animals who are considered to put on their own winter ceremonials. Third, they travel in groups, both in search of food and in attack. Fourth, they are heavily armored warriors with fearsome weapons, attacking both small and large prey fearlessly. Fifth, wasps are the hunters of the insect world, as men are the hunters of the human world. And sixth, they are brightly colored, which mimics men's wearing of clothing and body paint. The black masks on hornets' faces are mimicked in some of the facial paintings on human warriors (Boas, 1966:335; 1898b).

Flies, however, seem to have little significance in Kwakiutl myth, either as beings or as images of corruption. We might attribute this to the fact that flies are in no way active agents of bodily dissolution, for this task is attributed to ravens, eagles, and wolves. Flies, therefore, feast only on dead, soulless matter, and are not, in any way, the killers of the body or the sappers of its blood and power.

The ocean world of the fish and the air world of the birds and spirits are both organized along the same principles as the human world.[11] The denizens of these worlds are considered to be human in their own worlds, but when they appear in man's world, they put on masks, which alter their identity. In their own worlds, however, and without these masks, the inhabitants are human; they live in houses in villages, perform rituals

[10] The image of mosquitos as cannibals is clearly stated in the myth of their origin (Boas, 1887:425) in which they are the ashes of the incinerated body of Man Eater. The image of mosquitos as ashes is an interesting one, not only because both mosquitos and ashes are ubiquitous, but because as is always the case when food is cooked over a wood fire, ashes get into the food and are then eaten. Thus, at every meal humans eat part of the transformed inner substance (ash) of cedar as their food; mosquitos round out the cycle by being ashes that feed on man. As humans feast on the blood of cedars, mosquitos (symbolically equivalent to cedar ashes) feed on humans' blood.

[11] Presumably, the world of small animals is structured along lines similar to those of humans, birds, and fish. However, almost no information on the world of small animals was recorded by Boas, even though many rituals involving the bodies of small animals were recorded. I have had to exclude consideration of this particular world from my discussion simply because there is so little data about it in the texts.

and winter ceremonials, and have social organizations similar to those of humans (see Goldman, 1975:177-209).

The species that inhabit each of these two worlds must be divided into two subgroups: those who are true dwellers of that world and who visit man's world only under supernatural circumstances, and those who are actually of man's world and who visit the ocean or sky only when they put on masks.[12] In each case, the species primarily of man's world are those that inhabit the same area of the earth that man does. Ground-living or low-flying birds such as wrens, sparrows, owls, ravens, and sea gulls are considered part of man's world, while high-soaring birds such as hawks and eagles are part of the world of the sky; intertidal or surface-feeding species of fish (sculpins, rockfish, and trout, for example) belong to the human world, whereas pelagic species belong to the ocean world. Of course, those species that live near humans but are not land-locked are considered to travel frequently and easily across the borders between man's world and that of the sky and ocean; those species that are truly residents of the other worlds appear in man's world as sacred, magical beings whose presence is accompanied by the noumenon of supernatural power.

Both the sky world and the sea world are organized along the lines of man's, and both birds and fish perform important roles in Kwakiutl thought and ceremonial. The world of birds is more closely associated with the winter ceremonials, and much of the ritual involving birds takes place during that time. However, it is of the sea world, from which humans must wrest their food during the secular summer season, that they have more direct empirical knowledge. And as was the case in Kwakiutl interpretations of the land animals in their own world, the characteristics and behavior of fish reinforce both the supernatural awe that the Kwakiutl feel and the emphasis placed on the potency of hunger as the main motivating force of the universe against which the only defense is sociality.

Though the Kwakiutl take their livelihoods from the ocean, it remains to them a mysterious, unknown world of which man gets only occasional glimpses. Sea water on the Northwest Coast is murky, containing a high density of suspended particles that deflect light. Underwater visibility is limited, at best, to the top foot or two near the surface; below that there is no visibility at all, and the ocean realm is cut off from man's view.

Within that realm live a handful of familiar fish species that will become the food of men; but there are also hundreds of other species whose forms appear monstrous and terrible: ratfish, tubesnouts, sturgeon, prick-

---

[12] There is a myth that assigns each animal, bird, or fish to primarily one world or another. In addition, the social affiliation of each species is determined by where they go to celebrate the winter ceremonials. Like humans, animals form ritual communities (cf., Goldman, 1975: chaps. 2 and 3).

lebacks, poachers, warbonnets, big skates, giant sharks, and the hide-ously-toothed fish of the very deepest waters. These fish are the monsters of the ocean world, just as *tsonoqua* and *bukwis* are the monsters of man's world. Other marine species are symbolically equivalent to familiar terrestrial animals: eels are underwater serpents, dogfish are comparable to wolves, sea lions are like bears, and most importantly, herring are the salmon of the sea world.

Just as salmon is the staple food of the terrestrial world, where it is eaten steadily by men, bears, and eagles and occasionally by ravens, owls, wolves, weasels, otters, and gulls, so herring is the staple food of the sea. Herring is eaten by salmon, seals, sea lions, dogfish, lingcod, whales, and waterfowl.

The ocean world, like the human one, is united in its universal hunt for food. Man is reminded of this fact in many ways. Fish are generally lethargic animals until they sight prey. Then they put on sudden bursts of speed, opening huge mouths and swallowing large amounts of food. (The feeding frenzy we associate with sharks is actually an almost universal feature of the feeding behavior of carnivorous fish.) Some fish, such as the ten-ounce sculpin and the one-hundred-pound lingcod, seem to be all mouth. Many fish, such as salmon and sharks and the mesopelagic and bathypelagic fishes that occasionally appear dead at the surface (Robison, 1976), have rows of ferocious-looking teeth. Some fish, notably the sculpins and the plainfin midshipman, are vocal. Other species have particular features that emphasize their mouths: many species, for example, keep their mouths open constantly; other species open their mouths widely when they are attacking prey or defending themselves. The frequently seen rockfish, when removed from water, reacts by protruding its swim-bladder from its mouth and enlarging its eyes greatly. Octopi have sharp beaks, sometimes giving painful bites to people who try to catch them, as well as tentacles containing hundreds of sucking "mouths."

A number of fish exhibit strong metamorphic capabilities, both changes in coloration corollated with age or, as in the case of flounder, sole, halibut, squid, and octopus, the ability to transform themselves through color changes—an ability that figures importantly in Kwakiutl ideas and rituals concerning these species.

However, the fish other than salmon that seem to figure most importantly in Kwakiutl rituals and myths are those that are most noticeably voracious: sculpins, dogfish, lampreys, and hagfish.

The sculpin's inclusion in the pantheon of Kwakiutl totems is traceable to its oral characteristics alone rather than to its economic importance. It is difficult to tell which of the many species of sculpin is represented by the Kwakiutl in their myth and art, though the anatomical features and behavior of the Tidepool sculpin (*Oigocottus maculosus*) most resemble those of the animal depicted. Tidepool sculpins are small goby-shaped fish three-and-a-half inches long, which frequent the tidal pools of rocky shores. Normally slow-swimming, shy creatures, they bury themselves at low tide in the sand so that only their eyes show above the surface. When threatened, however, either by predators or by the sudden presence of a human foot in their pool, they become highly aggressive, opening a tooth-lined mouth that seems many times too large for such a small creature. Their defensive reactions escalate in their ferociousness: first they blow bubbles of air from their mouth; then they make grunts and whistling sounds; and finally, if neither of these methods has scared off the intruder, they attack, biting repeatedly and viciously. Thus, as in the case of other animals, the sculpin is important to the Kwakiutl because it is a graphic example of how the most meager of creatures conceals an overweaning destructive orality. In a sense, the sculpin has all the traits of a Kwakiutl monster: it appears from nowhere; it is ugly; it conceals its orality, but when revealed that orality is tremendous; it is aggressive; and it is hostile to humans. In a way, then, the character and behavior of sculpins is highly analogous to man's, thus justifying their inclusion among Kwakiutl totems.

The spiny dogfish has a peculiar place in the ocean world, being in some ways equivalent to and in other ways the enemies of salmon. Dogfish seem to be more common than the salmon. Since they eat the same food as salmon, they are often caught on trolling hooks that have been baited for salmon. Like all sharks, dogfish are voracious animals and feed frenziedly, normally attacking struggling fish. Frequently they attack salmon that have been hooked and are still struggling in the water. Their voraciousness is impressive, but it is also indicative of how uncontrolled hunger can bring about one's downfall, for in their frenzy to take bait they are caught and killed by the fishermen. Finally, dogfish, the only small species of shark on the Northwest Coast, are the individual "commoners" of a group of animals whose larger members are true monsters of the deep. Eight species of large shark have been sighted in British Columbia waters, though sightings are rare. What they lack in numbers, however, they make up in awesomeness: sharks such as the great white and the blue are large, aggressive, and dangerous to humans. (The great white shark will even attack small canoes.) Their hideously-toothed jaws can open wide enough to swallow a man whole. These large sharks are the chiefs of the shark-people, standing in relation to dogfish as human chiefs stand to commoners and Thunderbirds stand to eagles.

The hagfish and lamprey compose the third group of fish that figure importantly in Kwakiutl thought. Superficially finless and eellike (which makes them equivalent to snakes), these two animals have no jaws, but have instead a large, round, heavily-toothed sucking mouth at one end of their body. Both species are predators and parasites of other fish, but they have greatly different methods of feeding. The lamprey attacks its victim from the outside by attaching itself to its host's skin, boring a large hole in its host's body, and sucking body fluids and tissues through its mouth.[13] The hagfish, on the other hand:

> attacks its victim from the inside, having entered through the mouth or anus, and literally eats it from the inside out. It first digests the internal organs, then the muscle tissues of the living or dead host fish. Eventually all that remains is the victim's empty skin. Cod, lingcod, salmon and dogfish are commonly infested with this pest. One dogfish skin was found to contain four hagfish and, as the mature hagfish may be two feet in length, hosting four of these creatures is no small feat. Not surprisingly, the hagfish is a serious nuisance to fishing operations. (Hewlett and Hewlett, 1976:136-38)

The Kwakiutl fear that they themselves will be devoured from the inside by snakes, the terrestrial analogue of hagfish.

The four types of sea mammals found on the Northwest Coast (sea otters; harbor seals, sea lions, and elephant seals; killer whales, dolphins, and porpoises; and large whales) are also important in Kwakiutl thought, though they represent different aspects of orality than do the fish. All these sea mammals: are territorial; are voracious feeders; have noticeable teeth in their jaws; are solicitous of their young; and are noisy and vocal. Their most important shared characteristic, however, is that they live at the surface of the ocean and may even come onto land. Thus, they are free agents at breaching the boundary between worlds, a feat designating great power. This ability to transcend the boundary between the human and ocean worlds enables them to attend winter ceremonials in either world.

Sea mammals play an important role in Kwakiutl ritual for three reasons: first, as voracious animals they exemplify the eternal search for power; second, their voraciousness is tempered by sociality, as it must be in human society; and finally, two of the groups, the two most important ritually, have a superordinate/subordinate dyad inherent in them. Seals (which bark) are the dogs of sea lions, and are therefore subordinate to them, but sea lions are the commoners of a group whose chiefs are the sea elephants (equivalents to the slave, commoner, chief structure of human society); porpoises and dolphins are the common members of a tribe whose chiefs are the killer whales. The similarity between humans and these two groups of sea animals is enhanced by the fact that they feed on salmon and herring.

[13] This type of behavior forms the basis for some styles of Kwakiutl shamanic curing rituals (see Boas, 1930:1-56).

Another element of the sea, red tide, reinforces Kwakiutl ideas of birth and death through its connection with blood and vomit. Red tides, which appear and disappear with a numinous suddenness, are caused by the simultaneous deaths in massive numbers of specific microorganisms (in the Kwakiutl area, the phytoplankton *Gonyaulus catenella* is the agent) that create large patches and streaks of dark red or brown color in the waters just offshore. Red tides are highly toxic, and the toxins they produce are ingested by fish and shellfish, where they accumulate. When humans eat shellfish or fish taken from red-tide-infected waters, they suffer extreme pain, nausea and vomiting, the spitting of blood, and dizziness; if the amount of toxin eaten is great enough, the result is coma and eventually death.

In conclusion, though we have considered only a small number of the animals that inhabit the Kwakiutl world, and those only briefly, the identities and actions of other animals could be analyzed within the same *metaphorical system as that already presented.* Metaphors of orality underlie Kwakiutl conceptions of the organization of the natural world and the place of humans and nonhumans within it. Every living creature in the Kwakiutl universe, from the largest whale to the smallest phytoplankton, despite differences in size, shape, and habits, is linked in a great chain of being, links of which are formed by the universal need for food, by the power of hunger, and by the role each species plays as predator and prey. For the Kwakiutl, to be is to be hungry, and the characteristics of an animal's hunger metaphorize and summarize the characteristics of its being. And as we shall see in the next chapter, the choice of animals as actors in myth and ritual is never arbitrary or fortuitous; it is always determined by the qualities of that animal's hunger, by its role in the food cycle, and by the relationship between its hunger and man's.

As animals are metaphorized by hunger, so is hunger delineated by the animals it metaphorizes; every living being presents a small commentary on hunger, a small realization of the myriad forms hunger can take. Indeed, ultimately it is through nonhuman beings, and them alone, that man is able to describe and delineate his own hunger, his own being. Animals provide the reference point for human hunger, the visible manifestation of those profound desires found in the depths of every human's soul. As the Kwakiutl hide those desires from each other by a system of formal etiquette and by food-related rituals, so they hide, as well as express, the images of their own desires from themselves by putting the mask of animal identity upon them. Everything that is profound needs a mask, and for the Kwakiutl animals are the masks of human desires, and humans are the masks of animal desires. Animals and humans metaphorize each other, and thus they are ultimately as linked symbolically as they are ecologically, dependent on each other, reflecting each other's existence, mirror images of a single identity.

Myth, Metaphor, and the Ritual Process

Das Ziel alles Lebens ist der Tod.
—Freud, Jenseits des Lustprinzips

IN THE PAST THREE CHAPTERS we have seen how the Kwakiutl use oral/ assimilative metaphors to envision themselves and their identities, how these same metaphors provide the primary mode of sociality in Kwakiutl life, and how humans and animals are related in the natural world through their sharing of these metaphorical qualities. In this chapter I shall show that these metaphors also constitute the fundamental basis for Kwakiutl philosophy, religion, morality, and ceremonialism and that when the Kwakiutl envision the structure, nature, and operation of their world, they metaphorize it in oral terms. For the Kwakiutl the universe is founded on principles of omnipresent hunger, and man has the moral responsibility to be the master, not the slave, of that hunger.

We could limit our study of Kwakiutl worldview to their views of the spatial structure of the universe in which they live. But that is not in itself a sufficiently complete picture of the Kwakiutl universe, for since man is a moral being, the universe can be described correctly only in terms of its morality. For the Kwakiutl it is far less important to know how the universe was created, a topic about which they seem to have no myths and few hypotheses, than it is to know how the universe was made moral, a topic about which they have myriad myths and unlimited ideas. For the Kwakiutl the physical universe and the moral universe are a single unit of existence, coterminous and coextensive.

In such a universe, the Kwakiutl envision themselves as having a special, critical position. They are the fulcrum upon which the moral universe rests. They are the Archimedean level long enough and strong enough to move the world with their action. They are the people on whom the spirits have placed the burden of upholding the order of the universe. They are the chosen people, the people of the covenant.

Hunger is the energy, the force, that motivates the world, but ultimately it is morality that is the source of power. Hunger is powerful, but the knowledge of how to control hunger, to use it to move the world in the direction one wants, is a far greater power, and the man who masters hunger is the real master of power. Morality is the true property, the true wealth, of humankind. Morality is the gift the spirits have given to humans, the gift humans celebrate in their ceremonies, the gift they cherish above all others, the gift that manifests itself in myriad guises. One thanks the animals not only for giving their bodies for food but also for giving their bodies so that humans may have the chance to perform the proper rituals upon them. The spirits give not freedom from hunger but the knowledge needed to conquer and tame hunger. Knowledge, power, and moral choice are the same; to know is to control. The power of hunger is blind, but the power to conquer hunger is not; it is the result of consciousness, awareness, will, choice, action.

The fundamental moral basis of Kwakiutl myth may be observed in any of the many myths recorded by Boas. Kwakiutl myth and ceremonialism are pervaded by an emphasis on available moral choices, on their acceptance of that moral covenant. As an example I would like to discuss the first myth in *Kwakiutl Tales I* (Boas, 1935b:1-5), for in it is encapsulated the basic moral charter of Kwakiutl culture. Just as Freud postulated in *Totem and Taboo* that morality arose out of a single Oedipal instant in early human history, so the Kwakiutl believe that morality arose from the actions of *Q!aneqelaku*, the Transformer, the being who transforms the world from its past, amoral, hunger-dominated condition to its present, moral, hunger-controlling state.

The myth can be summarized as follows: Transformer, his younger brother (Only-One), his father, and his stepmother, living in the village *K!eyai'l*, are hungry. Transformer's father and mother go fishing and catch salmon. Not wanting to share food with their children, they falsely report that warriors are coming, and while the children are hiding, eat all the food they have obtained. Transformer discovers the deceit, says that his stepmother obviously hates the two children and that he is going to get revenge. He throws his father out of the house and transforms him into Heron, and throws his stepmother against the housepost, where she is changed into Woodpecker.

Transformer and his younger brother move to another place, *Ax^udE'm*. During the trip, Transformer sees and kills a *sisiutl*, which he keeps as a belt. He builds himself a house (Wind-Blowing-from-End-to-End) and one (Place-of-Rolling-Down-in-the-House) for his younger brother. He instructs his younger brother to sit in the house, provisions him with four whales he has killed with a sling, and then leaves to "set things right in the world" (p. 2).

Transformer then goes through a series of encounters with other beings whom he transforms. The first is a man sharpening a mussel shell as a fighting tool. When Transformer asks him what he is doing, the man laughs and says, "Are you the only one who does not know what is known by us? It is said that he will set everything right, Lord *Q!aneqelaku*" (p. 2). Transformer takes the mussel shells, turns the man upside down, and transforms him into Deer.

The second encounter is a repeat of the first, with the slight difference that the man is sharpening a lance, and the same verbal exchange takes place. Transformer takes the man, turns his head "the other way" (p. 2), transforms the lance into a tail, and smears the dust from the sharpening on the face and buttocks of the animal, transforming him into Raccoon.

The third encounter involves a visit to a village of many houses, which has only one inhabitant, a little girl. She feeds Transformer, and when he is finished, he asks for a drink of water. Thirst, says the girl, has been the cause of the death of her tribe. Transformer tells the girl not to be needlessly afraid, but to put on his *sisiutl* belt and to draw water from the lake. The child does so, but as soon as she enters the water, the sea-monster opens his mouth and devours her. Transformer then repeats four times the phrase "Snake in belly" (p. 3) and the sea monster opens its mouth and vomits first "very many bones of men" (p. 3) and then the child, still alive. Transformer then says to the child, "Help me . . . to gather the bones that we may revive them" (p. 3). Transformer sprinkles his water of life on the bones and the people all come back to life, but they are all deformed, shortlegged and short-armed. These are the first Koskimo, "who were pitied by Transformer" (p. 3).

Transformer's fourth encounter is like the first two, though the object being sharpened is not stated. Transformer takes the object, makes it into a tail, and changes the man into Land Otter.

Transformer's next encounter is with four blind (eyeless) women who are sitting on a beach steaming clover roots. Transformer steals part of their clover root, but they detect him by his odor. Transformer rubs their eye sockets with his thumbs, and they can see. Transformer throws them up into the air and transforms them into Mallard Ducks.

Transformer's sixth encounter involves a man wearing red cedar bark who is lying on his back with his knees drawn up, in a canoe on the water. The man is singing a song, "Do not touch me on the water, *Ō'lala* uninitiated./ Hai, I am made to be a thrower, *Ō'lala* uninitiated, Hai." Transformer is afraid, and says "Friend, you must be a shaman." The man answers, "I just wish to be a shaman. I just feel good because it is easy traveling." Transformer asks the man to come ashore; the man does, and then Transformer "streaks down" (p. 4) (streamlines) the man's body and throws him into the water, where he becomes Codfish.

Transformer then journeys on to Nimkish, where he meets another man. He announces himself to be Transformer, tells the man he is going to set him right, and asks him what he wants to be. The man responds that he wants to be a river, and Transformer makes him into a large river, the river of time, that will run forever. As a river, the man's name changes.

Transformer returns home, where he finds only the bones of his younger brother, who has died, remaining. He sprinkles the bones with the water of life and they are transformed into his revivified younger brother. Transformer then creates a tribe to live at his village. The men come from one of Only-One's house's posts. Transformer informs the post when the number of men is sufficient, and the post stops producing them. Transformer then instructs Only-One to go to the north end of the world, where he will control bad things, but without too much verve, so that Transformer will not have to work too hard to keep making things right. Transformer then goes to the south end of the world. Here this version of the myth stops (see also Boas, 1935: 133-40).

As noted earlier, in this myth is outlined the entire Kwakiutl cosmology. Originally, the world consisted only of amoral beings, people ruled by hunger (as indicated by the opening line of the myth: "Hungry were [Transformer and his family]"), destruction (indicated by the warriors), and hatred and antagonism, rather than the close bonds of sharing and cooperation that constitute kin relations.

In such times, parents did not want to share food even with their own children. It might seem to us, with our folkloric tradition of stepmother/stepchild antagonism, that Heron's wife is antagonistic toward her stepchildren because they are not her natural children (a second version of this myth [1935b:5-12] simply identifies Woodpecker as Heron's wife, not a stepmother). In fact, however, in a patrifocal society, all mothers are in a sense stepmothers, distanced from their children by the kinship and residence principles of their society.

The state of hunger that characterized the pre-Transformer world is a state that was a difficult one for its inhabitants. Only after Transformer sets up the rules for meals and reincarnation can there be an assured supply of food. Before that time, everyone would have lived with the constant threat of imminent starvation, obtaining food by his own limited means, though not in dependable quantities. To begin the myth with the idea of hunger emphasizes the agony of life without the organizing powers of the spirits. So today do people who deny the hegemony of the spirits live in a world of constant hunger, a world of undependable resources, a world of poverty.

It is difficult to pinpoint the differences between the era before Transformer's first act and after. We might distinguish between the two on the basis of chaos versus order, that before Transformer there were no kin principles, no animals, no sociality, no world order, and that now all these things exist. Yet this idea is so fundamental to Western mythos that I hesitate to ascribe it to Kwakiutl mythos. We might differentiate between stasis and flux. This idea seems more relevant to Kwakiutl thinking, in which time and the river flowing to the north end of the world are equivalent. Transformer does create the first river. Yet for two reasons this idea may be questioned. First, if the pre-Transformer world was not chaotic, then it must have had order and form. There is no geometry in a void; chaos is the most definitive type of stasis. And second, even today events do not take place in historical succession but in cycles. (Again, the historical tradition is so essential to Western thought that I hesitate to see it in Kwakiutl thought.) Furthermore, several aspects of Kwakiutl thought indicate an ahistoricity to that thought: the idea that time stops during the winter ceremony; the cyclic nature of birth, death and reincarnation; and the repetition, the reenactment, year after year, of the very events that occurred when the world in its present form was first begun.

We might see the difference between pre- and post-Transformer time in terms of control versus helplessness. Certainly, in pre-Transformer times the beings who were alive were not in control of events. They were ruled by their passions, especially by hunger, and were unable to obtain food with any regularity. In the post-Transformer world, humans do have some control over the way the world will go. Or at least we may say that now that some of the principles by which the world works are known and some people have been able to obtain the cooperation of the spirits by seeing that the world is maintained according to those principles, there is the ability to control some aspects of events.

Nor can the difference be ascribed to a presocial versus a social universe, an idea that appeals to anthropological predilections. For Transformer lives in a family, and there are villages, in the time when he first is alive. Still, there are some indications that Transformer does not live in a social world as we know it, for his father seems ignorant of his son's origin, asking him where he came from, and yet seems to accept Transformer as a coresident of his house. Nor can we infer from the fact that Transformer has a younger brother that kinship is already in existence at that time, since it is possible that the storyteller was merely translating for the ethnographer the relations of beings in premythic times, interpolating modern categories of kinship into times when there were no kin relations.

In short, I do not think it possible to come to any conclusions about the nature of the pre- and post-Transformer eras, between the time before the myths took place and the time since. What is important is the realization that the basic break in time lies not between mythic and modern times, but between premythic and mythic times. The essential changeover occurs at the point where the first myth begins; time today, on the other hand, is exactly like mythic time. It is the same time. The Kwakiutl have always lived, since their creation as a tribe by Transformer, in the same time as the mythic beings. They are living now in mythic time.

Thus, the first incident in the myth outlines the structure and dynamics of Kwakiutl family life. First, it is natural for parents to resent their children because these children eat food the parents want for themselves, and thus children are in competition with their parents. Second, parents are expected to provide food for their children, thus establishing a superordinate/subordinate relationship, which is replicated in the relationship of older siblings to their younger siblings. Third, the interests of the two dyads of husband/wife and parent/child are in conflict. Fourth, since by requiring food children in a sense demand food, parents are forced to evaluate the relative merits of keeping food (or power, status, names, dances, or any other valuable item) for themselves or of passing it on to their heirs.

The conflict between Transformer and his parents is the primeval prototype for the dynamics of succession in the Kwakiutl family. Because of Transformer's acts, it is now the normal course of events for children to transform, destroy, and supersede their parents. Parents control food and power, yet ultimately they will become subordinate to and dependent upon the children who are their heirs and who will take from them their food, power, wealth, status, and even the very energy of their being. It is a moral requirement upon parents that they permit the orderly progression of human events, that they willingly cede to their children their children's birthright. Transformer, in transforming and banishing his parents, makes it as much a moral obligation to relinquish wealth, power, and even life itself at the proper time as it is to possess them.

The world's first moral act, the transformation of Heron and Woodpecker, is not made as a matter of choice. Instead, Transformer acts out of hunger and anger, out of passion. In the heat of the moment he seeks revenge, and having obtained it, is forced to act in a world in which keeping food for oneself is now an immoral act. The way the world works has been revealed to Transformer; the knowledge of good has made itself manifest to him. He accepts his vision and goes out into the world to act upon its principles. So today does each person find the nature of the universe revealed through visions, dances, ceremonies; he chooses to accept the knowledge imparted in them, to live in concord with the power revealed to him, or to live in antipathy to it. The events that occur in Transformer's life, then, are mythic not because they occurred in distant times, for they are still occurring today, but because they occurred for the first time.

The revenge Transformer visits upon his parents is peculiarly apt. First, he throws them out of the house to which they, as his parents, had brought him and welcomed him. (This idea is far more obviously stated in the second version of this tale, which immediately follows the first in Boas, 1935b:5). So do all children, as they adopt the names and statuses once held by their parents, figuratively throw them out of their own houses. Humans are reminded of this by the behavior of herons and woodpeckers, which are associated with human villages, but which are shy and flee from humans, living on the peripheries of human habitation and activity, eternal exiles.

Second, the particular two avian identities of Transformer's parents stand as symbols for the omnipresent search for food. Both herons and woodpeckers are constant, active, avid feeders and it is mete that they should be punished for having hoarded food by being forced to search for it constantly. Nor is their hunting for food made easier by the fact that their food is hidden. Heron, eater of frogs (symbols of life), a fisherman, a creature of this earth, must find his food underwater; Woodpecker, an eater of insects (symbols of death), a creature of this earth who must find her food under the bark of dying trees, is a tree killer.

Yet there is another aspect of Heron and Woodpecker's transformation that is even more important. The basis of Kwakiutl ritual is dance and drumming, controlled, ordered movement and sound, and in creating Heron and Woodpecker, Transformer creates ritual. The food hunting methods of both birds are similar to those of ritual performance. Woodpeckers, the drummers of the avian world, always drum on and peck away at trees before they can get to the insects that live underneath. Herons, the most superb dancers of the Northwest Coast bird world, have complex and fascinating dances as part of their courtship rituals. These dances also occur in part during the heron's stalking of prey, when the heron walks slowly through the waters, its wings upraised like a dancer's arms so that the shadow of the wings will lull the fish and amphibians, which are its prey, into thinking they are safe.

Thus, though they are always drumming and dancing, always performing ritual, and though it is ritual and not hunting skill that is the ultimate source of food, neither of these birds is ever satisfied although both create food. Like some of the tormented beings of Classical Greek myth—Tantalus, Sisyphus, Prometheus—they are forever reenacting the same fruitless endeavor and are forever being punished.

Furthermore, since it is ritual that links the entire universe, Heron and Woodpecker are links with the entire universe because they are land birds that eat creatures of the sea, the underground, and the trees. Thus, the entire world becomes suffused with ritual, and the entire universe is linked both through a cycle of moral ritual and food. And since eating necessitates killing, death becomes part of this ritual cycle.

In this Transformer has created something even more important than ritual. He has created transformation. He has created the links that ensure eternal life through the proper treatment of death. He has created the process by which one being becomes another, through which change can occur, through which the spirits become humans and humans become spirits, through which dead people become live fish, and dead fish become live people. And since change implies differences between entities, Transformer has thus also created hierarchy, a series of identities by which humans, animals, and spirits progress.

Finally, Transformer has done something to the nature of names, for he names his parents, giving them identity, then proceeds to name the beings and places in the world. Thus, Transformer creates differentiation, the basis for hierarchy, the basis for structure. To name something is to create it, to give it existence through identity; so Transformer, as Nominator, is also Creator.

Armed with the power he has obtained by his moral act, Transformer begins to alter the world outside his family. His first adventure involves the killing of a *sisiutl*. To the Kwakiutl the *sisiutl* is one of the most terrifying of all beings, a giant two-headed serpent with a face in the middle of its body. We have already seen that snakes are frightening to the Kwakiutl because they are symbols of great oral destruction and because they have the potential, being creatures of the underground, to enter human beings through their anuses and devour their insides. Even so, snakes are not monsters because their digestive process is unidirectional, the food they eat being digested and excreted. Not so for the *sisiutl*. Since it has a head at both ends, it cannot have an anus. Therefore the prey of the *sisiutl*, once eaten, is trapped forever in its body, unable to escape, unable to be reborn.

The face in the center of the *sisiutl* is a very interesting example of simultaneous metaphorical expressions of orality. First, it represents the anus of the *sisiutl*—but an anus that does not expel but, like other mouths, ingests. Second, the face is often shown with horns of power radiating from its forehead, a symbol also found on the *sisiutl*'s major predator, the Thunderbird; prey and predator are thus shown to be related. Third, *sisiutl* masks are worn in ceremonies so that the mask's face covers either the face or chest of the dancer. In the former, the *sisiutl* face replaces that of the dancer, changing his surface identity, since the image is that of a mask. In the latter, the *sisiutl* face covers the soul of the dancer, changing his inner identity; in addition, the serpentine bodies of the *sisiutl* become analogues of the dancer's arms, and the motion of the dancer's arms indicates the motion of the *sisiutl* "moving all around," one of the Kwakiutl's most cogent expressions of omnipresence and powerfulness. This image of the arms as analogues of the ever-hungry *sisiutl* is repeated in the *hamatsa* dance, where the dancer frequently extends his arms outward and then brings them back in toward his body. The *sisiutl's* hunger and the *hamatsa's* reinforce each other.

The conquering of the *sisiutl* by Transformer is the first step for the development of morality, for as *sisiutl* metaphorizes all-pervading hunger, and morality consists of the ability to localize hunger in time and space, Transformer must conquer hunger before he can be a true moral being. He kills *sisiutl*. However, instead of relegating the killing to a mere act of violence, he takes the additional step of skinning the animal and of using the skin as a belt. Thus he simultaneously creates three important moral acts: the mechanism by which humans cause death, the dismemberment of the body; the act of saving the skin as an earnest of the being's life; and finally, the wearing of the first costume. Transformer becomes both the killer of *sisiutl* (i.e., Thunderbird) and *sisiutl* itself. Thus men become what they kill, a fact most clearly exemplified by the belief that hunters become their prey after their deaths. Of course, if men inherit the right to kill an animal because their fathers had that right, and their fathers become those animals upon their death, then men may be said to hunt their own fathers. Moreover, since the souls of their future children reside in the bodies of the animals they are hunting, men may be said to hunt their own children. This is why a hunter, when he dreams of copulating, immediately gets out of bed and goes hunting, because hunting (death-bringing) and copulating (life-bringing) are simultaneous occurrences—a soul must be released through death so it can be reincarnated in another form. The hunter's dream tells him that a soul is ready to be released and reborn, and it is his responsibility to see that it can obtain its freedom (Boas, 1921:642ff.).

The wearing of the *sisiutl* belt may be seen to symbolize several other key ideas. The belt is a phallic image, and the power of the *sisiutl* may be related to the potency of the penis. This image is reaffirmed by the use of coppers, in that when a copper is held in front of the body, the T-ridge's horizontal bar is analogous to the holder's waist, and the vertical bar is analogous to his penis. Thus, the wealth (of souls) that the copper represents is associated with the wealth of future lives that the penis represents; and the *sisiutl*, which represents all-pervasive hunger and death, is transformed through the actions of men into the all-pervasive power of fertility and rebirth.

Transformer, having killed and mastered hunger (*sisiutl*), is now able to find food easily. He immediately captures four whales. Having built a house for himself and one for his brother, he gives the whales as provisions to his brother and instructs him to sit in the house. As Transformer is guardian and benefactor to his younger brother, so is he to his other wards and younger brothers, men. He gives them a place to live, a house with a name, an identity, an eternal existence. In building a house Transformer gives the world geography; he changes it from a state of flux to one of constancy. He has stopped not time, but place. He has created stability.

As we have seen, the house is the Kwakiutl metaphor for physical space, and thus in building a house Transformer is bringing physical space into his new world. In naming the house he creates another dimension of space, that of identity. As the universe is an infinite space, composed of an infinite number of geometric spaces, it can achieve identity only when it has a limit, a boundary. And once a space has boundaries it also has an identity. A triangle has as much of an identity as a person, the principles for defining each of them being equal. For Transformer to create space he must simultaneously create identity. Thus, he gives his house a name, and the name a house.

The house Transformer builds for his brother is a further definition of the geography of the universe. From this point in the myths, Transformer will go about changing beings from their primal form into their present form, and then naming them. The creative power of Transformer comes not just from his ability to change, for every shaman has that power, but from his ability to make those changes permanent. The names he gives to his houses, to the animals, to the places of the world still remain. They are the identities by which the universe is denoted and described, and thus by which the universe is experienced. Transformer is also the creator of names, of identities, the Definer. He is the being who gives words the power to create, to define, to control. He is the being who makes talk meaningful, who makes words have meaning (identity), thus granting them eternal existence and power. Humans have the ability to assume names, to dress in them as if in a costume, to become them and participate in their attributes, but they do not have the power to create names. Thus, the creation of the first house and the first name are unified by their shared characteristics. As the house provides boundaries, which define and create physical space, so the name provides boundaries, which define and create nonphysical space.

This episode also presents the first example of a morally proper superordinate/subordinate relationship, an example of which stands in opposition to that of Transformer and his parents. Transformer, the superordinate, provides food in abundance as well as a house for Only-One, the subordinate. Only-One need only live in that house. Similarly, humans need only live in the universe Transformer has built for them, and food in abundance will be provided. Conversely, so long as humans reside within the structures the spirits have built, the spirits are constrained to provide them with food. Thus, the building of the house for Only-One symbolizes the creation of the superordinate/subordinate relationship. Indeed, in the last section of the myth, people arise out of the very poles of the house itself. The existence of people may thus be seen as a direct result of the morally correct relationship between Transformer and Only-One.

An interesting series of corollaries arises here. Existence occurs when a soul inhabits a box: a person comes to life when a soul inhabits his body, a house comes to life when people reside in it. The house of Only-One comes to life when Only-One resides in it. Finally, the house of Transformer, that is, the present moral universe, can come to life only when it is inhabited by its own soul—humans. The moral universe is dead—an empty shell, a vacant house—unless humans inhabit it and bring it to life.

Transformer next sets off to "set things right in the world." His first stop involves a meeting with a man still ruled by destructive impulses who is seeking to kill Transformer before his new moral universe can spread. The man is sharpening a pair of mussel shells into spear-carving tools, but Transformer takes them and, turning the man upside down, puts them on him to form his ears. The man is transformed into Deer. While deer are not eaten by the Kwakiutl, because the eating of venison is believed to induce forgetfulness, they are hunted and their skins used for clothing and their antlers for tools and armor. So, in creating deer, Transformer is creating the materials with which his descendants will costume themselves, as well as the tools, such as needles and awls they will need for making costumes.

Transformer then goes through a similar interaction with Raccoon. He takes the dust remaining from Raccoon's spear-sharpening and paints his face and backside with it. Thus, Transformer has created the first mask. Boas points out in many places (1897:passim; 1898; 1955) that every line painted on a face mask was meant to have some interpretive meaning. Although the meanings of particular face paintings have now been lost to us, we can nevertheless perceive that the acts of face painting and creating identity go hand in hand.

Transformer's next encounter, with the child in the deserted village, is one of the most complicated incidents of this myth. It is the incident in which Transformer is first able to bring the dead back to life, and it is rich in metaphorical expression. The village to which Transformer comes is filled with houses, but they are empty. Since houses need inhabitants to be made to live, they are dead. Such is the fate of the premoral person, for death is a final act, a one-way trek from this world to the bellies of the monsters that kill and eat them. Without reincarnation, the world would soon be emptied of humans. Though the village is one ruled by etiquette, evidenced by the propriety with which Transformer is served a meal without water, propriety is not in and of itself sufficient to conquer death. The meal the child serves Transformer is the first feast, and Transformer is the first guest. Yet, because of the sea monster, the feast cannot end, as it properly should, with a drink of water.

To protect the child, Transformer gives her his *sisiutl* belt, his power over hunger. When the child is eaten by the sea monster, Transformer is able to wield the power of the *sisiutl* belt to force the monster to vomit up the bones he has entrapped in his stomach. Transformer does this through the use of words, through the power he had previously given to speech. The *sisiutl* is a "snake in belly," a graphic image of hunger and its painful power. Yet, Transformer is able to take that power and use it to create matter from the ejection of the stomach contents, to change destructive hunger to creative hunger. The regurgitated bones, the vomit, the substance of creation itself, which is the seminal fluid of an oral culture, are the materials from which the newly created men will be formed. With the bones gathered by the child of the village (the bones are, of course, those of her ancestors), as the bones of the older generation are today gathered and treated for burial by their children, Transformer is able to reconstitute and revive them by sprinkling the "water of life" upon them. Water is both the cause of their death and the cause of their rebirth. So the power of the spirits is still able to revivify the dead as Transformer's water of life first revived the bones. Yet the *sisiutl* belt, the belt of potency, is worn not by Transformer but by the human child; so today, the power of reincarnation is given to one's descendants by the spirits, but it must be wielded by the children. Spirits and humans must work together if the dead are to be reborn.

The three mammals Transformer creates are linked in several ways. First, they all reject Transformer's new world, and seek to destroy him. Second, they are all ignorant of his identity. Third, they all depend on sheer physical strength for their victory over him. In these ways the dialectic of Kwakiutl militarism is expressed: it is in and of itself a rejection of moral values, a state, ultimately limited in its scope, in which knowledge (and the power inherent in it) is absent. Moral power is far greater than pure military strength. Only within the moral system does warfare gain power. As the *sisiutl* has fallen to Transformer's power, so do the warriors of the world. And as their punishment, Transformer uses the very weapons they would use against him to mark them—the mussel shells of Deer become his ears; the spears of Otter and Raccoon (and in the second version of the tale, Mink) become their tails. Thus forever men will immediately recognize these distinctive markings and know that these animals rejected the vision of Transformer. Indeed, the punishment for these animals is to remain outside the reincarnation system, for though all of them are hunted for their skins, and their skins are made into clothing, none of them is eaten. Therefore, none of them is treated in the ritual way that ensures rebirth. In creating these mammals, then, Transformer has both created food taboos and shown that the power of his moral system can control that of sheer strength, that the knowledge of how to live right is a greater power than any other.

Played off against the three mammals who are transformed because of their ignorance into nocturnal animals are the women who are transformed into Mallards. Though blind, a condition that might seem to render them incapable of perceiving Transformer and might therefore be said to symbolize ignorance, they know when he has stolen just one clover root from them and they are able to identify him immediately. They have a gift greater than sight, the ability to perceive and to know intuitively, a gift for which they are rewarded by being made diurnal birds, which can traverse the boundaries between the underwater and the surface of the water, between water and land, and between land and air, and which are also eaten by men, and thus treated in such a way as to be eligible for rebirth. And though the last line, "And so that is the reason why ducks do thus being thrown up when they first start to fly" (1935b:4), may seem to change the story into a "just-so" explanation of duck behavior, it is really a statement that the power of Transformer evidences itself in many specific ways, even in the way in which ducks start their flight standing upright, their wings spread, like women dancing with their arms spread at their sides to display their ceremonial costumes.

Transformer meets a man who is traveling on his back, his knees drawn up, in a canoe. The image, an important and ubiquitous one in Northwest Coast cultures, is both the image of a dead man in his coffin and the image of a baby at its birth. It is found on rattles, sculptures, feast bowls, and other items of ceremonial importance. Birth and death are both journeys, mirror images of each other. Both are the province of shamans, who have the power to achieve a temporary deathlike trance for themselves so that their souls may journey to other lands and discover knowledge they can use to cure and kill. And insofar as chiefs have control over food, and thus over the cycle of life and death, they too are shamans. Thus, the dead man/shaman of this myth warns the uninitiated with his songs to stay away from him. Only he has the power to deal with death safely; the uninitiated, ignorant of the knowledge they need to die properly and be reborn, must avoid death. Those who are initiated can die safely—for them, death is "easy traveling" (1935b:4). Thus, Transformer changes this man into a codfish, streamlining his body ("streaked down his body to the tail" [p. 4]) so that his travel through the water may be easy. So do men who treat other beings correctly find death, the journey between one identity (one existence) and another, to be easy.

Transformer then creates, in the form of a river, the motion that gives the world time. The Kwakiutl believe that the world consists of beaches and a great river, which forever runs northward. As physical space is a flowing river, so is temporal space. By creating a river, Transformer brings time to the world, but by ensuring that the river never runs dry he also makes it permanent, giving eternalness to his creations. As long as there is time, as long as there is a river, then Transformer's creations will exist.

Finally, after having created time, Transformer performs his last great act. Finding Only-One dead, Transformer, using Only-One's bones and the life-giving power he now possesses, is able to bring him back to life. Thus Transformer creates the cycle of reincarnation. Then, he and Only-One decide exactly how many people shall inhabit the earth, and when that number are brought into existence, they limit the human population. The cycle of reincarnation shall always deal with that finite number of souls.

Transformer then gives Only-One his first bit of knowledge, the definition of his role and purpose on the earth. Only-One is to reside in the north end of the world where he will create "bad sickness" (p. 5) but not so much that he overtaxes Transformer's ability to "set things right" (p. 5), a role Only-One accepts. Thus Transformer establishes the final basis for morality, which is that morality is meaningful only in a context of immorality. No one can be truly moral in a world in which there is no choice. Morality comes from the conquering, not the ignoring, of evil thoughts and desires. The accomplishments of Transformer would be meaningless if there were no longer a choice between right and wrong behavior. Consequently, it is Only-One's moral responsibility to provide the foil for Transformer's beneficial actions, to provide contrast and context for human moral action. Thus Only-One exhibits both the supposed good and bad traits of younger brothers, who are thought to bewitch their elder brothers in order to take over their identities and roles, and yet who also help their older brothers in the proper performance of their ritual responsibilities.

In summary, we have seen that this myth expresses the charter of Kwakiutl society, and that the charter is characterized by the importance of controlling hunger in the successful running of the universe. The incidents in the myth all center around hunger; the images of transformation are all oral images; and man's purpose is to affirm the actions of Transformer, to play out the eternal cycle of death and rebirth he established. Hunger is the force that motivates the world, and the control of hunger gives man and spirit the ability to control the world's motion. This knowledge was created by Transformer out of a single act that all humans beings are fated to reenact: the desire to keep food for themselves rather than share it, even with their own children.

Kwakiutl rituals enact the ideas embodied in this myth. Boas states innumerable times that the purpose of rituals is to present in dramatized form the myths that stand at the foundation of Kwakiutl culture and society. We must therefore conclude that Kwakiutl ritual is meant to reenact this primal conflict between hunger and its submission to ritual. Certainly, we can now see that the purpose of the Cannibal (*hamatsa*) ritual is exactly that, to embody in ritual the primal conflict between narcissistic desire and socialization.

Transformer created rightness; he made it possible for humans to act morally. However, every human must reaffirm his covenant with the spirits by personally displaying his desire to act correctly, by personally performing acts showing that, though the chance to act immorally is still available, though the world is ruled by hunger, he is going to tame his hunger, and thus conquer the forces of immorality. This is the purpose of the winter ceremonial. The winter ceremonial is a moral statement by the man who gives it and those who attend. The giving of the winter ceremonial is a reaffirmation of one's willingness to live by the rules and the principles set down by the ancestors and a rejection of the chaos of uncontrolled desires.

The time of the winter ceremonials is in every sense a special time, when men put aside the mundane concerns of daily life, when, like the true philosopher in Plato's cave, they turn from the flickering images they see before them and move out of the darkness of their cave into the blinding power and light of the truth. It is the time when the motion of the universe is brought to a stop, when all events become coterminous, when the Mouth of Heaven opens and the powerbeings come from their worlds dressed in their costumes, the blinding light of their power streaming from their bodies as from the sacred quartz crystals and filling the room as does the eagle down trailing from their headdresses. This is the time when the spirits display their beauty and their power before the men of their covenant, and when they give to men the knowledge necessary to rule the world.

During the winter ceremonials, time stops. The principles of sociality associated with the summer, the secular food-gathering season—the time when the migrations occur, when hunting takes place, the time of change and motion, when the river of time flowing past the village brings with it the salmon who give life—are suspended. There is no more fishing, no more food gathering. The round of daily activity comes to a halt. From now on all food will come not from the waters, but from a box.

Perhaps the most powerful symbol of the stoppage of time comes from the representation of the universe as a house. The Kwakiutl measure time by the motion of the stars through the sky, by the changing patterns of the constellations, by the position of the Milky Way. During the secular season, when a house is only a house and the sky is the roof of the world, the seasons pass. But during the winter ceremonials, the ceremonial house becomes the universe; their boundaries are contiguous, and the central beam of the house becomes the Milky Way. Yet the central beam of the house is a fixed point in space, standing in a constant geographical relationship to the beach and the river of time flowing past it. When the house is transformed into the universe, then the rotation of the sky is stopped; the motion of the heavens is halted. Thus, from the first blowing of the ceremonial whistles until the concluding speech, there is only a single instant. All acts during that period, though they may seem from a historistic viewpoint to precede or postdate one another, are considered to occur simultaneously.

Furthermore, since this is the time of year when men give up their positions in favor of their sons, the permanence of the name is made more important than the identities of the individuals who successively personify those names. One man leaves a name and another man takes his place; but, since this occurs in the same instant, we cannot perceive it. We see only the name, existing before and after that instant. The identity of the specific actor who animates that name is secondary, imperceptible to us.

The Kwakiutl contextualize their feasts and ceremonies, simultaneously heightening their dramatic impact, through the contraposition of images of voracious hunger with images and rituals of moral control. The special seal feast that is part of the winter ceremonials (Boas, 1966:182), at which large amounts of food are displayed and distributed, provides a good example. The participants go to their homes to put on their face paintings; when they return to the ceremonial house for the feast, their painted faces clearly indicate that the rituals of the feast have been elevated to a sacral level. The singing of sacred songs and the strict ritualization of food distribution and consumption at the feast bracket the various dance societies' ritually exaggerated expressions of hunger, signifying the power of the social order to contain the force of voraciousness and demonstrating that in a moral universe abundance is not an excuse for a lack of self-restraint.

The way in which Kwakiutl feasts are structured internally so as to continually contrast hunger and control is illustrated by a feast given by the father of a new Bear Dancer (Boas, 1966:182-83). This feast is preceded by the appearance of *tsonoqua* (whose characteristics provide one of the most obvious statements of oral desires in the pantheon of Kwakiutl spirit beings), Fool Dancers, Killer Whale Dancers, dancers who spread their blankets and imitate the motions and voices of ducks, and finally a man carrying his small son who is to be initiated as a Fool Dancer. Only after all these imges of hunger have appeared do the people eat their meal, thus opposing the dancers' hunger-created power with the greater power of sociality and etiquette. Then, after the first course, a Bear Dancer appears. The people, filled with the power given them through meal sharing, are able to pacify him with sacred songs. The dancer goes out and the people then reaffirm their power by eating the feast's second course, after which they go home.

The war between hunger and morality may be directly stated in and enacted through song. During one ceremony involving a Koskimo Cannibal Dancer (Boas, 1966:190), the people first sing a song meant to create the power of Man Eater and the Cannibals: "I have been all around the world eating with [Man Eater]/I give nobody time to escape me, going around in the house with [Man Eater]. . . ." Since, as we have seen, song is a form of prayer, and prayer forces the spirits to act, this song is thereby creating the presence of Man Eater in the house. Thus, the taming songs, which immediately follow, act not just upon the Cannibal Dancer, who is Man Eater's cohort, but upon the cosmic force of hunger itself as well.

Many of the songs of the winter ceremonials are meant specifically to point out the interrelationship between men, animals, and spirits, and to act as reaffirmation of man's moral covenant. The song of the Salmon Dancer is a good example:

1. The salmon came to search for a dancer.
2. He came and put his supernatural power in him.
3. You have the supernatural power. Therefore the chief of the salmon came from beyond the ocean. The people praise you, for they cannot carry the weight of your wealth.

$$\text{(Boas, 1897:474-75)}$$

Here the idea that the salmon need someone to perform their reincarnation ritual is stated clearly in the song's first verse; the giving of power to the dancer by the salmon is stated in the second verse. Both these ideas are reinforced in the third verse, which also states the benefits this dancer's covenant brings to the rest of humanity. The implication that the chief of the salmon sends his people to die solely because the dancer has agreed to perform the dance required to recreate their bodies is easy to see. It is even more clearly stated in the other song of this ceremony:

1. Many salmon are coming ashore with me.
2. They are coming ashore to you the post of our heaven.
3. They are dancing from the salmon's country to the shore.
4. I come to dance before you at the right-side of the world, overtowering, outshining, surpassing all; I, the salmon.

$$\text{(Boas, 1897:475)}$$

The imagery of this song aptly metaphorizes the man/salmon bonds, bonds made of ritual dancing. The dancer brings the salmon with him.

He is the chief of the salmon, and he leads them to human lands, as human chiefs lead their own tribesmen. The dancer's actions force the chief of the salmon to bring his tribesmen with him, for in a sacred setting, the song sets up the relationship between human and spirit, and the dance, which imitates the swimming of salmon, causes the salmon to swim. The dancer calls the salmon to him: as the embodiment of the salmon chief, he is the "post of heaven" to the salmon, just as human chiefs are the means of access to the world of spirits for their human tribesmen; as human dancer, he is "post of heaven" for the chief of salmon, for he is the link all salmon have with the world of humans. And just as the human dancer dances to reaffirm his pledge to the salmon that they will be reborn, so the salmon "dance" their way from their own country to man's, reaffirming their pledge.

The *hamatsa* rituals exist in varied forms, as should be expected in a society where every ritual is determined in part by the ritual privileges of the individual members of the sponsoring group. The particular rites in each *hamatsa* ceremonial differ according to the tribes involved and their acquisition by the Cannibal Dancer. These rites can be complicated and confusing, and in the welter of chapters and sections about the *hamatsa* ceremony it can be nearly impossible to pick out even the simple chain of events involved. Boas details the various ceremonies and rites of approximately a dozen different *hamatsa* rituals (1897; 1966). Yet despite their variations, all the ceremonies share the basic characteristics involving the idea of taming the initiate, of returning him, as Boas says (1966:173), to a secular state.

The ceremony commences after the initiate returns from his sojourn in the realm of Man Eater, which is considered to take four days in spirit-time no matter how long that may seem to be in human time, whether months or years. At the end of this period, as the sacred beings return to live among humans, the *hamatsa* initiates, who form part of the retinue of Man Eater, return from his realm. They can be heard from afar, their cries and the sound of their sacred whistles heralding their approach.

The ceremonials have been underway for some time. The people have been performing their songs and dances expressing their ties with the spirits and reaffirming their suppression of hunger. The master of ceremonies periodically sends men to see if the *hamatsa* dancer is near the village, especially after a well-performed ritual, when the power the tribe possesses has been amply demonstrated. Early the next morning, the Ghost Dancer appears, and the singing of his song excites the old *hamatsas*. His song is replete with images of death and automatically establishes an analogic relationship with the *hamatsas* that forces them to action, just as all spirits are forced to act when the words of prayers expressing their analogic relationships to humans are sung. The *hamatsas'* cries and whistles are heard from outside the house, and they enter the house from all sides (thus symbolizing the omnipresence of hunger). They dance around the fire four times, at which point the sound of their cries (which functions as does a song) and the motion of their dance causes the new initiate to come to the house. He appears on the roof, circles it clockwise four times, pushes the roof boards aside four times and then jumps down into the house. Since the roof of the house is the sky, the hole in the roof becomes the Mouth of Heaven, and the *hamatsa*'s entry through the Mouth of Heaven symbolizes his return from the world of the spirits. Now that the *hamatsa* is in the world of men, all his future entrances and exits will be from the doors on the ground level of the house, except when he acts as messenger to the spirits.

The people try to hold him, but he escapes into the secret room; only the hemlock branches, which were his only clothing, are left behind. Eventually, the hemlock branches, symbol of the wildness of the woods, will be replaced with a woven cedarbark head ring, symbol of the ritual bond between man and the universe (see Curtis, 1915: illus. facing pp. 172, 182).

Much of the *hamatsa* ceremony involves travel from one level of existence to another. Pathways to other worlds are represented in several fashions. We have already seen how, in the winter ceremonial, the central housebeam serves as the Milky Way, and the central rear post (*hams'pek*), called the "cannibal pole" or "eating pole" (Curtis, 1915:175), forms a pathway by which the Cannibal Dancer descends from the roof (or sky). Sometimes paths are represented by totem poles. The totem poles of the Haida village of Skedans (Smyly and Smyly, 1973) represent various forms of paths in a highly concise fashion. There is one type of pole that has only one or two carved figures beneath a long ascending pole without figures, but that is sometimes ornamented with concentric, equidistant circles. These poles, seen by most scholars merely as totemic crest insignias, are usually interpreted in terms of a strong identification with the crest animal represented. But the differences in the two variants of this type of pole, ringed and plain, seem, at least in the case of Skedans, to be associated totally with the distinction between land and sea animals. Land animals can ascend to the next level only on a ladder, and thus land animal poles are ringed (runged); sea animal poles, representing animals who ascend without ladders but in smooth-sided whirlpools, are unringed. The ladder aspect of the rings is emphasized in other poles by the placement of rings within the body cavity of an animal, thus forming its backbone (Smyly and Smyly, 1973:52, 54), i.e., the ladder by which the soul moves up and down within the body. The rings are often interpreted only as rings on a potlatch hat (supposedly indicating the number of potlatches given by the wearer), yet the rings on the hat are another ladder, for property is the ladder by which man ensures his passage from this world to the next.

Thus many Haida memorial poles are capped by figures with ringed potlatch hats. The cannibal pole, the totem pole, the potlatch hat rings, and the backbone are all analogues of each other.

The next stage in the winter ceremonials involves the ritual explanation for the *hamatsa* dancer's escape, and the inability of the dancers and the rituals to capture him (p. 526). Boas gives two examples of possible explanations, both of which involve transgressions of the rules of propriety during ceremonial occasions. In the first case, a person who has laughed earlier in the ceremony must both call his daughter to dance and give a feast; in the second case, a woman brings some uninitiated children into the ceremonial house, and they are forced to be initiated. In both instances, transgressions are followed by a reforging of the bonds of human and spirit, signaled by a ritual performance and a feast.

The congregation then adjourns for a few hours rest in preparation for the return of the Cannibal Dancer during the next day. The sound of the *hamatsas'* sacred whistles are heard constantly coming from the woods.

The next day, when the Seal Society members gather, they are led down to the beach by the female assistants, always kinswomen, of the *hamatsa* dancers. These assistants sing their taming songs: "1. Yiya ham yiyaha. I am the real tamer of [Man Eater]. 2. Yiya ham yiyaha. I pull the red cedar bark from [Man Eater's] back," and, "It is my power to pacify you, when you are in a state of ecstasy" (p. 527). In doing so they set up a situation in which their actions automatically fall within the rubric of taming the Cannibal.

The people go to a special sacred place on the beach, some boys are sent to gather hemlock branches, from which neck and head rings are made. The *quē'qutsa*, or people not presently possessed by a spirit, form a row, all join hands and, preceded by the members of the Seal Society, move forward while singing their new sacred songs.

The novice appears suddenly and escapes three times. Then all, Seal Society members and *quē'qutsa*, join hands and form a line. One man takes off his clothes and goes before them. He is called "the bait of the tribe." As soon as the *hamatsa* sees him, he rushes up to him, seizes his arm, and bites it. Then the people catch the *hamatsa* and lead him toward the ceremonial house, singing the new songs "meant to tame him" (1897:527-28). When the captors all arrive at the house, they find the family of the *hamatsa* dressed in ceremonial costumes on its step. Family members bring boards for the captors of the *hamatsa* to beat on, and the captors then sing, "Woe! you are making your parents poor, *naualak!*" (p. 528). All the people except the *hamatsa* dancer and his assistants then enter the house.

The preceding sections of the taming ceremony point up the parallelisms between the capture of an animal and the capture of a dancer. Both captures involve the use of prayers expressing the relationship of hunter and hunted, which "tame" the quarry enough that he will be willing to be caught. The people first set up a relationship of similarity between themselves and the *hamatsa* by putting on the hemlock head and neck rings, which symbolize the wildness of the *hamatsa* (see p. 528). In doing so, they also reaffirm the idea that all men carry within them the wildness the *hamatsa* possesses in greater abundance. Once they have done this, the people are able to affect their relationship with the *hamatsa* by linking together, an expression of cooperation not only because their hands are linked, but because with their hands linked they form a net within which the *hamatsa* can be caught. This human net will snare the *hamatsa* as the cedar-twine nets snare fish, and as the womb snares the souls of children.

At first the net is composed only of people who are not possessed by spirits, but they fail to catch the *hamatsa*. Only when possessed and unpossessed join hands can their net succeed, and then only when they perform the first symbolic sacrifice of the ceremony, the presentation of a human being whose flesh will feed the uncontrolled hunger of the dancer. The *hamatsa*'s hunger is so great that he fails to see the net in his rush to get food. Thus by first proclaiming their own wildness, the people are able to make the *hamatsa* wild enough to lose his fear of them (as an animal may be tempted to recklessness and frenzy and then trapped) and wild enough that he fails to see the trap of sacred, cooperative power they set up.

The appearance of the *hamatsa*'s relatives at the door of their house dressed in their regalia is a statement of their willingness to assume the burdens incumbent upon them, that is, to spend their wealth in the proper performance of the rituals and to follow the practices the spirits have required of them. The giving of the boards is a metaphor for the dissolution of a house, for when a community moves, the boards of a house are taken down and carted off. The *hamatsa*, like all children, is dispossessing his parents of their house, "making them poor." One may cry, "Woe," as one does in mourning for a dead person, because one is essentially mourning the symbolic deaths of the *hamatsa*'s family, yet at the same time these deaths are necessary if *naualak*, a word used to denote supernatural power and treasure, is to be brought to the world of humans. Thus, the return to the house is a critical transitional moment in *hamatsa* ritual. It is the moment when the members of Kwakiutl society formally announce for the first time their willingness to perform the rituals that go along with the hunting, capture, and "killing" of a being in order to obtain the supernatural benefits.

The relationship of pregnancy and hunting is reaffirmed in the combination of the two sets of symbols used in this part of the ceremony: a hunter must first capture the soul that will become the child; and the parents must evidence their willingness to perform and then must perform the rituals that transform that animal soul into a human one.

The ceremony continues as the *hamatsa*'s female helper tries to lure the *hamatsa* into the house (p. 528). She dances naked before him, but he does not respond. The symbolism is obvious: women are not alluring to a spirit. He cannot be tempted by sexuality, even if the sexuality is that most powerful of sexual enticements, incestuous desire (the helper is the *hamatsa*'s kinswoman, with whom intercourse and marriage are taboo). The message is clear: hunger is the only means by which a spirit being can be enticed and captured.

The people then raise the two sacred devices of the *hamatsa* dance, the cannibal pole and the screen that covers the sacred room at the back of the house. Both involve a great deal of oral symbolism. The cannibal pole consists of a vertical series of faces with wide mouths upon which the *hamatsa* climbs between roof and floor, that is, between heaven and earth. (See Andrews, 1960:52-53 for a picture.) In climbing the pole, the *hamatsa* goes through the mouths in such a way that he is symbolically passing through a series of transformations, a series of swallowings and vomitings forth. The screen is often designed as a face, the mouth of which forms the opening to the inner room (Boas, 1897:plate 29). Sometimes, the image of the mouth is presented as a genital orifice by making the opening of the screen occur as a mouth but at the location of the genitals, a substitution that is common in Kwakiutl art (cf. Fowler, 1972:125; Boas, 1897:377).

Once these devices have been raised, and the scene set for the series of transformations that the *hamatsa* must go through, the *hamatsa* is no longer reluctant to enter the house. He enters, going counterclockwise to the rear of the house, climbs the pole to the roof, runs around it once, returns and rushes over to a man, biting the man's arm and pulling the man once around the fire while his arm is still in the *hamatsa*'s mouth. This is repeated four times, during which time the people again try to calm the *hamatsa* with their new songs. They are unsuccessful, for the *hamatsa* dances as wildly as ever, out of his senses. He enters the sacred room, at which time the people remove their hemlock paraphernalia and burn it, an act called "smoking the wildness of Man Eater" (Boas, 1897:528). By burning the branches, they both remove the wildness from themselves and send it back to the world of the spirits from whence, before Transformer, it originally came.

With the wildness gone, they now sit down according to the strict rules of the ceremonial (Boas, 1967:229), and the distribution of property—the presentation and exchange of souls the man and his numaym have captured, which constitutes their wealth—begins.

As noted earlier, the winter ceremonials often juxtapose images of wildness with images of control. Such a juxtaposition occurs in that portion of the ritual just summarized. Here the *hamatsa*'s wildness contrasts with the orderly distribution of wealth that follows, his frenzied motion with the static seating of the guests, his uncontrollable passion for taking in food with the numaym's carefully regulated desire to give it away.

Another aspect of Kwakiutl symbolization is at work here. As we saw in the first chapter, transformation is equivalent to the action of placing material into, or removing it from, a box. Since the preceding ritual involves a number of acts of traveling into and out of boxes, we can conclude that these motions are not arbitrary, but indicate transformations. The *hamatsa* dancer first leaves the greater universe and enters the house; four times he leaves it, taking with him the flesh of four men to the spirit world, where he vomits it up. These are pledges that stand as an earnest payment to the spirits who will claim them upon the death of each of the four men. The *hamatsa*'s taking of the men around the fire symbolizes the burning, and thus the sending upwards, of their flesh; but the *hamatsa* still acts as messenger to the spirits. The *hamatsa*'s retirement into the sacred room counteracts his movement from the house to the outside, larger box; here he goes into a smaller box, where he will remain in storage until the next time he is called forth to perform his ritual responsibilities. The removal of coppers and bracelets from their storage boxes to the larger box of the house and then to the even larger box of the village balances the diminishing of the *hamatsa*'s universe. As he is tamed, as hunger is contained, wealth emerges. The gift of flesh to the spirits is reciprocated with the gift of wealth to men.

The eating, and subsequent regurgitation, of human flesh presents a critical issue in an analysis of the meaning of the *hamatsa* rites. In Western thought, vomit is a disgusting substance of filth, and Western scholars have brought this ethnocentric conception to their interpretations of the *hamatsa*'s actions. For example, Benedict (1934:178) sees the vomiting as a rejection, a renunciation of cannibalism, while Drucker and Heizer (1967:32, 87) explain away the vomiting as merely another indication, along with the *hamatsa*'s frequent sequestering in the sacred room and his payment of small gifts to the people he has bitten, of the overall staginess and fakery of the *hamatsa* ceremony.

For the Kwakiutl, vomit is not a substance of filth. Vomit is to a culture with oral metaphors what semen is to a culture with sexual metaphors: an important category of material existence, a symbol of undifferentiated matter with no identifying features and a total potential for becoming. All the power of vomit is potential, not realized. Vomit is the first stage of causality, the state of existence that precedes order and purpose. All things about to begin the process of becoming—fetuses, corpses, the universe before Transformer changed it—are symbolized by vomit. The act of vomiting is not an act of rejection but a positive act of creation, a necessary step in the process of transformation.

Vomit is the transformed identity of that most precious of spirit gifts—food. All food, even though it may not be regurgitated, becomes vomit at one stage in the digestive process. Food and vomit are complementary aspects of a single substance: the bodies of animals transformed into, respectively, cultural and spiritual forms. Vomit is thus the symbol of transformed substance; and the cycle of ingestion, digestion, and regurgitation is a metaphor for the cycle of death, metempsychosis, and rebirth.

The act of creating vomit from food is an important part of the *hamatsa* ritual. After entering the house and eating flesh bitten or cut from the arms of living people, the *hamatsa* enters the sacred room in the rear of the house. There he takes emetics to ensure that he regurgitates every bit of the flesh he has swallowed. The *hamatsa*'s eating of human flesh symbolizes the unity of the tribe and its role in the cycle of reincarnation. Each of the people the *hamatsa* has bitten has given a piece of his flesh so that the *hamatsa*, who has received from Man Eater the knowledge of the proper way to devour men, can transform that flesh into a creative substance. Each bitten person thus gives to the *hamatsa* a partial, token, payment—an earnest, or perhaps an interest payment—on the real debt he owes to the spirits: his own body. The *hamatsa* must completely regurgitate the flesh so that the earnests with which he has been entrusted can be paid in full to Man Eater.

In the payment of flesh to Man Eater, as in any repayment of debts in Kwakiutl culture, there is a careful accounting of who has given and how much they have given. The *hamatsa*'s assistants keep a careful record of who was bitten by the *hamatsa*, and the *hamatsa* gives return payments to these people. Since the *hamatsa* is intermediary between the spirits and humans, these payments can be seen as earnests on the part of the spirits who thereby reaffirm their reciprocal responsibilities towards mankind. Just as in the Kula exchange, where large, important valuables are exchanged only rarely but partnerships are kept active by the frequent exchange of small gifts, so in the *hamatsa* ritual the large gifts, exchanged only once in a lifetime, are pledged and repledged dozens of times, verified and reaffirmed by the gifts of small amounts in kind. Only one of the many agents of Man Eater, the *hamatsa*, through his feedings, collects these small pledges and thereby reaffirms man's ultimate destiny.

It is completely consonant with the symbolism of the house and the sacred room that the *hamatsa* should retire to the sacred room in order to regurgitate the flesh he has eaten, for the room forms the special spirit abode within the universe of the house. It is the womb from which the spirits emerge, the mouth from which new life comes, the entrance to the world of creation. It is entirely appropriate that the digestion of the food the *hamatsa* has eaten in the larger world of the house should take place in a room that is analogous to the hidden transforming parts of the body. *That room is the stomach where the human flesh is turned into the vomit* from which the spirits and humans will later be born. Such symbolism is reinforced by the painting of the entranceway of that room, which emphasizes the mouth/anus/vagina character of the passageway (see Boas, 1897:plate 29). The sacred room forms the rest of a large box/body, the front side of which is the face. While in that room, the *hamatsa* is both sacred treasure kept in a box and the food of that box to be digested, transformed, and reborn. From this room *hamatsas* emerge as from the mouth vomit spews forth or from the vagina babies emerge.

The distribution of property is an essential part of the winter ceremonial, but its purpose has often been misinterpreted as being competitive. Since the Kwakiutl associate both marriage and the giving of property with war, it is easy for us to see Kwakiutl marriage and property exchange as warlike. However, through some ethnocentric prejudices we hold, we fall into ethnographic error here. In our case, marriage is seen as a war between the sexes and business as war between competitors. Because in our society these activities carry with them the aspect of hostility, we assume that it is this hostility about which the Kwakiutl draw their analogies between war, marriage, and exchange. In actuality, these three acts are war because all three are part of the same system of creating, destroying, and distributing souls, not merely the acting out of interpersonal hostilities or competition. It is thus appropriate that the final payment of the marriage exchanges should take place at a winter ceremonial, that the winter ceremonial should be performed by dancers with warrior status and power, and that the primary actions—the Cannibal Society dances and the exchange of coppers—should be part of both marriage payments and winter ceremonial rites, and should require or be brought about by death, for in the last analysis marriage, war, property distribution, and ceremonial dancing are all four aspects of a single creative act, the act of renewing life.

Furthermore, an examination of the symbolism of coppers should serve to prove that it is not property as property that is being distributed here, but instead that the distribution of property sets up a concomitant distribution of souls. As in all Kwakiutl rituals within a sacred context, peoples' motions impel similar motions by the spirits. People make the pathways that spirit action follows; they "make the traveling easy."

Coppers are metaphors of individual beings, which is immediately obvious from the fact that they are named. But the ways in which coppers are held and destroyed are also metaphors of their life history. There are two ways of holding coppers: in both cases they are held in front of the body, but in one case they are held obliquely to the axis of the backbone (Boas, 1895: plate 6) and in the other they are held parallel to that axis (Keithahn, 1963:46, 78, 126, 145). The analogy between copper and human is furthered by the fact that many figures are shown clutching humans in the same position as coppers (Keithahn, 1963:160). In the case where the axis of the copper is parallel to that of the holder's spine we can see a number of substitutions occurring. First, the copper is itself an entire being, for it has a definite head and backbone (and in some instances, the ribs are shown descending from the backbone, as in Hawthorn, 1967:161, fig. 155 and 156). Yet when held in front of the human body, the face of the copper is at the level of the human's chest, and thus it becomes the analogue of the human's soul; the crossbar of the copper is at the level of the human's belt, which is associated with his power, as we have seen in the Transformer myth; and the vertical axis of the T-bar is parallel to the penis of the holder, the two side pieces being parallel to his legs. The copper, in front of the body, becomes the body, and thus the copper and the human become one. The human becomes the box over which the copper is placed like a lid. The human becomes a costume and mask the copper is wearing like a skin. The human face is like a frontlet worn above the head of the copper-being. The copper-soul animates the human body. Thus, the man who sells a copper is, in a way, also selling his identity.

The destruction of a copper, in keeping with its human identity, mimics the destruction of the human body: the first piece removed is the head, after which the body is cut up. While it is honorable to sell a copper without breaking it up (killing it), this is an incomplete act—a transfer of identity, not a rebirth. The destruction of the copper through burning or throwing it into the sea is more admirable, because this enables it to return to other realms, where the souls it represents will replenish the numbers of the dwellers of that realm. However, killing the copper by dismembering it is most honorable. The act of buying back the pieces of the copper for more than they were originally worth increases the number of souls the copper represents. The act of riveting the pieces together again reincarnates the copper as a living being. In this instance, since the pieces of the copper all remain in the world of humans, all the souls it contains also remain in the world of humans. But even more important is the fact that the man who buys a copper's pieces and reassembles them thereby reaffirms his ever-growing commitment to the maintenance of the world order, and asserts his ability to create life, for he gives to the copper the same life that the copper will give to the beings to which it is finally sent.

One of the most important aspects of the sale of coppers and the closing of the marriage debt is the giving of box lids by the father-in-law to his son-in-law. These might seem to us to be insignificant and slightly miserly—after all, why not give an entire box? Yet the lids of boxes are the most crucial part. They are the souls, whereas the sides are equivalent to skins.

We can best see this analogy between the lid of a box and the soul of an individual if we look at a Chilkat blanket (figure 2), a type of Tlingit ceremonial robe that, because it so eloquently and concisely expresses the general tenets of Northwest Coast belief, was adopted by tribes other than the Tlingit. The Chilkat blanket has several variants, but in its most typical form it shows a three-dimensional box in two-dimensional representation. The structure of a Chilkat blanket depicts a box as if seen from above, with the joins on the bottom removed and the other panels folded upward into the same plane as the lid. In figure 2, the face of the crest animal is depicted in section a, which is equivalent to the front panel of the box; the two flanks of the animal are shown on the two lateral sections of the blanket (section d) as they would be on a box; and the hindquarters of the animal are shown on the rear panel of the box (section c). These sections of the blanket are clearly demarcated by lines indicating the edges of the boards of the box. Section b, usually known as a humanoid face, is the representation of the lid of the box. And since the lid of a box is the means of access to the box, the means of revealing the box's contents, section b also shows a picture of the contents of the body of the animal depicted—that is, its soul, shown in its proper location within the body cavity. Some blankets also show the soul as it would be seen from the side of the box, in profile or half-face (Hawthorn, 1967: fig. 183-85). Thus, we can see that the Chilkat blanket graphically demonstrates the identification of the lid of a box with the soul of that box (see also Boas, 1897:421).

The Chilkat blanket expresses cogently another important tenet of Northwest Coast belief—that an individual possesses separate human, animal, and spirit identities, all related analogically. Since humans are animals that have shed their skins, a person wearing a Chilkat blanket is wearing his discarded animal skin on his back, and the image on the blanket denotes his own alternate animal identity. In addition, since animal identity is composed of a human soul contained within an animal skin, the image of the crest animal depicts the human soul in its proper location within the animal's body. Yet since a human soul is also an owl soul, the soul of the animal is depicted simultaneously in its human and avian forms. For example, in figure 2 the avian form of the soul—with the soul face shown above the body of a bird standing upright and with its wings outstretched—is shown in sections a and b (see figure 2b). When these blankets are worn at ceremonies, the various components of identity are united analogically by placing the soul face of the blanket over that spot on the upper back under which the wearer's soul resides, the blanket thus acting as a symbolic lid for the box of the human body.

Since boxes must be used to contain sacred paraphernalia, and since the ownership of those contents passes totally to the son-in-law with the final marriage payments, the father-in-law must also pass along the boxes to hold the paraphernalia. However, it would be incorrect to pass along entire boxes, for this would not indicate a succession, a cycle of reincarnation. Instead, the father-in-law "kills" his boxes by removing their souls, destroys their empty "skins," preserves the lids (souls) as is necessary, and then passes them on to his heir, who then has the souls "reborn" in newly carved boxes. Since the soul of the two boxes is the same, the result is that the old box is reincarnated in a new body. The proper inheritance acts have thus been performed, mimicking the same process that occurs when a person dies and has to be reborn. Therefore, it is entirely appropriate that a man pass on only the lids of boxes to his successor.

The passing on of wealth by a still active person to an heir seems an alien act to our materialistic minds. For example, it seems odd that, in Kwakiutl myths, the powerbeings are readily convinced to give their powers to the man who comes to their home. Indeed, in some myths, the beings offer or give powers to the person before they are asked. It would be incorrect, however, to compare the willingness to give with what we see in our own folktales, where various potent figures may offer lesser powers to their conqueror in hopes of either being able to escape or preventing them from asking for their really important powers. Yet, in Kwakiutl life, the spirits are faced with a dilemma that Rumpelstiltskin is not: they need to have human beings perform their rituals for them, to keep their sacred objects, to free their souls for rebirth. The powerbeings are as dependent on humans as the humans are on them. Thus, when a human appears at the home of a powerbeing, he is automatically proving that he wishes to set up a ritual relationship with that powerbeing, that he was moral and strong enough to reach the world of the powerbeing, and thus that he is willing and able to be the human counterpart of the powerbeing's existence. Thus, it is natural to expect that in Kwakiutl myth the powerbeings should pass power readily to their human counterparts. They have been shown, as Yahweh was shown by Abraham's willingness to sacrifice Isaac, that the covenant they create will be upheld, no matter what the cost. In fact, in some ways the extravagance of the potlatch is a direct proof that humans will be willing to impoverish themselves totally if such a cost should be necessary for the maintenance of their covenant with the spirits. The man who passes his wealth on to his heir thus acts as do the spirits when they give their power to men—they give willingly,

Figure 2. This drawing of a Chilkat blanket shows a mythical animal, probably one called the Sea Bear. The separate components of the blanket are seen in figure 2a. The two panels constituting the avian soul of the being (see text) are seen in figure 2b. For clarity, the design has been simplified slightly from that of the original.

Figure 2.

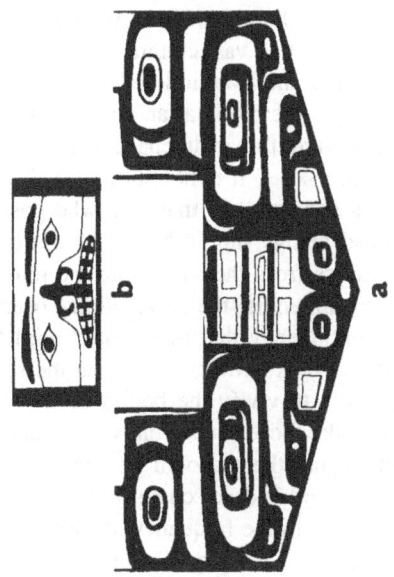

c

d

a

b

d

Figure 2a.

Figure 2b.

with the understanding that the wealth and its power will be used correctly for the benefit of all.

We can better understand the reactions of the Kwakiutl to historic forces if we keep this last idea—the willingness to distribute property for the benefit of others—in mind. Two important aspects of Kwakiutl culture, central to the motivating forces of their history, remain almost totally unexplored in the literature. The first is that the Kwakiutl suffered a loss of almost 90 percent of their population during a very brief period (1830-1900). The ramifications of this population decline were so vast that death became the primary subject of interest, the primary focus of their rituals, the primary condition of their existence. Second, they believed in reincarnation, in a system of metempsychosis, in the eternal nature of existence. Boas barely mentions the topic, and I can think of no major work of Kwakiutl ethnography that explores Kwakiutl ideas of reincarnation. Yet the Kwakiutl, like other peoples in this vast culture area, believed in reincarnation. When we remember that the Kwakiutl believed in metempsychosis and reincarnation, that they were dying at an alarming rate, and that their rituals were oriented toward the maintenance of population through the distribution of souls and skins, it is not surprising that there should be an increased potlatching activity, and that men who possessed boxes filled with the relics of dead beings should be all the more ready and determined to release those relics from their care into the reincarnation system. For centuries, perhaps millennia, the Kwakiutl had been storing souls and skins against the contingency that they would need them. It was the responsibility of righteous men, who believed that the souls of the dying Kwakiutl were being taken to vivify the bodies of an ever increasing number of white men, to take those souls from storage and to be extravagant in their distribution so that there should be enough to reincarnate all those Kwakiutl who had died and not come back to life.

Thus, the well-documented increase in the frequency and extravagance of potlatches at the end of the nineteenth century (Codere, 1950) can be attributed to the population decline rather than to the end of warfare. It is not surprising that a ritual whose purpose is to maintain the balance of human souls in the world should increase in importance at a time when the balance of human souls has gone completely awry. If we can say that the Kwakiutl did "fight with property," that fight was not against other Kwakiutl but against the invasion of white men who were taking a disproportionate number of the world's supply of souls.

We return now to the *hamatsa* ceremony (Boas, 1897:529ff.). On the evening of the third day, two sets of four messengers call the people to come to the ceremonial house. Each messenger is given a button blanket. The first messengers say: "Shamans [*pēpaxalai*, "powerful ones" (p. 529)]. We will pacify this supernatural one. We will soften [Tamer of *hamatsa*'s Mouth] by means of our songs." After people have had time to prepare, the second set of messengers gives the signal for everyone to come at once to the house: "The fire is going out. We have no fuel. Come quick, shamans" (p. 529). The imagery here reasserts the idea of the Kwakiutl as the smoke-makers of the world, the people who burn their wealth to supply the spirits.

The pacification of the *hamatsa* begins with all the women dancing (p. 530). Then come four of the greatest of the power dancers: a *hamshamtses*, or female cannibal (see Boas, 1897:463ff.); *hai'alikima*, a spirit associated with the ferocity of war whose dance involves suspension from the wall or roof by ropes, which are threaded through the dancer's skin in a manner reminiscent of that of the Plains Indian Sun Dance (Boas, 1897:495-98); the *to'xuit*, a female spirit associated with *sisiutl*, whose dance involves either the killing of a *sisiutl* or a scene in which the dancer is killed and reborn; and the *ki'nqalalala*, the *hamatsa*'s female assistant. All are associated with blood and war. They blacken their faces—an act which resembles putting on a mask but which does not, as does a mask, change the identity of the dancer—put eagle down on their heads so that power may be present in the room (p. 530), and dance. The *hamatsa* is drawn by the ritual power and enters the room, but only for a single circuit of the fire before he returns to the inner room. The *hamatsa*'s departure is attributed to the breaking of a ritual taboo, and a messenger is sent to the sacred room, returning later to say that there was not enough eagle down in the room and that the people were too noisy. Dishes of eagle down are brought out, thus expressing the metaphor of food as power, for both are brought out in dishes.

When the down has been spread throughout the room, the *hamatsa* again appears, but retreats as before to the inner room after a single circuit. The messengers go to him and learn that the four dancers did not sing their secret songs. The four dancers are given four button blankets, which make them equivalent to the messengers at the start of the ceremony, and they then enter the sacred room. When they return to the room, it is with the *hamatsa*, as earlier the messengers had returned with the rest of the people. The *hamatsa*, dressed only in hemlock, bites two of them as he dances around the house. He returns to his room, is again brought out, and bites the other two. Now the four dancers block the entrance to the room so the *hamatsa* cannot escape again.

The people begin singing their taming songs. After the first one, the spirits associated with Man Eater appear. The *hamatsa* dances once and reenters the sacred room; Raven of Man Eater immediately appears and dances. The Raven disappears; the *hamatsa*, now entirely naked, briefly returns and then goes back to the sacred room, at which point Man Eater himself appears. When Man Eater goes into the sacred room, the *hamatsa* reappears, now dressed in cedar bark clothing and a bearskin. The *hamatsa* has acted as a messenger to Raven of Man Eater and Man Eater himself, and he has been given a new set of clothes symbolizing the ritual of this world, not the wildness of the other. The bearskin cloak he wears is the only outward symbol of his violent desires. A new mat is spread for the *hamatsa* to sit on, thereby providing him with space in this world. More taming songs are sung.

A man is called forward to tame the *hamatsa* using the new method (p. 531). He asks for four pieces of the white inner bark of the cedar. He puts "the secret of the winter dance" in them by crying "hoip, hoip" (p. 531) and then ties each to a long pole. The *hamatsa*'s helper, repeating the words "hoip, hoip," removes the *hamatsa*'s clothing. The man gives a signal, the people begin drumming, and the man puts one end of the cedar bark into the fire. He passes the burning bark over the head of the *hamatsa*. The *hamatsa* begins to dance, constantly squatting and turning. The sequence is repeated four times. The four dancers lift the *hamatsa* and carry him into the sacred room. A further distribution of wealth takes place.

It is at this point that the real taming of the *hamatsa* begins. The symbolism of the previous dance is relatively clear. At first the *hamatsa* is not convinced that the people are really willing to tame him, to perform the rituals correctly, but they show that they are. The *hamatsa* then allows himself to be brought back, his change in clothing symbolizing the changing in character that he will go through. He abstracts an earnest of flesh from each of the four dancers who bring him. With these four morsels he dances into the sacred room and calls forth first the Raven of Man Eater—the symbol of death, the messenger of Man Eater—and then the spirit-chief himself, Man Eater, the lord of death. Their acceptance of the earnest is thus confirmed. They are willing to give up their spirit-helper, the *hamatsa*, because in return for him they will receive the bodies of the four dancers whose flesh they have just been given. Man Eater has returned the *hamatsa*'s soul to men, an act symbolized by the *hamatsa*'s wearing of cedar bark. From this point on, no more spirits appear, and the taming of the *hamatsa* involves humankind alone.

The name of the second section of the previous ceremony, *nawa'qamā* (p. 532), gives us a better clue to its meaning. Although Boas does not seem to translate this term, Curtis, who spells it "nanakawalihl," does (1915:158). He points out that:

> The word refers to the middle portion of the house, the significance lying in the fact that this dancer in his song uses alternately the words of a hamshamtsus and those of a haiyalikyilahl, being thus midway between the two.

At this point, the *hamatsa* is himself halfway between the world of spirits and the world of humans. Although he is no longer quite in the world of spirits, having been released by Man Eater, he is not yet tamed and transformed into a moral human being. However, Curtis overlooks part of the meaning of the name, in that the image of the middle of the house is one in which the identity of the house changes. The house previously had been the entire human world; the sacred room at its side had represented that part of the world where the spirits reside. Now, however, the house represents the immediate environment of the tribe, and the room is part of that environment. When he enters that room, the *hamatsa* no longer travels to the spirit world, but to a part of the human world. Therefore, he can at all times be said to be in the house.

Thus, the means of taming the *hamatsa* now change. The power of ritual, of morality, of the winter ceremonials is emphasized. The inner bark of the cedar, white and soft like eagle down but from this world, not that of the spirits, is used as a pathway for the introduction of the power of the winter ceremonial. The bark acts like a box, the secret (i.e., the knowledge) of the ceremony is placed within it, and then it is burned, as all wealth is burned. The smoke fills the room until everything is imbued with the power of righteousness and of ceremonial performance, i.e., right thinking and right action. The *hamatsa* is covered with the smoke of the burning cedar bark just as all babies are cleansed with cedar bark and with the smoke of its burning.

As a ceremony about coming into being, the *hamatsa* ritual shares a common metaphorical structure with other Kwakiutl ceremonies—such as those surrounding the birth of a child or the maturing of a girl at puberty—about coming into being. The birth-oriented symbolism of the *hamatsa* ceremony is that of an initiation rite, of a symbolic rebirth.

In a number of ways, the taming of the *hamatsa* mirrors the socialization of a child: all children come from the spirit world to which Man Eater had taken them; all children come into the world naked, as does the *hamatsa* (since his clothes are removed); all children have a female assistant, their mother, who has to accept them, feed them, and help them through the ritual process of becoming socialized; all children dance in the womb, kicking and turning like a *hamatsa*; all children are hungry and cannot be denied food; all children threaten to devour their parents' wealth and eventually their identities; all children are ignorant of morality and proper action, as is the *hamatsa*; and finally, all children are cannibals, not only because they will devour the wealth of their parents, but because they actually live off the flesh of their mothers while in the womb. Thus in Kwakiutl thought all humans are cannibals.

Every human must go through the same taming process as the *hamatsa* dancer, for every human carries within him vestiges of his previous identity as an animal. Each comes into the world directly from the world of animals. A number of myths (such as the Bear Mother myths of the Haida, captured so vividly in argillite sculptures) encapsulate this idea. However, in the last analysis all children can be said to come from beast-fathers, to retain within themselves the qualities of the animal their soul last inhabited, and to need restraining as a human being. Kwakiutl child-rearing techniques attempt to "tame" the child, to restrict its movements, to extinguish its bestial hunger. Through swaddling, denial of food, ritual fasting, magical charms, songs, lullabies, and other actions, parents transform their child from a cannibal into a moral human being.

The *hamatsa* ceremony recapitulates the entire process of birth. The *hamatsa* is as much in a state of preexistence as is the soul of an unborn child. In their spirit forms, both the *hamatsa* and the soul wander hungry, carrying with them their essential energy and power encapsulated in a desire for food. The *hamatsa* enters the house from the roof as the soul of a baby enters the human world from its spirit home. Both are essentially destructive beings, requiring human flesh to achieve substantiality. Both require that humans should first reaffirm their willingness to die so that the cycle of reincarnation can be maintained before they will permit themselves to be captured.

The actions by which the *hamatsa* is captured and tamed recapitulate the rituals by which a soul is captured, tamed, and reborn. Once humans have reaffirmed their willingness to allow this spirit to live among them, the *hamatsa* retires to the sacred room and vomits up the transformed flesh, an act symbolic of his transformation from a destructive to a creative being. The *hamatsa*'s eating of the flesh of a mummy symbolizes the soul's gathering of the ancestral substance necessary to form its new body. During all this time, the members of the group sing their songs designed to tame the *hamatsa*, to bring him within their moral universe, just as pregnant women sing lullabies and perform rituals so that the souls of their unborn babies may be tamed. The *hamatsa* is finally tamed when he is made to inhale the smoke of a burning blood soaked menstrual napkin, the transformed substance of the womb. At this point, the *hamatsa* has undergone the entire birth process and begins to act like a newborn baby—unable to walk, speak, feed itself, and so forth.

Several aspects of the nature of souls are symbolized in the ways in which the audience reacts to the *hamatsa* dancer. In his original spirit form he is essentially dangerous and destructive, as is any soul seeking to be reborn, for since birth also requires a death, so the *hamatsa* may bring about death in his attempt to find a body to inhabit. The tribe members sing their sacred songs, attempting to use the social power they possess to tame him, but the songs have no effect; the destiny of the soul is to be reborn, and songs will not keep it from hungering for that destiny.

The *hamatsa* is opposed by the forces of pure energy and amoral hunger, the Bear and Fool dancers. These beings represent hunger in its primal form, both as it existed in premoral times (Fools) and as it exists today (Bears). Even this power is insufficient against the force of the soul's destiny. Finally, the soul is tamed by the one power that is greater than its own, the power mothers have because they are willing to give up the very flesh of their own bodies that they may bear children. This motherly sacrifice is the act that satisfies the soul's desire for food while simultaneously placing it in a moral universe governed by human willingness to sacrifice.

The creative purpose of the *hamatsa* dance is restated and reinforced by the Kwakiutl in the songs that precede it; for example:

The Cannibal spirit made me a winter dancer.
The Cannibal spirit made me pure.
I do not destroy life, I am the life maker.
(Boas, 1966:253)

The ceremony continues (Boas, 1897:532ff.). All the profane people must leave the house and the house is closed up. The purification of the *hamatsa* begins. This section of the ceremony involves four dancers called: the washer, the rubber, the tongsmaker, and the timebeater. All motions are performed four times. The tongsmaker splits a plank off the board the timebeater is using for a drum and carves some tongs from it; he also cuts a small piece of white cedar bark, which he gives to the rubber. The rubber takes a fresh mat and the cedar bark and makes a ringed figure representing a human being (1897:533). During all this time they do not sing songs. They say only the sacred word of the winter ceremonial, "hoip."

The next part of the ritual involves the handling of the cedar bark human figure. It becomes an analogue of the *hamatsa*, and the actions performed upon it cause the first part of the *hamatsa*'s taming, just as all human actions in a ritual context cause spirit action.

The rubber picks the figure up with the tongs and carries it to the east side of the house, where he hangs it on the wall. He takes four stones, which he heats in the fire, a new dish, and a bucket of water. He pours the water into the dish, at which point the *hamatsa* and his helper, both naked, come out from the sacred room. Before they sit down on a new mat next to the dish, the helper dances around the fire four times, the *hamatsa* following her and repeating her every move (1897:534). This symbolizes the journey of *hamatsa* from the spirit world; the helper leads him, as Orpheus led Eurydice, back to the world of humans. The path she makes is the path he must follow. The place, the mat, set for him is where he must sit (as Only-One sat in the house made for him by Transformer). The rubber then takes the cedar bark figure off the tongs, puts it on a short stick, and carries it around the fire. The stick that held the tongs open is struck with a baton, and its trajectory acts as an omen about the life of the *hamatsa*: if it flies out the door, he will live a long time. The symbolism here is a bit complicated. The stick acts as a soul catcher, like a shaman's soul catcher. With it the figure is symbolically carried to the house; if the stick holding the tongs open does not fly out of the house, the tongs can be opened again, and the *hamatsa*'s soul can easily be recaught; but if the stick flies out of the house, the tongs remain closed and useless, and thus the *hamatsa*'s soul will remain in the human world for a long time.

With the figure now on the stick and no longer in the soul catcher, the *hamatsa* can no longer be taken back to the land of the spirits. He is now firmly lodged in the world of humans.

The stones are placed in the water, heating it. Then the washer dances around the fire and takes down the figure from the wall where it was hanging. He dances, with the figure in his hands, around the fire, stopping near the *hamatsa*. The washer's hands tremble like Man Eater's (Boas, 1897:535), because he is now a man eater himself, having taken the body from its resting place on the wall. Indeed, he even carries it like a corpse.

The washer next takes the heated water from the bucket and washes the heads of the *hamatsa* and his helper. This act ceremonially cleanses the two dancers. Then the rubber takes the figure, dances with it, and places it around the neck of the *hamatsa* dancer. At this point the shared identity of figure and *hamatsa* is made obvious. Thus, the rituals performed upon the figure are transferred to the *hamatsa*. The figure acts like a new skin, like a costume. It gives the *hamatsa* a new surface identity, a new persona. The figure is passed down the body of the *hamatsa* from head to feet, and then he steps out of it; the same is done with the *hamatsa*'s helper. The people sing the only song of this part of the ritual: "In olden times you went all around the world with the supernatural being" (Boas, 1897:535; 724). This song emphasizes the fact that the *hamatsa* once went with the supernatural being, but no longer does, and so with it the close relationship of *hamatsa* and Man Eater is severed.

The rubber then takes the ring outside the house and burns it; inside the house he burns the tongs. The *hamatsa* leaves the house and runs around the village. The people who had not been present during this last part of the ceremony now reenter. There is a property distribution of small food-preparation items. The four dancers then announce a large feast, the last one of the winter ceremonials.

The *hamatsa*'s mistakes are tallied up, the dancers and singers are paid, and the people who had been bitten receive compensation. All these presents must be returned with interest the next year (Boas, 1897:536).

The *hamatsa* still runs about biting people; after the fourth day, the final ceremony takes place. Only a few dancers are allowed in the house, which is totally closed. The doors are nailed shut; even the holes in the wall are filled. Each dancer sings his song and makes his peculiar cry. The *hamatsa* initiate, excited, dances around the fire four times, at which point the cannibal pole and the screen of the sacred room are pulled down and burned. For four days they all remain in the house singing the initiate's power songs. On the fourth day they dress in red cedar bark, cover their heads with feathers, and blacken their faces, all symbols of ritual performance. The *hamatsa* has been tamed. He is then given his first meal since his return from the bush after a period of no less than eight days has transpired. The entire group goes to another house, where they all eat a meal. The last symbol of the *hamatsa*'s taming has occurred—he can now eat a meal in an ordinary human house.

The sacred paraphernalia is then collected and, after someone pledges to give the next year's winter ceremonials, it is thrown into the fire and burned. The batons for beating time are also burned, and the winter ceremonials come to an end (Boas, 1897:537).

The *hamatsa* must observe many taboos and perform a large number of rituals after his taming ceremony (Boas, 1897:537-38). Most involve eating and defecation. The rituals of defecation (1897:537) are especially interesting, in that they show that every aspect of the *hamatsa*'s digestive process is now ritualized. For *hamatsas*, defecation is a social act rather than an individual one. All the *hamatsas* go out together and perform exactly the same motions. Other rituals limit the *hamatsa*'s ability to eat: he must sip water through a straw rather than place a cup to his lips; he must eat with a spoon, thus not getting too much into his mouth; he must show that he can control his hunger and thirst by going through the motions of picking up food and water four times before he actually eats or drinks. Like a baby, he eats from his own special food dish, with his own special spoon; he wears soiled cedar bark; he pretends to have forgotten all the ways of humans and "has to learn everything anew" (Boas, 1897:538); and he is always hungry.

Although the particular version of the *hamatsa* ceremonies we have just examined underscores the separation of the *hamatsa* from his spirit associates and his reintegration into human society, it is not the best account of the ceremony for the analysis of the symbolism of the *hamatsa* as fetus. The version Benedict chose (1934:177-81) is better suited. Benedict's account from page 177 to the first paragraph of page 180, seems to be an account of the very ceremony we have just studied. However, the description in paragraph two of page 181 differs greatly from that of the end of the ceremony we have just examined. That descriptive paragraph deserves our attention.

In this example the *hamatsa* is finally tamed when the menstrual blood of four women of high status is placed on a cedar bark menstrual napkin which is then set on fire. The burning napkin is passed in front of the *hamatsa*, the smoke surrounding his face. This symbol is an especially cogent statement of the *hamatsa* as fetus, because it is an offering to the *hamatsa* of the one food a woman gives to her children, her own flesh. Every human being enters the world nourished by the blood and flesh of his own mother. We might even ask where the menstrual blood of a woman goes once she becomes pregnant; obviously, it enters the body of the fetus, which is feeding on it. By taking menstrual blood, making it spiritual by burning it (and thus sending it to the spirits), and by using the sacred smoke, the Kwakiutl offer the last statement of their willingness to die for the benefit of the spirits. They had previously given their dead, represented in the winter ceremonials by the mummy fed to the *hamatsa* and by parts of their living bodies meant to act as pledges to the spirits for future gifts of their dead bodies. Now they pledge something even greater, the blood from their living bodies, the "water of life" itself.

The cycle is complete. A new Kwakiutl can come into the world because his fellow tribesmen have pledged to feed him and ultimately to replace him—to fill the hole left in the spirit world created by his birth into the human world. Man Eater need no longer keep his soul mates in his own world, in his own box. He can give them away; he can distribute them, secure in the knowledge that in the future they will be returned to him, and with interest.

Benedict (1934) emphasized the power the *hamatsa*'s wildness gives him. But an even more important point lies at the very foundations of Kwakiutl thought: hunger is power, but the knowledge of how to control hunger is an even greater power. The *hamatsa*'s hunger is fearsome; but it is the same hunger felt by every human, and thus every human has the power to learn how to control it. Ultimately the *hamatsa*, and the bestial ferocity he embodies, can be conquered. Morality, the force of controlled social action, the strength of ritual, can conquer even a Cannibal's hunger. In fact, ritual can totally alter the impetus of the Cannibal's hunger, changing it from a destructive act to an affirmation of self-control, an act of creative power. The winter ceremonials prove that no matter how terrible the power of hunger, no matter how many fearsome guises it assumes, no matter how many masks it wears, and no matter how many voices it speaks with, morality will be the ultimate victor. So long as humans have the knowledge to use food correctly, they need never fear hunger nor its awful accompaniment, death.

Ultimately, Kwakiutl ritual results in a fundamental change in the role of humans in the world, for at some ineffable point they discover that they need no longer kill for food, no longer kill because they are hungry.

Instead, a human kills because it is his responsibility to kill, his responsibility to eat, his responsibility to be the vehicle of rebirth for those beings, human and otherwise, with whom he has a covenant. At such a point, he may truthfully say:

I have the magical treasure
I have the supernatural power
I can return to life.
(Boas, 1897:373)

Wä, lawēSLa ǧwāł lāxēq.

The First Salmon Rites

THERE IS A sacral and ceremonial character to all Kwakiutl meals. However, because of the ways in which Boas dissected, recombined, and published his textual materials, it is often difficult to perceive the overall ritual process of Kwakiutl meals. The following texts present a recollated version of a series of texts relating the sequence of events of a single ceremonial meal—the First Salmon Rites for silver salmon.

The First Salmon Rites are ceremonies that take place in the spring, at the beginning of the secular season, and that involve the first four fish of each species caught that year by each individual fisherman. As the first meals of the season, they are the template, the metaphor, the archetype for all other meals. Because of the importance of these meals, the Kwakiutl are careful to delineate and perform correctly every step of the ritual procedure. Thus, these ceremonies provide the most complete and straightforward examples of the structure of food collection and preparation.

It should be remembered that a meal is only a spatially and temporally localized ceremony in the larger ceremonial cycle. Although the following texts detail an entire bounded ritual sequence, the First Salmon Rites are only the first step in the longer ceremonial process by which humans define their relationship to the animals upon whom they feed. Many other textual materials not included in this appendix—from the myths that tell of the silver salmon's sacrificing of its body to humans, to the songs that are sung during the meal and the winter ceremonials that deal with the acting out of the human/salmon relationship—are directly relevant to a complete depiction of the character of these rites and to their contextualization within the greater scheme of Kwakiutl ceremony.

The first silver-salmon of the season is caught by trolling It is cut in a ceremonial manner, head and tail being left attached to the backbone These are roasted and eaten at once. . . . The meat of the silver-salmon is boiled. (Boas, 1921 348)

The trolling hook is generally used for catching salmon. After the hook has been baited, the fisherman says to it, "Now go at it, go ahead, it has been put on well!" Then the hook is thrown in the water, and the fisherman continues to paddle. As soon as he has a bite, he says, "Hold fast, hold fast, salmon!"[1] and the line is hauled in slowly. While hauling in the fish, he says "Pfff!" in the same way as dogs are called. When the salmon comes in sight, it is struck with a short pole to the end of which a harpoon-point is attached. Then it is hauled in and struck on the head.[2] The salmon are placed in the canoe with head turned towards the bow. (Boas, 1909:485)

When the salmon-fisher gets home, and when he has caught many[3] salmon, he goes into the river house and immediately prays to his house to be good when he dries his salmon.[4] He only prays to it when he has many salmon. He does not pray when he does not get any salmon.

This is the prayer of the salmon-fisher, when he catches the first salmon with a hook: "Welcome, Swimmer. I thank you because I am still alive at this season when you come back to our good place; for the reason why you come is that we may play together with my fishing tackle, Swimmer. Now, go home and tell your friends that you had good luck on account of your coming here and that they shall come with their wealth bringer, that I may get some of your wealth, Swimmer; and also take away my sickness, friend, supernatural one, Swimmer." Thus he says, while he is praying.

This is only the prayer for the first salmon caught by trolling or the first one caught with the hook in the river. All the wise salmon-fishermen have different prayers, and there are salmon-fishermen who are not wise, who do not care about the salmon they have caught. The numayms are not the owners of the prayers of the salmon-fishermen, for the prayers belong to those who work on the salmon. (Boas, 1921:610)

When they go trolling for silver-salmon and when they first go out to sea, as soon as a man has caught four silver-salmon, his wife goes down to meet him when he arrives at the beach of his house. When she first sees what was caught by her husband, she prays to the silver-salmon. (Boas, 1921:610)

(Woman's prayer to dog salmon)[5] The woman says as she is praying: "O Super-

[1] This statement can be seen both as a direct causal act making the salmon stay on the hook and as a statement addressed to the salmon assuring it that if it will hold fast to the line, the fisherman will ensure the proper treatment of its body.

[2] Here Boas neglects to mention that it is struck on the head only once. In accounts of the rituals surrounding the catching of sockeye salmon, which follow the same pattern as that for silver, the texts very carefully note the fact that the fish is struck only once (see Boas, 1921:205-7).

[3] "Many" is equal to four or more in Kwakiutl counting.

[4] Since he is about to perform a consecrated act, he must ensure that the house's sacred state is activated. The phrase "to be good" means both "to be lucky" and "to be correct," both of which are associated with the presence of sacred power.

[5] Boas fails to include here the particular prayer said by the woman. However, those women's prayers he does list for other salmon are so similar to one another that we can assume that the prayer a woman makes to silver salmon would be similar to them. A woman's prayer to sockeye salmon can be found in Boas, 1930:206-7. I have chosen a woman's prayer to dog salmon (Boas, 1921:609) as an illustration.

natural-Ones! O, Swimmers! I thank you that you are willing to come to us. Don't let your coming be bad,[6] for you come to be food for us. Therefore, I beg you to protect me and the one who takes mercy on me,[7] that we may not die without cause, Swimmers!" Then the woman herself replies, "Yes," and goes up from the bank of the river. (Boas, 1921:609)

After she has prayed, she picks up with her fingers the four silver-salmon and goes with them and puts them down on the beach in front of the house. Then she takes her fishknife and cuts the four silver-salmon; the head and the tail are left on the backbone. Then she takes the roasting-tongs and puts them on the beach, where she is sitting. Then she takes what she is going to roast and puts the salmon-tail and the backbone between the roasting-tongs. Then she pushes it down, so that the ends of the tongs reach to the eyes of the salmon-head. After she has done so, she gathers the slime and throws it into the sea. (Boas, 1921:610-11)

As soon as they finish cutting up the speared salmon, the woman at once gathers the slime and everything that comes from the salmon, and puts it into a basket and pours it into the water at the mouth of the river; for it is said that the various kinds of salmon at once come to life when the intestines are put into the water at the mouths of the rivers, and therefore they do this; and they [usually] break off the intestines at the anal fin of the speared salmon but they cut off the intestines at the anal fin of salmon caught with a hook, for, if the intestines were broken off from those caught with a hook, then the fish-line of him who does so would always break. Therefore the woman takes care in breaking it off. (Boas, 1921:609-10)

As soon as she comes up from the beach, she picks up the roasting-tongs with the eyes in them, that had been put over the fire, for there are four of them, and she places them by the side of the fire of her house. Then she watches them until the skin of the head is blackened; and when it turns black, she takes it away and puts it over the fire. Then her husband at once invites his numaym to come and eat it, for he must take care not to keep it over night in the house; for the first people said, that, if the roasted eyes were kept over night in the house when they are first caught, then the silver-salmon would disappear from the sea. Therefore they do in this way. As soon as the guests come in, they sit down in the rear of the fire, on the mat that has been spread out for them. When all the guests are in, the woman takes a new food-mat and spreads it in front of those to whom she is going to give to eat. Then she takes down the four roasting-tongs with the eyes in them that had been over the fire and places them before her guests. Then she takes the salmon out of the roasting-tongs. After she has done so, she gives water to them to drink; and after they finish drinking, then the one highest in rank prays to what they are going to eat. He says: "O, friends! thank you that we meet alive. We have lived until this time when you came this year. Now we pray you, Super-

---

[6] That is, unlucky, devoid of supernatural import

[7] That is, her husband; note the superordinate/subordinate structuring.

natural-Ones, to protect us from danger, that nothing evil may happen to us when we eat you, Supernatural-Ones! for that is the reason why you come here, that we may catch you for food. We know that only your bodies are dead here, but your souls come to watch over us when we are going to eat what you have given us to eat now." Thus he says; and when he stops, he says, "Indeed!"

As soon as he stops speaking, they begin to eat, and his friends also eat. Then the man takes up a bucket and goes to draw fresh water after they have eaten; and when he comes back, he puts down the water that he has drawn, and waits for them to finish eating. After they have eaten, the water is put in front of them, and they drink. Then his wife picks up the pieces of bone and skin and puts them on the food-mat; and when she has them all, she folds up (the mat) and goes to throw the contents into the sea; and the guests only rub their hands together to dry off the fat from their hands, for they are careful not to wash their hands, and not to wipe their hands with cedar-bark. After they have done so, they go out. (Boas, 1921:611-12)

In the evening the man invites the chiefs to come and eat with spoons the fresh silver-salmon. When all the men are in the house, he takes his kettle and pours water into it. Then he puts it on the fire. His wife takes four fresh split silver-salmon and slices their meat crosswise. When the water in the kettle is boiling, she puts the four fresh silver-salmon into it. The woman only stirs it when it has been boiling for some time, to break it into pieces. After she has finished stirring it, she takes three dishes, when there are twelve men who will eat with spoons the fresh silver-salmon, and she takes twelve spoons which are really new, and the large dipping-ladle. As soon as they have all been put down, she washes out the three dishes and the spoons; and after she has done so, she puts the meat of the silver-salmon into the dishes. When the dishes are filled, she spreads a food-mat in front of [the men]; and the man takes up the dishes and places them before four men, and he places another before four others, and again one dish before four others. After all the dishes have been put down, he distributes the spoons to them; then he gives them water to drink. After they have finished drinking, the one highest in rank prays the same prayer that they said when they first ate the roasted eyes; and after he stops speaking, they begin to eat with spoons. When they begin to eat, the man takes up a bucket and goes to draw fresh water; and when he comes back, he puts down the bucket with water in it, and waits for them to finish eating. After they finish eating, the man takes up from the floor the bucket with water in it and puts it in front of his guests. Then they drink, and the man takes up the dishes and puts them down at the place where his wife is sitting. Then he takes the spoons and puts them down at the place where his wife is sitting. As soon as this is done, the guests go out. They do the same with the dog-salmon when it is caught for the first time. They also do the same thing with the dog-salmon when it is dried for winter, when they are going to keep it in the same way as the silver-salmon. They do not pour oil over it, because it is really fat: therefore they give it to eat only in the evening. This is also the way when silver-salmon caught by trolling is eaten with spoons in the morning. He who eats it is never strong; he always feels sleepy the whole day, and he is not strong:

therefore it is first eaten in the evening. As soon as the dog-salmon coming from the upper part of the river is eaten, they pour much oil over it, for it is dry; and there is never a time when they do not eat it in the morning, at noon, and in the evening. They are afraid to eat it in the morning, when it just jumps at the mouth of the river, for it is really fat. That is the cause of making [those who eat it] sleepy. That is the end of this. (Boas, 1921:348-50)

Index to
Boas's Kwakiutl Texts

Art	1955:	186-298.
	1966:	318-46.
Baskets	1909:	382-95; 418-20.
Birth	1921:	644-99.
	1966:	358-68.
Blankets	1909:	395-99.
Body Signs	1921:	603-5.
Boxes	1909:	342-44; 417-19; 447-50.
Canoes	1909:	344-69; 444-46.
	1921:	615-16.
	1966:	20-21; 31-32.
Cedar Trees	1921:	616-19.
Coppers	1897:	344-53.
	1925:	282-89.
Cradle	1909:	458-60.
Crests	1897:	323-28.
Cries of the Raven	1921:	606-7.
Death	1921:	705-13; 1329-31.
Dishes (bowls)	1897:	390-93.
	1909:	420-24.
Dishes (feast)	1921:	805-20.
Eagles	1921:	784.
Fire	1921:	1331-33.
Food Collection	1909:	461-516.
	1921:	173-222; 607-17.
Food Preservation	1921:	223-304.
Gestures	1966:	372-76.
Houses	1897:	367-71.
	1909:	414-17; 425-26.
	1925:	310-57.
	1966:	33-35.
Hunting Taboos	1921:	637-44.

Industries	1921:	57-172.
Life Cycle	1966:	358-71.
Meals	1909:	427-43.
	1921:	607; 750-76; 778-93.
Medicine and Curing	1966:	376-88.
Mythological Concepts	1930:	175-81.
Myths	1910.	
	1935b.	
(Boas and Hunt)	1905:	7-446.
Myths (analyses)	1935.	
Names	1921:	785-87; 820-35.
	1925:	112-357.
	1934.	
Origin Myths	1897:	371-90.
	1921:	802-4.
Potlatch	1897:	341-58.
	1966:	77-104.
Prayers	1921:	620-37; 1318-29.
	1930:	182-245.
	1966:	155-65
Pregnancy and Birth	1921:	644-99.
	1966:	358-68.
Property	1921:	1333-58.
	1925:	132-236.
Property (destruction or distribution of)	1897:	353-55.
	1925:	132-236.
Property Rights	1966:	35-36.
Rank, Property, and Inheritance	1925:	56-357.
Recipes	1921:	305-601.
Religious Terminology	1966:	165-70.
Shamanism	1921:	728-33.
	1930:	1-56.
	1966:	120-48.
Social Organization (basic)	1897:	328-40.
	1966:	37-76.
Social Organization (winter)	1897:	418-31.
Songs	1921:	1279-1315.
	1966:	346-52.
(Boas and Hunt)	1905:	475-84.
Souls	1921:	713-28.
Spirit/Man Rituals	1897:	393-418.
Time and Space	1909:	410-13.

Winter Ceremonials	1897:	431-632.
	1930:	57-174.
	1966:	171-298.
Witchcraft	1966:	148-55.

─────────────── ◄ **REFERENCES** ► ───────────────

Adams, John
1973   *The Gitskan Potlatch.* New York: Holt, Rinehart & Winston.
Andrews, Ralph W.
1960   *Indian Primitive.* New York: Bonanza Books.
artscanada
1974   "Stones, Bones and Skin: Ritual and Shamanic Art." *artscanada*, Nos. 184-87.
Attenborough, David
1977   *The Tribal Eye.* New York: W. W. Norton & Co.
Barnett, Homer G.
1938   "The Nature of the Potlatch." *American Anthropologist* 40:349-58.
1957   *Indian Shakers.* Carbondale: Southern Illinois University Press.
1968   *The Nature and Function of the Potlatch.* Eugene, Ore.: Department of Anthropology, University of Oregon.
Barnouw, Victor
1973   *Culture and Personality.* Homewood, Ill.: Dorsey Press.
Benedict, Ruth
1934   *Patterns of Culture.* Boston: Houghton Mifflin Co.
Beston, Henry
1928   The Outermost House. New York: Rinehart & Co., Inc.
Bettelheim, Bruno
1976   *The Uses of Enchantment.* New York: Alfred A. Knopf.
Bierhorst, John
1976   *The Red Swan.* New York: Farrar, Straus & Giroux.
Birket-Smith, Kaj
1964   "An Analysis of the Potlatch Institution of North America." *Folk* 6:5-13.
Blackman, Margaret B.
1973   "The Application of Photogrammetry to Photographic Ethnohistory." *Newsletter of the Society for the Anthropology of Visual Communication* 5, No. 1:9-15.
1973b   "Totems to Tombstones: Culture Change as Viewed Through the Haida Mortuary Complex, 1887-1971." *Ethnology*, XII, pp. 47-56.
1976   "Northern Haida Ecology: A Preliminary Discussion." Paper read at the Northwest Coast Studies Conference, May 1976, Vancouver, British Columbia.

References

Bledsoe, Wade T., Jr.
1975   "The Social Life of an Unsociable Giant." *Audubon* 77, No. 3:2-17.

Boas, Franz
1887   "Notes on the Ethnology of British Columbia." *American Philosophical Society, Proceedings* 24:422-28.
1888   "The Houses of the Kwakiutl Indians, British Columbia." *United States National Museum, Proceedings* 11:197-212.
1892   "Vocabulary of the Kwakiutl Language." *American Philosophical Society, Proceedings* 31:34-82.
1897   *The Social Organization and Secret Societies of the Kwakiutl.* United States National Museum, Report for 1895:311-738.
1898   "Facial Paintings of the Indians of Northern British Columbia." *Publications of the Jesup North Pacific Expedition*, I, pp. 13-24.
1909   *The Kwakiutl of Vancouver Island.* American Museum of Natural History, Memoirs, 8, Pt. 2:301-522.
1910   *Kwakiutl Tales.* Columbia University Contributions to Anthropology, 2. New York: Columbia University Press.
1911   "Kwakiutl." In *Handbook of American Indian Languages*, Franz Boas ed., Bureau of American Ethnology, Bulletin 40, Pt. 1. Washington, D. C.: Government Printing Office.
1916   *Tsimshian Mythology.* Bureau of American Ethnology, Thirty-first Annual Report (1909-10). Washington, D. C.: Government Printing Office.
1921   *Ethnology of the Kwakiutl.* Bureau of American Ethnology, Thirty-fifth Annual Report, Pts. 1 and 2 (1913-14). Washington, D. C.: Government Printing Office.
1925   *Contributions to the Ethnology of the Kwakiutl.* Columbia University Contributions to Anthropology, 3. New York: Columbia University Press.
1928   *Bella Bella Texts.* New York: Columbia University Press.
1930   *The Religion of the Kwakiutl Indians.* Columbia University Contributions to Anthropology, 10. New York: Columbia University Press.
1930b   *The Religion of the Kwakiutl Indians* (Kwakiutl language volume). Columbia University Contributions to Anthropology, 10. New York: Columbia University Press.
1932   "Current Beliefs of the Kwakiutl Indians." *Journal of American Folklore* 45:176-260.
1932b   *Bella Bella Tales.* American Folklore Society, Memoirs, 25. New York: G. E. Stechert.

1933   "Review of Locher's 'Serpent in Kwakiutl Religion.' " *Journal of American Folklore* 46:418-21.

1934   *Geographical Names of the Kwakiutl Indians.* Columbia University Contributions to Anthropology, 20. New York: Columbia University Press.

1935   *Kwakiutl Culture as Reflected in Mythology.* American Folklore Society, Memoirs, 28. New York: G. E. Stechert.

1935b   *Kwakiutl Tales, New Series.* 2 vols. Columbia University Contributions to Anthropology, 26. New York: Columbia University Press.

1938   *General Anthropology.* New York: Johnson Reprint Company.

1940   *Race, Language and Culture.* New York: The Free Press, 1966.

1947   "Kwakiutl Grammar with a Glossary of Suffixes." in *Transactions of the American Philosophical Society*, New Series, edited by H. B. Yampolsky and Z. S. Harris, Pt. 3:203-377.

1955   *Primitive Art.* New York: Dover Publications.

1966   *Kwakiutl Ethnography.* Edited by Helen Codere. Chicago: University of Chicago Press.

1966b   "Representative Art of Primitive People." In *The Many Faces of Primitive Art*, edited by D. Fraser, pp. 4-9. New York: Prentice-Hall.

1973   *The Kwakiutl of British Columbia.* Film edited by Bill Holm. Seattle: University of Washington Press.

Boas, Franz, and George Hunt

1905   *Kwakiutl Texts.* Memoir of the American Museum of Natural History, 5.

1908   *Kwakiutl Texts, Second Series.* Memoir of the American Museum of Natural History, 10.

Borror, Donald J., and Richard E. White

1970   *A Field Guide to the Insects North of Mexico.* Boston: Houghton Mifflin Co.

Brockman, C. Frank

1968   *Trees of North America.* New York: Golden Press.

Brown, Vinson

1976   *Sea Mammals and Reptiles of the Pacific Coast.* New York: Macmillan.

Buber, Martin

1958   *I and Thou.* New York: Scribner's.

Bultmann, Rudolf

1961   *Kerygma and Myth.* New York: Harper Torchbooks.

1962   *History and Eschatology.* New York: Harper Torchbooks.

Burris, Fred, and Dora Burris

1974   "Death of a Cottontail." *Audubon* 76, No. 6:36-37.

Burt, William H., and Richard P. Grossenheider
1964 *A Field Guide to Mammals*. Boston: Houghton Mifflin Co.
Burton, John A., ed.
1975 *Owls of the World*. New York: A & W Visual Library.
Caras, Roger
1974 *The Private Lives of Animals*. New York: Grosset & Dunlap.
Cassirer, Ernst
1953 *The Philosophy of Symbolic Forms*. 3 vols. New Haven: Yale University Press.
Chapman, A.
1965 *Mâts Totémiques: Amérique du Nord, Côte nord-ouest*. Paris: Catalogues du Musée de L'Homme.
Chapman, Abraham, ed.
1975 *Literature of the American Indians*. New York: Meridian.
Chasan, Daniel J.
1975 "Salmon." *Audubon* 77, No. 6:8-23.
Clark, Ella E.
1966 *Indian Legends of the Pacific Northwest*. Berkeley: University of California Press.
Clark, Ian C., and Dominique Darbois
1971 *Indian and Eskimo Art of Canada*. Toronto: Ryerson.
Clarke, Herbert, and Arnold Small
1976 *Birds of the West*. New York: Barnes.
Clement, Roland C.
1973 *American Birds*. New York: Bantam Books.
Codere, Helen
1950 *Fighting with Property*. Monographs of the American Ethnological Society, 28. New York.
1956 "The Amiable Side of Kwakiutl Life: The Potlatch and Play Potlatch." *American Anthropologist* 58:334-51.
1957 "Kwakiutl Society: Rank without Class." *American Anthropologist* 59:473-86.
1959 "The Understanding of the Kwakiutl." In *The Anthropology of Franz Boas*, edited by W. Goldschmidt, pp. 61-75.
1961 "Kwakiutl." In *Perspectives in American Indian Culture Change*, edited by E. S. Spicer. Chicago: University of Chicago Press.
1966 Introduction to *Kwakiutl Ethnography* by Franz Boas. Chicago: University of Chicago Press.
Collins, Henry B.; F. de Laguna; E. Carpenter; and P. Stone
1973 *The Far North*. Washington, D. C.: National Gallery of Art.
Conant, Roger
1958 *A Field Guide to Reptiles and Amphibians of Eastern North America*. Boston: Houghton Mifflin Co.

Curtis, Edward S.
1914 *In the Land of the War Canoes.* Film edited by Bill Holm and George Quimby. Seattle: University of Washington Press, 1973.
1915 *The North American Indian,* 10 (Kwakiutl). New York: Johnson Reprint.
1915b *In the Land of the Headhunters.* Yonkers-on-Hudson: World Book Company.

Dauenhauer, Richard
1976 "Yuwaan Gageets: A Russian Fairy Tale in Tlingit Oral Tradition." Paper read at the Northwest Coast Studies Conference, May 1976, Vancouver, British Columbia.

Dawson, George M.
1887 "Notes and Observations on the Kwakiool People of the Northern Part of Vancouver Island. . . ." *Proceedings and Transactions, Royal Society of Canada,* 5, Section 2.

de Laguna, Frederica
1954 "Tlingit Ideas about the Individual." *Southwestern Journal of Anthropology* 10:172-91.
1960 *The Story of a Tlingit Community.* Bureau of American Ethnology, Bulletin 172. Washington, D. C.: Government Printing Office.
1972 *Under Mount Saint Elias.* Smithsonian Contributions to Anthropology, 7, Pts. 1-3. Washington, D. C.: Government Printing Office.

de Laguna, Frederica; F. A. Riddell; D. F. McGeein; K. S. Lane; J. S. Freed; and C. Osborne
1964 *Archaeology of the Yakutat Bay Area, Alaska.* Bureau of American Ethnology, Bulletin 192. Washington, D. C.: Government Printing Office.

De Menil, Adelaida, and William Reid
1971 *Out of the Silence.* New York: Harper & Row, Publishers.

Densmore, Frances
1943 *Music of the Indians of British Columbia.* Anthropological Paper No. 27, Bureau of American Ethnology, Bulletin 136:1-99. New York: Da Capo Press, 1972.

Donald, Leland, and Donald H. Mitchell
1975 "Some Correlates of Local Group Rank among the Southern Kwakiutl." *Ethnology,* XIV, No. 4:325-46.

Driver, Harold F.
1961 *Indians of North America.* Chicago: University of Chicago Press.

Drucker, Philip
1939 "Rank, Wealth and Kinship in Northwest Coast Society." *American Anthropologist* 41:55-65.
1940 "Kwakiutl Dancing Societies." *University of California Anthropological Records* 2, No. 6:201-30. Berkeley: University of California Press.
1953 *Indians of the Northwest Coast*. Garden City: Natural History Press.
1958 *The Native Brotherhoods*. Bureau of American Ethnology, Bulletin 168. Washington, D. C.: Government Printing Office.
1965 *Cultures of the North Pacific Coast*. San Francisco: Chandler.
Drucker, Philip, and Robert F. Heizer
1967 *To Make My Name Good*. Berkeley: University of California Press.
Duff, Wilson
1964 *The Impact of the White Man*. The Indian History of British Columbia, 1. Anthropology in British Columbia, Memoir No. 5. Victoria: Provincial Museum of British Columbia.
1967 *Arts of the Raven*. Catalogue to the Exhibition, The Vancouver Art Gallery.
1975 *Images Stone B.C.* Saanichton, B. C.: Hancock House.
Dumont, Louis
1974 *Homo Hierarchicus*. Chicago: University of Chicago Press.
Edwards, Paul, ed.
1967 *Encyclopedia of Philosophy*. New York: Macmillan and The Free Press.
Eliade, Mircea
1964 *Shamanism: Archaic Techniques of Ecstasy*. London: Routledge & Kegan Paul.
Elman, Robert
1976 *The Living World of Audubon Mammals*. New York: Grosset & Dunlap.
Elmendorf, William
1967 "Soul Loss Illness in Western North America." In *Indian Tribes of Aboriginal America*, edited by S. Tax, pp. 104-14.
1971 "Coast Salish Status Ranking and Intergroup Ties." *Southwestern Journal of Anthropology* 27:353-80.
1976 "Coast and Plateau Salish Power Concepts, Rituals and Social Structures." Paper read at the Northwest Coast Studies Conference, May 1976, Vancouver, British Columbia.
Everett, Michael
1975 *Birds of Prey*. New York: G. P. Putnam's Sons.

Falk, Randolph
1976 *Lelooska*. Millbrae, Cal.: Celestial Arts.
Feder, Norman
1969 *American Indian Art*. New York: Harry N. Abrams.
1971 *Two Hundred Years of North American Indian Art*. New York: Praeger, Publishers.
Fischer, David H.
1970 *Historians' Fallacies*. New York: Harper Torchbooks.
Ford, Clellan S.
1941 *Smoke from Their Fires*. Hamden, Conn.: Archon, 1968.
Ford, Clellan S., and Frank A. Beach
1951 *Patterns of Sexual Behavior*. New York: Ace Books.
Fowler, Don D.
1972 *In a Sacred Manner We Live*. Barre, Mass.: Barre Publishing Co.
Freeman, John E., and M. E. Smith
1968 *A Guide to Manuscripts Relating to the American Indian in the Library of the American Philosophical Society*. Memoirs of the American Philosophical Society, 65.
von Frisch, Karl
1974 *Animal Architecture*. New York: Harcourt Brace Jovanovich.
Garfield, Viola E., and Linn A. Forrest
1961 *The Wolf and the Raven*. Seattle: University of Washington Press.
Garfield, Viola E., and Paul S. Wingert
1966 *The Tsimshian Indians and Their Arts*. Seattle: University of Washington Press.
Geertz, Clifford
1973 *The Interpretation of Cultures*. London: Hutchinson.
Gladwin, Thomas
1957 "Personality Structure in the Plains." *Anthropological Quarterly* 30:111-24.
Goldman, Irving
1937 "The Kwakiutl of Vancouver Island." In *Cooperation and Competition Among Primitive Peoples*, edited by M. Mead. Boston: Beacon Press, 1961.
1975 *The Mouth of Heaven*. New York: Wiley-Interscience.
1976 "Ritual Distribution and Exchange among the Southern Kwakiutl: A Cosmological Perspective." Paper read at the Northwest Coast Studies Conference, May 1976, Vancouver, British Columbia.
Goldschmidt, Walter, ed.
1959 *The Anthropology of Franz Boas*. Memoir No. 89, American Anthropological Association, 61, No. 5, Pt. 2.

Gooders, John
  1975   *The Great Book of Birds.* New York: The Dial Press.
Graybill, Florence Curtis, and Victor Boesen
  1976   *Edward Sheriff Curtis.* New York: Thomas Y. Crowell Company, Publishers.
Grossman, Mary L., and John Hamlet
  1964   *Birds of Prey of the World.* New York: Clarkson N. Potter.
Grzimek, Bernhard, ed.
  1972-75   *Grzimek's Animal Life Encyclopedia.* New York: Van Nostrand Reinhold.
Gunther, Erna
  1962   *Northwest Coast Indian Art.* Seattle: World's Fair.
  1966   *Art in the Life of the Northwest Coast Indian.* Portland: The Portland Art Museum.
  1972   *Indian Life of the Northwest Coast of North America.* Chicago: University of Chicago Press.
Haberland, Wolfgang
  1968   *The Art of North America.* New York: Greystone Press.
Halpern, Ida
  1967   Notes accompanying the sound recordings, *Indian Music of the Pacific Northwest Coast.* New York: Folkways Records.
Harris, Marvin K.
  1968   *The Rise of Anthropological Theory.* New York: Vintage Books.
  1974   *Cows, Pigs, Wars, and Witches.* New York: Thomas Y. Crowell Co.
Harrison, Hal H.
  1975   *A Field Guide to Bird's Nests.* Boston: Houghton Mifflin Co.
Hatch, Elvin
  1973   *Theories of Man and Culture.* New York: Columbia University Press.
Hawthorn, Audrey
  1967   *Art of the Kwakiutl Indians.* Vancouver: University of British Columbia Press.
Hays, H. R.
  1975   *Children of the Raven.* New York: McGraw-Hill.
Helm, June, ed.
  1966   *Pioneers of American Anthropology.* Seattle: University of Washington Press.
Hewes, Gordon W.
  1948   "The Rubric 'Fishing and Fisheries.' " *American Anthropologist* 50:238-46.
Hewlett, Stefani, and Ronald Hewlett
  1976   *Sea Life of the Pacific Northwest.* Toronto: McGraw-Hill Ryerson.

Hillyer, William H.
1931 *The Box of Daylight.* New York: Alfred A. Knopf.

Holm, Bill
1970 *Northwest Coast Indian Art.* Seattle: University of Washington Press.
1972 *Crooked Beak of Heaven.* Seattle: University of Washington Press.
1972b "Heraldic Carving Styles of the Northwest Coast." In *American Indian Art: Form and Tradition.* New York: E. P. Dutton.
1973 "Notes" for the film THE KWAKIUTL OF BRITISH COLUMBIA by Franz Boas. Seattle: University of Washington Press.

Holm, Bill, and Bill Reid.
1976 *Indian Art of the Northwest Coast.* Seattle: University of Washington Press.

Honigmann, John J.
1973 *Handbook of Social and Cultural Anthropology.* Chicago: Rand McNally & Co.

Hunt, George
1906 "The Rival Chiefs." in *Boas Anniversary Volume, Anthropological Papers*, pp. 108-36. New York: G. E. Stechert.

Hymes, Dell
1965 "Some North Pacific Coast Poems: A Problem in Anthropological Philology." *American Anthropologist* 67:316-41.

Inverarity, Robert B.
1971 *Art of the Northwest Coast Indians.* Berkeley: University of California Press.

Jacobs, Melville
1959 *The Content and Style of an Oral Literature.* Chicago: University of Chicago Press.

Karalus, Karl E., and Allan W. Eckert
1974 *The Owls of North America.* Garden City: Doubleday & Co.

Keithahn, Edward L.
1963 *Monuments in Cedar.* New York: Bonanza Books.

Kew, Michael
1976 "Salmon Abundance, Technology and Human Populations on the Fraser River Watershed." Paper read at the Northwest Coast Studies Conference, May 1976, Vancouver, British Columbia.

Kierkegaard, Søren
1941 *Fear and Trembling.* Princeton: Princeton University Press.

Kimball, Yeffe, and Jean Anderson
1965 *The Art of American Indian Cooking.* New York: Avon.

Kirk, G. S.
1970 *Myth.* Berkeley: Cambridge/ University of California Press.

Laplanche, J., and J.-B. Pontalis
1973 *The Language of Psychoanalysis*. New York: W. W. Norton & Co.
Lévi-Strauss, Claude
1971 *The Raw and the Cooked*. New York: Harper Torchbooks.
1975 *La Voie des Masques*. Geneva: Albert Skira.
Line, Les, and Franklin Russell
1976 *The Audubon Society Book of Wild Birds*. New York: Harry N. Abrams.
Lowie, Robert L.
1918 *Myths and Traditions of the Crow Indians*. Anthropological Papers of the American Museum of Natural History, XXV, Pt. 1.
MacQuitty, William
1976 *Island of Isis*. New York: Scribner's.
Maranda, Pierre, ed.
1972 *Mythology*. New York: Penguin Books.
McClellan, Catherine
1954 "The Interrelations of Social Structure with Northern Tlingit Ceremonialism." *Southwestern Journal of Anthropology* 10:75-96.
McFeat, Tom, ed.
1967 *Indians of the North Pacific Coast*. Seattle: University of Washington Press.
McLuhan, T. C.
1971 *Touch the Earth*. New York: Promontory Press.
Mead, Margaret
1959 *An Anthropologist at Work*. New York: Avon.
1974 *Ruth Benedict*. New York: Columbia University Press.
Mead, Margaret and Rhoda Métraux, eds.
1953 *The Study of Culture at a Distance*. Chicago: University of Chicago Press.
Menzel-Tettenborn, Helga, and Günter Radtke
1973 *Animals in their Worlds*. New York: Grosset & Dunlap.
Miller, Polly
1967 *Lost Heritage of Alaska*. Cleveland: World Publishing Co.
Milne, Lorus; Margery Milne; and Franklin Russell
1975 *The Secret Life of Animals*. New York: E. P. Dutton.
Mochon, Marion J.
1966 *Masks of the Northwest Coast*. Publications in Primitive Art 2, Milwaukee Public Museum.
Mozino, José Mariano
1970 *Noticias de Nutka*. American Ethnological Society, Monograph 50. Translated and edited by I. H. Wilson. Seattle: University of Washington Press.

Murie, Olaus
1954 *A Field Guide to Animal Tracks*. Boston: Houghton Mifflin Co.
Naroll, Raoul, and Ronald Cohen, eds.
1973 *A Handbook of Method in Cultural Anthropology*. New York: Columbia University Press.
Newcomb, William W., Jr.
1974 *North American Indians*. Pacific Palisades: Goodyear.
Oberg, Kalervo
1973 *The Social Economy of the Tlingit Indians*. American Ethnological Society, Monograph 55. Seattle: University of Washington Press.
Olson, Ronald L.
1940 "The Social Organization of the Haisla of British Columbia." *Anthropological Records* 2, No. 5:169-200. Berkeley: University of California Press.
1954 "Social Life of the Owikeno Kwakiutl." *Anthropological Records* 4, No. 3:213-59. Berkeley: University of California Press.
Oswalt, Wendell K.
1966 *This Land Was Theirs*. New York: Wiley.
Otto, Rudolf
1939 *The Idea of the Holy*. London: Oxford University Press.
Palmer, Ralph S.
1954 *The Mammal Guide*. Garden City: Doubleday & Co.
Parker, Derek, and Julia Parker
1976 *The Immortals*. New York: McGraw-Hill.
Parker, Seymour
1964 "The Kwakiutl Indians: 'Amiable' and 'Atrocious'." *Anthropologica* 6:131-58.
Pearson, T. Gilbert
1936 *Birds of America*. Garden City: Garden City Publishing Co.
Perrins, Christopher, and Ad Cameron
1976 *Birds*. New York: Harry N. Abrams.
Peterson, Roger T.
1961 *A Field Guide to Western Birds*. Boston: Houghton Mifflin Co.
1967 *A Field Guide to the Birds*. Boston: Houghton Mifflin Co.
Piddocke, Stuart
1965 "The Potlatch System of the Southern Kwakiutl: A New Perspective." *Southwestern Journal of Anthropology* 21:244-64.
Platt, Joseph B.
1976 "Bald Eagles Wintering in a Utah Desert." *American Birds* 30, No. 4:783-88.

Pough, Richard H.
1949   *Audubon Land Bird Guide*. Garden City: Doubleday & Co.
1951   *Audubon Water Bird Guide*. Garden City: Doubleday & Co.

Quimby, George
1948   "Culture Contact on the Northwest Coast, 1785-1795." *American Anthropologist* 50:247-55.

Reed, Chester A.
1951   *Bird Guide: Land Birds East of the Rockies*. Garden City: Doubleday & Co.

Robbins, Chandler S.; Betel Bruun; and Herbert S. Zim
1966   *Birds of North America*. New York: Golden Press.

Robison, Bruce H.
1976   "Deep-Sea Fishes." *Natural History*, LXXXV, No. 7:38-45.

Rohner, Ronald P.
1966   "Franz Boas: Ethnographer on the Northwest Coast." In *Pioneers of American Anthropology*, edited by J. Helm, pp. 149-212.
1967   *The People of Gilford*. National Museum of Canada, Bulletin 225, Ottawa.
1969   *The Ethnography of Franz Boas*. Editor. Chicago: University of Chicago Press.

Rohner, Ronald P., and Evelyn C. Rohner
1970   *The Kwakiutl*. New York: Holt, Rinehart & Winston.

Rosman, Abraham, and Paula Rubel
1971   *Feasting with Mine Enemy*. New York: Columbia University Press.

Ruyle, Eugene E.
1973   "Slavery, Surplus and Stratification on the Northwest Coast." *Current Anthropology* 14, No. 5:603-31.

Sagan, Eli
1974   *Cannibalism: Human Aggression and Cultural Form*. New York: Harper & Row.

Sanderson, Ivan T.
1967   *The Continent We Live On*. New York: Random House.

Scheffer, Victor B.
1976   *A Natural History of Sea Mammals*. New York: Scribner's.

Scherer, Joanna C.
1973   *Indians*. New York: Crown Publishers.

Schwiebert, Ernest
1970   *Salmon of the World*. New York: Winchester Press.

Smith, Ian
1973   *Vancouver Island: Unknown Wilderness*. Seattle: University of Washington Press.

Smith, Marian W.
   1967   "Culture Area and Culture Depth." In *Indian Tribes of Aboriginal America*, edited by S. Tax, pp. 80-96.
Smyly, John, and Carolyn Smyly
   1973   *The Totem Poles of Skedans*. Seattle: University of Washington Press.
Spiro, Melford
   1951   "Culture and Personality: The Natural History of a False Dichotomy." *Psychiatry* 14:21-46.
Spradley, James P.
   1969   *Guests Never Leave Hungry*. New Haven: Yale University Press.
Spradley, James P., and G. E. McDonough
   1973   *Anthropology through Literature*. Boston: Little, Brown.
Stebbins, Robert C.
   1966   *A Field Guide to Western Reptiles and Amphibians*. Boston: Houghton Mifflin Co.
Stocking, George
   1966   "The Franz Boas Collection." In *The American Indian: A Conference in the American Philosophical Society Library*. Library Publication No. 2:1-19, Philadelphia.
   1968   *Race, Culture and Evolution*. New York: The Free Press.
   1974   *The Shaping of American Anthropology, 1883-1911*. Editor. New York: Basic Books.
Strathern, Andrew
   1971   *The Rope of Moka*. Cambridge: Cambridge University Press.
Sturtevant, William C., comp.
   1974   *Boxes and Bowls*. Washington, D. C.: Smithsonian Institution Press.
Suttles, Wayne
   1960   "Affinal Ties, Subsistence, and Prestige among the Coast Salish." *American Anthropologist* 62:296-305.
   1968   "Variation in Habitat and Culture on the Northwest Coast." In *Man in Adaptation: The Cultural Present*, edited by Y. Cohen, pp. 93-106. Chicago: Aldine.
Sutton, Myron, and Ann Sutton
   1973   *The Wild Places*. New York: Harper & Row.
Swanton, John R.
   1905   *Haida Texts and Myths*. Bureau of American Ethnology, Bulletin 29. Washington, D. C.: Government Printing Office.
   1909   *Tlingit Myths and Texts*. Bureau of American Ethnology, Bulletin 39. Washington, D. C.: Government Printing Office.

Tannahill, Reay
  1973 *Food and History.* New York: Stein & Day.
  1975 *Flesh and Blood.* New York: Stein & Day.
Tax, Sol, ed.
  1967 *Indian Tribes of Aboriginal America.* New York: Cooper Square.
Tedlock, Barbara
  1975 "The Clown's Way." In *Teachings from the American Earth,* edited by D. Tedlock and B. Tedlock, pp. 105-118.
Tedlock, Dennis, and Barbara Tedlock, eds.
  1975 *Teachings from the American Earth.* New York: Liveright.
University of Iowa, Museum of Art
  1973 *The Art of the Shaman.* Iowa City: University of Iowa, Museum of Art.
Vansina, Jan
  1961 *Oral Tradition.* London: Routledge & Kegan Paul.
Vaughan, J. Daniel
  1976 "Haida Potlatch and Society." Paper read at the Northwest Coast Studies Conference, May 1976, Vancouver, British Columbia.
Vayda, Andrew
  1968 "Economic Systems in Ecological Perspective: The Case of the Northwest Coast." In *Readings in Anthropology,* edited by M. H. Fried, II:172-78. New York: Crowell.
Wagner, Roy
  1972 *Habu: The Innovation of Meaning in Daribi Religion.* Chicago: University of Chicago Press.
Waite, Deborah
  1966 "Kwakiutl Transformation Masks." In *The Many Faces of Primitive Art,* D. Fraser, pp. 266-300. Englewood Cliffs: Prentice-Hall.
Walker, Ernest P. *et al.*
  1975 *Mammals of the World.* Baltimore: Johns Hopkins University Press.
Walker, Lewis W.
  1974 *The Book of Owls.* New York: Alfred A. Knopf.
Wardwell, Allen
  1964 *Yakutat South.* Chicago: The Art Institute of Chicago.
Waterman, T. T.
  1923 "Some Conundrums in Northwest Coast Art." *American Anthropologist* 25:435-51.

Waterston, A. R., ed.
1975 *Larousse Encyclopedia of the Animal World.* New York: Larousse & Co.
Wherry, Joseph H.
1969 *Indian Masks and Myths of the West.* New York: Apollo.
White, Leslie A.
1963 *The Ethnography and Ethnology of Franz Boas.* Bulletin 6 of the Texas Memorial Museum. Austin: University of Texas Press.
Wike, Joyce
1952 "The Role of the Dead in Northwest Coast Culture." In *Indian Tribes of Aboriginal America*, edited by S. Tax, pp. 97-103.
1957 "More Puzzles on the Northwest Coast." *American Anthropologist* 59:301-17.
Williams, F. E.
1938 *Orokaiva Magic.* Oxford: Oxford University Press.
1940 *Natives of Lake Kutubu, Papua.* Serialized in *Oceania*, 11 (1940-41).
Willis, Roy
1974 *Man and Beast.* New York: Basic Books.
Wilson, Monica
1951 *Good Company.* London: Oxford University Press.
Wolcott, Harry F.
1967 *A Kwakiutl Village and School.* New York: Holt, Rinehart & Winston.
Wyss, Dieter
1973 *Psychoanalytic Schools.* New York: Jason Aronson.
Young, Michael W.
1971 *Fighting with Food.* Cambridge: Cambridge University Press.

Library of Congress Cataloging in Publication Data

Walens, Stanley, 1948-
  Feasting with cannibals

  Bibliography
  Includes index
    1   Kwakiutl Indians—Religion and mythology
  2. Indians of North America—Northwest coast of
  North America—Religion and mythology   3   Kwakiutl
  Indians—Rites and ceremonies   4   Indians of
  North America—Northwest coast of North America—
  Rites and ceremonies.   I   Title
  E99 K9W34   299'.72   81-47161
  ISBN 0-691-09392-X   AACR2

Made in the USA
Monee, IL
10 June 2026

52191938R00118